CLASSICALLY
ROMANTIC

CLASSICALLY ROMANTIC

Classical Form and

Meaning in Wagner's *Ring*

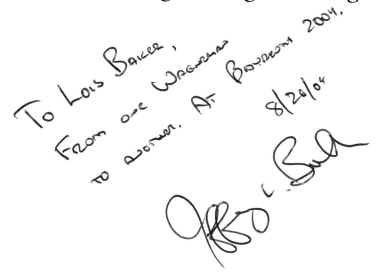

To Lois Baker,
From one Wagnerian
to another. At Bayreuth 2004.
8/26/04

Jeffrey L. Buller

To order additional copies of this book, contact:
Xlibris Corporation
1-888-7-XLIBRIS
www.Xlibris.com
Orders@Xlibris.com

CONTENTS

Sola una cosa tiene mala el sueño, según he oído decir, y es que se parece a la muerta, pues de un dormido a un muerto hay muy poca diferencia.

—Sancho Panza in Chapter 68 of *Don Quixote*, Part II

PRELUDE

Heinrich Porges once said that the characters of *Götterdämmerung* looked "as though the poet had conjured up from their graves the ancient Germans of Tacitus."[1] Porges, perhaps Wagner's most perceptive critic during preparations for the first *Ring* festival, may have been closer to the truth than he realized.[2] Despite the well-known influence that the *Ring* demonstrates from the *Nibelungenlied*, the *Volsunga Saga*, the *Prose Edda*, and several other German and Scandinavian poems, Wagner—like many of his generation—received his first impressions of the ancient Europeans, not from northern epic, but from the Greek and Roman classics. By the early nineteenth century, the histories of Tacitus, like the tragedies of Aeschylus, Sophocles, and Euripides, had become standard texts in German schools.

Wagner's ideas about German nationalism thus may have begun with the idealism of the Romantics, but they were always focused through the lens of classical literature. His belief in the social importance of drama, his attitudes about plot and character, many of his themes, his conviction that the form of a drama should serve to underscore its meaning, and several aspects of his most basic philosophy were all shaped by the epics, tragedies, and philosophical works of the early Greeks and Romans. Norse myth and German saga, Greek epic and Roman history, Schopenhauer and presocratic philosophy were all woven together in the single fabric of the *Ring*.

The essays that follow explore this classical background to the *Ring*. In particular, they trace the influence that Wagner's ideas about the classics had on his cycle's form and meaning. Five of these essays were published in an earlier form in *The Opera Quarterly* between 1994 and 1998.[3] The others are newly written. The approach taken in them begins with specific questions arising from Wagner's score or libretto, and then seeks to answer these questions by exploring what we know about the composer's education, reading, and intellectual background. As a result, this book contains relatively little analysis of minor (and, in my opinion, mostly imaginary) similarities between the plot of the *Ring* and this or that work of ancient literature. Such an approach has already been taken many times, beginning with Robert Petsch[4] and reaching its fullest form in the studies of Hugh Lloyd-Jones[5] and Duane Roller.[6] My purpose, in other words, is not to argue that Wotan and Fricka were inspired by the characters of Zeus and Hera in the *Iliad* or that Brünnhilde is a Germanic version of Athena from the *Oresteia*. Others have already done this. Rather, I am interested in exploring how Wagner's entire approach to drama—from the most minute details of his work's structure to the most fundamental aspects of its meaning—was rooted in his beliefs about ancient Greek literature and society. Even such key Wagnerian concepts as the leitmotif and the *Gesamtkunstwerk* resulted, I believe, from the composer's mixed heritage of romantic idealism and devotion to classical principles.

Failure to recognize the connection between Wagner's classical and romantic elements has caused most scholars to take far too narrow a view of the *Ring*'s thematic integrity. As but one example, we shall have abundant evidence to suggest that the leitmotif, a device usually regarded as strictly *musical* in nature, has many parallels in the text, characters, and staging of the *Ring*. Because of Wagner's desire to re-create the perfectly "unified art" of Homer or Aeschylus (the classical part of his vision), he developed a completely new thematic approach (the romantic part of his vision) in which each element of his drama was conceived and developed in a manner closely paralleled by the conception and development of every other element.

Many individuals were generous in providing assistance during the development of this book. Bill Ashbrook and Tom Glasow of *The Opera Quarterly* were unfailingly supportive during the writing of the five essays that appeared there; Herbert Benario of Emory University, no admirer of Wagner himself, provided insight into German classicism and nationalism during the nineteenth century; Rebecca Duplantier of Wake Forest University and Lowell Bouma of Georgia Southern University supplied guidance in elucidating matters of Wagner's German text; Gregory Harwood of Georgia Southern University applied a critical eye to an important section of this work; Lisa Sherwin of Georgia Southern University reviewed the entire manuscript, making many valuable suggestions; Michael Braz of Georgia Southern University opened his Wagner seminar so that I could "road test" some of the ideas contained in this book; Brian Flynt of Georgia Southern University transcribed the musical examples; and Sandra McClain of Georgia Southern University proved to be an unfailing source of inspiration, guidance, and support. Without her, this book would not exist.

CHAPTER 1

Wagner's Romantic Classicism

Houston Stewart Chamberlain, Richard Wagner's son-in-law[7] and biographer, believed that "of all the really great masters of musical art Wagner is the only one who enjoyed a thorough classical education."[8] Chamberlain's brash statement was unlikely to go unchallenged and, as one might expect, it was ridiculed in many quarters. While Wagner did receive an education that included classical languages and literature, many critics have noted that he was hardly unique in this regard. Berlioz's study of Latin became nearly a lifelong obsession, Mendelssohn was proficient in both Latin and Greek, and Mozart had acquaintance, not only with the Latin language, but also with a large number of historical sites in central and southern Italy.[9] What Chamberlain ignored was that nearly every composer who studied in Germany or Austria from the late eighteenth to the early twentieth century received at least *some* exposure to the classics. Contrary to all his intentions, therefore, Chamberlain's exaggeration led some biographers to dismiss *any* claims that Wagner was particularly learned in the classics. William Wallace, for instance, derided the very notion that Wagner had attained "fluency" in ancient Greek. "This of the boy who [by his own admission] threw away his grammar in disgust! . . . Wagner's reputation as a classical scholar has been built up by friends who in their ignorance imagined that because he talked about Greek and the Hellenic drama he must of necessity have had a profound knowledge of the language."[10]

Chamberlain and Wallace represent the two opposing camps in

the question of Wagner's classical education. It is appropriate, therefore, to begin any study of the *Ring*'s classical background with this
question: Which of these two observers is closer to the truth? Did
Wagner, as Chamberlain states, enjoy "a thorough classical education"
as a boy—an experience that nearly made him a classicist instead of a
musician—and did this early training affect everything the composer
later produced? Or was Wagner, as Wallace believed, merely a dilet-
tante, absorbing a few facts here and there and claiming far greater
levels of expertise than he actually attained?

The first step in answering these questions is to realize that neither
Chamberlain nor Wallace was an impartial witness. Chamberlain's un-
critical support of Wagner caused him to portray his father-in-law as
the paragon of every virtue. To be sure, Chamberlain tended to idealize
any individual he regarded as providing the voice of absolute truth.
This inclination, coupled with his own anti-Semitism, caused Chamberlain late in life to seek a new hero in the rising young politician,
Adolf Hitler.[11] On the other side of the question, however, Wallace's
contempt for Wagner and his music sometimes made him careless
with the facts. Wallace was so intent on ridiculing the composer that
he, perhaps even intentionally, twisted a number of Wagner's statements to provide "evidence" that this supposed genius was nothing
more than a fraud.[12] For this reason, a complete answer to the question of Wagner's classical background cannot be found by accepting
either Chamberlain or Wallace uncritically. It must be found instead in
the text and score of the *Ring* itself, in Wagner's own statements about
these works, and in the observations of his contemporaries. The resulting approach will suggest that the composer's own view of antiquity
was both different from and far more interesting than either of his
early biographers imagined.

Many scholars have recognized that there are superficial similarities in plot and character between the *Ring* and major works of classical literature. Wagner's Siegfried shares much with Achilles.[13] His Wotan
shares much with Oedipus.[14] His Brünnhilde shares much with
Antigone.[15] Nevertheless, these parallels, interesting as they are, may
be nothing more than coincidence or a proof of the kinship that exists

among all great works of art.[16] The real influence of the classics on the *Ring*, if it exists at all, should not be sought among these few details of plot or character. As Richard Jenkyns rightly observed,

> The contrast [of ancient Greek literature] with Wagner, who admired Aeschylus deeply, is instructive. The mechanisms on which the plot of his tetralogy depends—a ring which makes its possessor all-powerful, a dragon's blood with miraculous properties, a Valhalla which collapses the moment that the ring is returned to the Rhinemaidens— are magical and arbitrary; they seem to be there to suit the convenience of the composer. The great Greek dramas, however strange or primitive the beliefs that they express may be, are rooted in the real world in a way that Wagner's story is not; this is true even of the *Prometheus*, in which every character but one is an immortal.[17]

Wagner's "classicism," as Jenkyns implies and as we shall discover, has a "romantic" core. For this reason, the place to begin an exploration of the classical influence on Wagner is not with specific details of plot (although a few of these will need to be addressed later), but with everything that the composer knew—or *thought* he knew—about ancient epic and tragedy and how these forms of literature were related to the operatic works of his own day.

Wagner's Early Classical Education

In his autobiography, *Mein Leben*, Wagner reports that his interest in classical antiquity began in earliest childhood. When Wagner was only seven years old, his father entrusted his education to a family acquaintance identified only as Pastor Wetzel, "a clergyman in the country of Possendorf near Dresden."[18] In the evening, Wetzel would read to the children, giving special attention to passages that might develop their interest in literary and cultural matters. Wagner mentions hearing, in particular, a synopsis of the Robinson Crusoe story, a brief biography of Mozart, and an account of the war between Greece and Turkey then still in progress. "[T]he newspaper and magazine reports of the contemporary events of the Greek War of Independence excited me dreadfully. My love for Greece, which later fell with enthusiasm upon the mythology and history of Ancient Hellas, thus originated in intense and painful interest in the events of the present."[19] Though a romantic (and quite possibly embroidered) tale, this episode does establish a theme that Wagner would repeat throughout his autobiography: his fascination with antiquity did not arise out of an interest in the past for its own sake. It was the contemporary world, Wagner claims, that drew him to study ancient Greece and Rome and to see parallels between those early struggles and events in his own day. This pattern would continue for Wagner. An interest in classical antiquity was always tied to a desire to understand and reform contemporary society.

Wagner's youthful preoccupation with ancient Greece caused him to stint other academic areas. "From the direction my mind was taking it is obvious that I did not devote much zeal to ordinary scholastic work. Greek mythology, legend, and, finally, history were all that interested me."[20] The "ordinary scholastic work" that the composer admitted slighting included mathematics, religion, French, natural philosophy, and (perhaps surprisingly) Latin.[21] Later in life, Wagner would confide to Friedrich Nietzsche that, "though Greek mythology and history were my chief attractions, I also felt drawn to the study of the Greek language itself with a power that made me almost unruly in my shirking of the Latin."[22] Similar comments in *Mein Leben* support this claim. Wagner indicates that, as a young student, he was "particularly attracted by Greek, because the stories from Greek mythology seized my imagination so strongly that I wanted to imagine their heroic figures speaking to me in their original tongue, in order to satisfy my longing for complete familiarity with them."[23] Roman history and the Latin language, it is clear, never had the same effect on him.

Despite the nonchalance with which Wagner approached Latin, he did demonstrate greater attraction to it than to another discipline he might be expected to have admired: music. In the "Autobiographical Sketch," first published in 1843, Wagner says that music "…was quite a secondary matter [in his early education]: Greek, Latin, Mythology, and Ancient History were my principal studies."[24] These subjects laid the intellectual foundation that was to shape his point of view for the rest of his life. Even years later, Wagner could say that "... people were amazed ... to hear me talk with particular vivacity about Greek literature and history, but never about music."[25] In his mind at least, reading the classics gave Wagner the basis for his most serious thoughts. As an all-consuming interest, music would arise only later.

The "Autobiographical Sketch" provides a few details about Wagner's early education in the classics. He claims that "I passed in my school for a good head '*in litteris*;' even in the 'Third Form' I had translated the first twelve books of the *Odyssey*."[26] This statement is elaborated a bit in *Mein Leben*. There he claims that, even as a child, he had produced "a *written* translation of twelve books"[27] of the *Odyssey*. This particular boast attracted the full intensity of Wallace's ire. Wallace dismissed Wagner's statement entirely, labeling it "an Homeric—and Wagnerian myth."[28] The reason for Wallace's incredulity was his refusal to believe that a thirteen-year-old boy, "without a hint of early training in Greek, could in a few weeks master the special idiom of Homer,"[29] thus translating more than six thousand lines of dactylic hexameter in approximately six months. Such a feat, Wallace suggests, would be roughly the same as a young speaker of a foreign language translating the first seven books of *Paradise Lost*.

Nevertheless, despite Wallace's claim, it must be remembered that minds far less capable than Wagner's achieved at least this level of proficiency in the German schools of the mid-nineteenth century. In his 1899 study of secondary education in Germany, James Earl Russell noted that, during the very period of Wagner's early education, there was a steady shift in emphasis away from mathematics to the study of classical literature.

> After the entrance of Johannes Schulze into the Education Department in 1818, Latin was again gradually advanced to first place. A plan of supplementary reading followed in the *Gymnasium* of Dantzsic (*sic*) was officially recommended

to all directors, the time of mathematics being soon after-
ward reduced a half in order to make it possible. In this
way the schools were able to read the following works [in
their original languages]: 'The entire *Iliad* and *Odyssey*, several dramas of Æschylus, Sophocles and Euripides, four
books of Herodotus, two books of Thucydides, the *Anaba-
sis* [of Xenophon], several of Plutarch's *Lives*, Demosthenes'
Oration on the Crown, Plato's *Phædo*, all of Vergil except
the *Georgics*, Horace complete, Ovid's *Metamorphoses* complete and selections from other poets, Cæsar's *Gallic War*
and *Civil War* complete, five or six books of Livy, all of
Sallust, Tacitus' *Annals*, many of Cicero's *Orations* and *de
amicitia, de senectute, de officiis, de diviniatione* and *de
natura deorum.*' The speaking of Latin, which was in common use in the schools at the beginning of the century,
gradually fell into disuse. In 1834, however, it was ordered
that the final examination in Latin should be conducted in
Latin.[30]

The remarkable complexity of this secondary-school reading list—
a requirement so daunting that Wallace dismissed it as impossible—is
supported numerous times by contemporary witnesses. Hugo
Münsterberg said that the reading required for successful passage of
the *Abiturientenexamen* (for entry into a university) meant that if any
student "in Dartmouth or Amherst takes his bachelor's degree with
that knowledge in mathematics, history, geography, literature, Latin,
Greek, French, and physics which we had on leaving [the Gymna-
sium], he is sure to graduate with honors."[31] Friedrich Paulsen likewise reports that "Amongst the requirements for [successful completion of the *Abiturientenexamen*] was . . ., in the first place and above all,
a complete mastery of the classical languages. In Greek, candidates
had to show by 'unseen' translations—even of dramatic dialogues—
that they were able to read Greek fluently; a written translation from
the German was further to testify to their proficiency in Greek grammar."[32] Even Stefan Zweig, who bitterly opposed the "treadmill" memo-

rization of nineteenth-century education in Germany and Austria, was compelled to give it its due. A "'general education' required French, English, Italian—the 'living' languages—together with classical Greek and Latin in addition to the regular school work—that is, five languages plus geometry, physics, and the other subjects. It was more than too much. . . ."[33]

Wagner completed his secondary school education during the very period when these expectations existed. Although his plans would later change, it was his intention as a young man to continue his education at one of the German universities. As a result, his extensive reading of Homer in Greek, while impressive, was neither unparalleled nor particularly rare. Most of his fellow students would do at least as much translation of Greek verse perhaps a year or two after him. Like any student whose enthusiasm for a single subject causes him to avoid others, Wagner was merely devoting the attention to Greek that his peers were dividing among all the other subjects of their curriculum.

To some extent, Wallace's skepticism towards Wagner's achievement may be accounted for by his misunderstanding of German pedagogical terms. Both English and German schools in the nineteenth century classified early education into six forms. Nevertheless, the English and the Germans numbered these forms *in the opposite order*. The "First Form" at that time (and still today) the lowest level in an English school was equivalent to the expression (*Ober-Prima*) for the *highest* level of a German gymnasium in Wagner's day. Wallace, therefore, made assumptions about the academic preparation of students in the "Third Form" (*Tertia*) that were simply not valid for Wagner. The future composer had completed at least one additional year of training in the fundamentals of the classical languages than Wallace had supposed. Though the biographer described Wagner as "without a hint of early training in Greek," Wagner had by the time he reached the "Third Form" mastered the language's basic grammar and the reading of simple prose.

Wagner remained in the *Tertia* for twenty-seven weeks at the Kreuzschule in Dresden. Reading the first twelve books of the *Odyssey* during this time would have involved a translation of fewer than fifty

lines a night, five times a week. Despite Wallace's misleading statements, the grammar and vocabulary of Homer are not particularly
difficult. Even today, students of Greek often begin reading Homer
with only a year or two of linguistic study, and several major series of
textbooks *introduce* ancient Greek by having students read the first
twelve books of the *Odyssey*.[34] In light of the amount of linguistic mastery required by German secondary schools of the nineteenth century,
a translation of fifty lines a night would have been well within the
abilities of most students.

Moreover, there can be little doubt of Wagner's dedication to the
task. Even Wallace himself admits that, when C.F. Glasenapp examined the Kreuzschule archives, he found a school record "inform[ing]
us of [Wagner's] diligence."[35] It should come as no surprise, therefore,
that the composer—an individual who all his life could perform prodi-
gious feats of labor whenever a challenge captured his interest—applied himself with vigor to reading Homer as a young student. This
was his opportunity to learn about Odysseus' encounter with the Cy-
clops, his seduction by Circe, his journey to the underworld, his temp-
tation by the Sirens, his passage through Scylla and Charybdis, and his
dalliance with Calypso . . . all episodes that occur in the first twelve
books of the *Odyssey*.

Wagner's Later Study of the Classics

After spending five years at the Kreuzschule in Dresden, Wagner returned to Leipzig where he enrolled at the Nicolaischule. There he was
disappointed to learn that he would be demoted to a lower form. "My
disgust at having to lay aside Homer . . . in order to take up again the
easier Greek prose writers, was indescribable and wounded me
deeply."[36] Despite his frustration, Wagner gradually worked his way
back to the upper forms. He claims that he produced an ode celebrating the Greek War for Independence *in classical Greek*,[37] a far more
difficult task than his mere translation of Homer. This time, however,
Wagner's claim should be approached with some skepticism. Two years
later when he left the Nicolaischule, he did so under a cloud because it

had become apparent that his teachers would not recommend him for graduation. Wagner's sudden lack of success seems unlikely if he was making the progress in Greek he later attributed to this very period. In any case, he sought the help of tutors, hoping to qualify for admission to the older, but less prestigious, Thomasschule. As a way of continuing his academic preparation, he "took private lessons in Greek from a scholar and read Sophocles with him. For a time, I hoped that this noble subject would reawaken my desire to learn the Greek language thoroughly; but it was all in vain: I hadn't found the right teacher; and besides, the living room in which we pursued our studies looked out upon a tannery, whose disgusting smell affected my nerves badly enough to spoil Sophocles and Greek for me completely."[38]

A similar effort to study Greek tragedy, this time with his uncle Adolf, enjoyed little more success. "My uncle was delighted to find in me a very willing listener for his readings of classical tragedies, having himself begotten a translation of *Oedipus the King*."[39] Unfortunately, Wagner's youthful devotion to ancient literature had its limits. "I remember once, when the two of us were alone and he was sitting at his lectern reading from a Greek tragedy, that, far from being annoyed when I fell fast asleep, he afterwards pretended not to have noticed it."[40] It is apparent that Wagner's attention was now being drawn in other directions. The nature of these new interests became apparent while he was still enrolled at the Thomasschule and then while he was briefly a student at Leipzig University. It was at this time that Wagner began to consider the possibility of a career in music. Outwardly, Wagner's devotion to classical literature continued even as he began to study composition. In an important examination of Wagner's intellectual life, L.J. Rather noted that, as late as Wagner's selection as Hofkapellmeister in Dresden in 1843, the books in his library "encompassed the cultural heritage of Western Europe. Homer, Pindar, Aeschylus, Sophocles, Euripides, Aristophanes, Xenophon, Horace, and Vergil have their places, at times in several different translations."[41] When Wagner fled Dresden in the uprisings of 1848, he abandoned this library to his creditors. By the time of his death, however, he had assembled a new library in Bayreuth consisting of copies of

Homer's *Iliad* and *Odyssey*, together with Anacreon, Pindar, Aeschylus, Sophocles, Euripides, Aristophanes, Lucian, Thucydides, Xenophon, Plato, Aristotle, Polybius, Plutarch, Diogenes Laertius, and Pausanias. Of the Latin authors, we find the comic poets Plautus and Terence, the historians Sallust, Suetonius, and Tacitus, and the poets Lucretius, Catullus, Vergil, Horace, Ovid, Tibullus, Propertius, Persius, Martial, and Juvenal, together with Caesar, Cicero, Seneca, Epictetus, Pliny, and Marcus Aurelius (in Latin, German, or both).[42]

Moreover, it must not be assumed[43] that Wagner was a mere collector of books. He read everything he collected, reread many works frequently, and discussed his favorite authors with members of his family and friends. Cosima Wagner's diaries include long lists of authors that her husband talked about with her or whose works they read aloud during their evenings together. "Homer—Sophocles—Aeschylus—Xenophon—Sappho—Plato—Aristophanes—Euripides—Thucydides—Plutarch—Herodotus—Demosthenes—Ovid—Lucretius" as well as "The Edda—The Volsunga Saga—The Nibelungen Lied."[44] The degree to which Wagner reflected on what he read may be judged from his frequent references to classical authors, ancient gods, and early historical figures appearing throughout his letters and essays. In his formal education, Wagner had come to view the classics as a model for all serious thought. As he turned to writing his own works, he wanted these creations, too, to have such complexity and depth that they could not be quickly admired and quickly set aside. Like the epics and tragedies he knew as a boy, Wagner's own productions were designed to be savored slowly. He wanted his music dramas to be "classics" in the best sense of the term: works that would stand the test of time, providing ever greater pleasure as appreciative audiences gained greater familiarity with them, and yielding new levels of insight and understanding with each new encounter.

Once Wagner's formal schooling ended, his contact with classical literature took a new turn. As his daily exposure to the Greek language ceased, he discovered (like countless others both before his time and since) that his ability to read Greek texts began to decline. As a result, he grew more and more dependent on reading his favorite authors in translation.

Reflecting on the books he assembled for his Dresden library, Wagner noted that "I took the easier way with classical antiquity and purchased those translations that have themselves become classics, because I had already found in perusing Homer, whom I bought in the original Greek, that I would have to count on more leisure than I could plausibly expect from my conducting duties if I wanted to find more time to polish up my former knowledge of the Greek language."[45] By the time he served as Hofkapellmeister in Dresden, Wagner had been away from the active study of Greek for thirteen years. Though his facility with the classical languages had declined, he retained his love for ancient literature and art, and enjoyed many of the other benefits that came from a classical education: he had developed a great degree of mental discipline, a broad knowledge of the humanities, a capacity to remember impressive amounts of detail, an interest in tracing developments to their earliest causes, a concern for the sweeping patterns of history, and a recognition that masterpieces are created, less frequently from blinding flashes of genius, than from long hours of infinite patience.

Periodically as an adult, Wagner would attempt to revive his acquaintance with the Greek language. Not all of these efforts resulted from his interest in the classical world itself, however. In 1847, when Wagner was 34 years old, he began a program of linguistic studies that drew him to the *Nibelungenlied* and, ultimately, to all the literary sources of the *Ring*. "In order to approach the real goal of these studies, Old and Middle High German, I began anew with Greek antiquity and was soon filled with such overwhelming enthusiasm for it that whenever I could be brought to talk, I would only show signs of animation if I could force the conversation around to that sphere."[46] From the very origins of the *Ring*, therefore, mediæval Germany and classical Greece were fused in Wagner's mind. In order to find his Siegfried, he knew that he must return to Achilles. The walls of Valhalla could only be built, Wagner realized, from stones originally mined in ancient Argos.

Wagner's reading of Greek literature continued even as he was completing final work on *Lohengrin*. By this time, the concept of the *Ring* had taken embryonic form. As a result, it was Greek tragedy—especially the grand, connected trilogies of Aeschylus—that attracted Wagner most. Nevertheless, tragedy alone did not account for *all* of his reading. The other texts that interested Wagner at this time provide an important insight into what the composer believed he was gaining from a study of classical antiquity.

> For the first time I now mastered Aeschylus with mature feeling and understanding. Droysen's eloquent commentaries in particular helped to bring the intoxicating vision of Attic tragedy so clearly before me that I could see the *Oresteia* with my mind's eye as if actually being performed, and its impact on me was indescribable. There was nothing to equal the exalted emotion evoked in me by *Agamemnon;* and to the close of *The Eumenides* I remained in a state of transport from which I have never really returned to become fully reconciled with modern literature. My ideas about the significance of drama, and especially of the theater itself, were decisively moulded by these impressions. After working my way through the other tragedians, I reached Aristophanes. When I had spent a morning industriously working on the music for *Lohengrin,* I used to slink away into the depths of the shrubbery in the part of the garden allocated to me to take refuge from the increasingly obtrusive summer heat; there I would read, to my boundless delight, the plays of Aristophanes, after having been introduced by *The Birds* to the world of this ribald darling of the Graces, as he boldly called himself. Side by side with him, I read the best of Plato's dialogues, and from the *Symposium* in particular gained such an intimate insight into the wonderful beauty of Greek life that I felt myself palpa-

bly more at home in ancient Athens than in any circum-
stances afforded by the modern world.[47]

Perhaps more than any other statement in Wagner, this passage
from *Mein Leben* summarizes the composer's view of the classics. In
the course of one long paragraph, three important principles emerge.
First, Wagner explains that reading the *Oresteia* deepened his understanding of not merely the *plots* of ancient tragedy, the way that *character* is developed, or the techniques of advancing *themes* and images, but
also the "*significance* of drama" itself. What this phrase meant to Wagner
was that classical tragedy, more than any other form of art, exemplified
the role that literature played in advancing an author's social agenda.
Classical literature thus fulfilled a major objective of reformers in the
Romantic Age. In their own time, according to Wagner, the classics
established a form of cultural identity that transcended class, wealth,
and political party. In Wagner's view, the works of Aeschylus, Sophocles,
and Euripides were significant, not only because they contained important philosophical ideas, but also because they conveyed these ideas
to the Athenian community *as a whole*.

Despite the divisiveness of ancient Athens, Wagner regarded tragic
festivals as a time when aristocrat sat elbow-to-elbow with commoner,
when the humblest peasant had access to the same cultural enrichment
as the most elevated priest of Dionysus. The value of tragedy, Wagner
believed, was its ability to transform Athens, for a few days each year,
into a harmonious state. Even if this idyllic situation could not last, it
nevertheless remained important because it demonstrated to the community that widespread unity was possible. As an added advantage, it
achieved this goal by providing examples of high moral achievement
for the masses to emulate and by encouraging individuals to leave behind the banality of their day-to-day lives through contemplation of
lofty, spiritual issues.

Wagner wanted his own works to unite nineteenth-century German society in the same way that he believed Attic tragedy had united
fifth-century Athens. In the patchwork of German states that were

struggling for unity, Wagner imagined a form of drama that would provide a focal point for restored German identity.

> I found [my model] in the theater of ancient Athens, where its walls were thrown open on none but special, sacred feast-days, where the taste of Art was coupled with the celebration of a religious rite in which the most illustrious members of the State themselves took part as poets and performers, to appear like priests before the assembled populace of field and city; a populace filled with such high awaitings from the sublimeness of the artwork to be set before it, that a Sophocles, an Æschylus could set before the Folk the deepest-meaning of all poems, assured of their understanding.[48]

In addition to seeing ancient tragedy as a model for music drama itself, therefore, Wagner also saw parallels between classical drama and the special status of the Festspielhaus, the role that the Wagner-Societies would play in promoting his artistic vision, and the fusion of art, folk belief, and religion that formed the basis of *Die Meistersinger*, *Parsifal*, and the *Ring*.

Second, Wagner traced his belief that drama had an important social function both to Greek tragedy and to the *comedy* of that time. Wagner had always been particularly fond of Athenian Old Comedy. Aristophanes was one of his favorite authors and he referred to him as "the greatest of Greek geniuses."[49] Copies of Aristophanes' plays were found in both Wagner's Dresden and Bayreuth libraries. Cosima reports that Wagner frequently spent evenings reading entire plays of Aristophanes aloud, always careful, however, to omit the most salacious passages.[50] During the Franco-Prussian War, Wagner even tried his hand at an Aristophanic satire entitled *Eine Kapitulation: Lustspiel in antiker Manier* ("A Capitulation: Comic Play in the Ancient Style"). Some early editions of this work were published under the pseudonym "Aristop Hanes."[51] In the play (a work that Wagner once hoped Liszt would set to music), Victor Hugo appears onstage as a character, with

Offenbach taking the role that Aristophanes himself assigned to Euripides: chief object of ridicule.

What attracted Wagner to Aristophanes, aside from sheer delight in the plays themselves, was the comic author's candor about his didactic purposes. In his earliest surviving comedy, Aristophanes described his literary function as "neither to flatter nor to praise my audience but to teach them what they need to know" (*Acharnians* l. 658). In the *Frogs*, he comments that "It is proper for the sacred chorus to advise and teach useful things" (ll. 686-87). This moralizing function was precisely what Wagner believed to be missing from the literature of his own day. Opera—and, to Wagner's mind, this particularly meant grand opera—too frequently delighted the senses without educating the mind. That composers like Offenbach and Meyerbeer could create grandiose works without considering the moral impact of their creations was reprehensible to Wagner. He envisioned a society in which all forms of art—not only tragedies like the *Oresteia* and *Oedipus*, but even the lightest and most popular fare enjoyed by the public—improved society and edified its citizens. He believed that, for Aristophanes no less than for Aeschylus, drama had once held great civic and moral importance. Inspired by these models, Wagner set himself the goal of writing a didactic, socially significant form of drama.

Third, Wagner states that classical literature has value in the modern world because it exposes readers to "the wonderful beauty of Greek life" (*die wunderbare Schönheit des griechischen Lebens*). Appropriately, Wagner mentions this idea in connection with the *Symposium*, the Platonic dialogue that dealt with the nature of love (a repeated theme in Wagnerian drama). The *Symposium* takes the form of a protracted conversation and debate, a form of communication known all too well by the composer's friends. Plato's theme in the *Symposium* is that all types of love are the product of a soul's attraction to beauty—physical, intellectual, or spiritual beauty—and that, in the end, "the beautiful" is another name for "the good itself." As individuals grow in an understanding of both love and life, their desire to approach ever purer forms of beauty intensifies. Finally, the most successful philosophers achieve love of "the good itself" or, we might say, of God. With a style that perfectly complements his content, Plato develops this argument in a dramatic form that is, in and of itself, an illustration of the beauty that his characters are discussing in the text. Each argument is perfectly balanced by its counter-argument in a structure so symmetrically perfect that, despite its almost mathematical proportions, it never becomes static. Each speaker's interpretation of beauty builds upon the last, subtly illustrating the process by which the mind advances through philosophical inquiry.

In this way, Plato's *Symposium*, like Aeschylus' *Oresteia,* provided Wagner with an important lesson about how the form and function of great literature should work together. A work's structure should *demonstrate* for the reader the same themes that the text was *explaining*. It is not enough to discuss lofty ideas. The true artist is the individual who can illustrate those ideas in the structure of the drama itself. Only such an individual can lead an audience to experience emotionally what is being taught intellectually. It was thus a combination of Classical ideals and Romantic passion that, Wagner believed, the drama of his day needed in order to transform society. Only through such a fusion could a new form of art emerge that had the same effect on Germany that the works of Aeschylus, Aristophanes, and Plato once had on the ancient Greeks.

Wagner's Attitude Towards Classical Education

In nearly all of Wagner's essays, study of the ancient world is so celebrated that it comes as something of a shock to find one passage in which he seems to be disparaging the very same type of classical education that he elsewhere admires. When Friedrich Nietzsche's *The Birth of Tragedy from the Spirit of Music* was first published in 1872, Ulrich von Wilamowitz-Möllendorff—by far the most eminent classicist of his day and still regarded as the founder of modern philology—criticized Nietzsche's scholarship and wrote a reply. Wilamowitz denounced the highly speculative nature of *The Birth of Tragedy* with a tone so condescending that it prompted Wagner to rise to Nietzsche's defense. In an open letter dated June 12th, 1872, Wagner criticized the emphasis that German education had come to place on classical philology, suggesting that his own intellectual development had occurred *in spite of*, not because of, the hours he devoted to learning Greek. Classical philology has no real value to the modern intellectual, Wagner argued. "[E]veryone among us who lays claim to the Muses' favour, our whole artistic and poetic world in fact, jogs on without the slightest recourse to philology. . . . [T]he Philology of nowadays exerts no jot of influence on the general state of German culture; while the theologic faculty supplies us with parsons and prelates (*Consistorialräthe*), the juristic with lawyers and judges, the medical with doctors—all practically useful citizens—Philology gives us nothing but philologists, of use to no one but themselves."[52] Even worse, as far as Wagner was concerned, it was not merely that classicists contributed nothing to society; they actually *knew* nothing at all and preserved only a pretense of knowledge. Teachers of classical philology, Wagner said, maintained their position through the sheerest *illusion* that they had a vast store of expertise. In fact, they were charlatans, interested only in protecting their privileged positions. Wagner compared classicists to Hindu Brahmins. "[O]ne therefore may await from them a sacred word from time to time. And indeed we are awaiting it: we await the man who for once shall step from out this wondrous sphere and tell us laymen, without learned terms and terrible quotations, *what* it is that the initiate perceive behind the veil of their incomprehensible researches, and whether it is worth the trouble of supporting so expensive a caste."[53]

This was a remarkable change of attitude for a man who, in *Mein Leben*, had presented classical education as the cornerstone of all his later development, describing his own "ideas about the significance of drama" as "decisively moulded by" classical literature. What caused Wagner to condemn so vehemently the very sort of linguistic education that he elsewhere claimed—and in the future would claim again—had shaped his entire approach to drama? What caused Wagner to turn his back on a type of education that, as he admits in the very same letter to Nietzsche, he had so recently championed, calling neglect of the classics "by our artists and writers" a source of "progressive deterioration of our national culture"?[54] Certainly, much of Wagner's anger may be traced to the tone of Wilamowitz's own attack. The classical scholar was merciless in his scorn for Nietzsche's work, a book that had lionized Wagner himself. Moreover, Wilamowitz was unsparing in derisive references to Wagner's "so-called poetry."[55] Wagner, of course, was not a man to suffer attacks upon himself or those close to him passively. At least part of his contempt for classical philology in his open letter to Nietzsche, therefore, must be traced simply to Wilamowitz's position as a philologist.

Nevertheless, it must be recognized that another reason for Wagner's rejection of classical scholarship in this letter is that he was, at the very time that he wrote this essay, developing his own highly *romantic* view of classical civilization. Wagner's romantic classicism, rooted in the sentiment and outlook of the nineteenth century, was diametrically opposed to the scholarly approach of Wilamowitz and other academics. Their discipline had its origin in the neo-classicism of the late eighteenth century. Though his period of historical interest was the same, Wagner had a perspective that was derived from contemporary society. As but one example, the philological method advocated by Wilamowitz required long and detailed study of historical linguistics, history, and the transmission of texts, disciplines that, it was believed, would improve a scholar's understanding of literature and other written material. To Wilamowitz, an appreciation of Aeschylus' *Oresteia* involved far more than reading the text and could not be accomplished at all if one merely read the text in translation. The scholar trained in philology was expected to have intimate knowledge of the dialects used in ancient Greek tragedy and to couple that knowledge with long study of Greek prosody, the cult practices of Greek religion, the historical context in which the *Oresteia* was first produced, the dramatic festivals of the ancient Athenians, the textual problems resulting from the transmission of Greek manuscripts, and the philosophical speculations of scholars during the mid-fifth century B.C. The philologist's method was, therefore, focused on recovering the *past*. It was the "science" (as that term was used in the nineteenth century) of devoting all the tools at one's disposal towards reconstructing the language, thought, history, and beliefs of a specific moment in history.

Wagner's romantic classicism, on the other hand, was a completely different type of intellectual pursuit. Rather than focusing on the past, its ultimate aim was the present. Wagner regarded the texts and ideas of antiquity, not as ends in themselves, but as useful models for transforming contemporary society into a more harmonious community. All the minutiae of a philological education—the study of particles and participles, paleography and epigraphy, sequence of tense and sequence of moods, epistolary aorists and all the rest—simply bored Wagner. He felt that such arcane pursuits distracted one from the only matter that was really important: *What do classical texts mean and why does this matter to us?* To denounce Nietzsche, as Wilamowitz had done, because he had committed a few errors of detail was, in Wagner's view, greatly to misunderstand why one studied classical literature in the first place. The enlightened individual read the classics, not because he wanted to gain the sort of abstruse knowledge that would allow him to read still more of the classics, but because he wanted to understand life. To Wagner's romantic spirit, the classics existed as models for later ages to build upon in their efforts to create a more perfect society.

With its emphasis on reform, Wagner's approach to classicism shared an outlook with several of the utopian movements then becoming common in western Europe. Yet, while other revolutionaries took inspiration from religious principles, plans of economic reform, or schemes for futuristic development, Wagner's brave new world of harmony, justice, and social equity was to be built on the model of classical Greece. This did not mean that Wagner thought it sufficient simply to imitate ancient society and copy its forms of art. The form and meaning of classical literature would be Wagner's starting point, but that form and meaning could certainly be surpassed. "Indeed, the foolish restoration of a sham Greek mode of art has been attempted already,—for what will our artists not attempt . . .? But nothing better than an inane patchwork could ever come of it. . . . No, we do not wish to revert to Greekdom; for what the Greeks knew not, and, knowing not, came by their downfall: that know *we*."[56]

Wagner believed that the downfall of the Greeks, in culture if not in history, occurred because they permitted the best feature of their early art—its unity—to degenerate into a plethora of unrelated skills. Aeschylus, Wagner argued, achieved lasting social importance because he created tragic cycles that combined every form of art known in his day. His successors failed because they had no interest in vast connected cycles like the *Oresteia* or the *Prometheus* trilogy but were content to stage three unrelated works. Even worse, they allowed each of the arts to develop in a vacuum, unaffected by the trends occurring in other areas of cultural development. "The Drama separated into its component parts; rhetoric, sculpture, painting, music, &c., forsook the ranks in which they had moved in unison before; each one to take its own way, and in lonely self-sufficiency to pursue its own development."[57] When the union of art disappeared from Greek society, tragedy could no longer be a source of unity for the *polis*. After all, Aeschylus' trilogies had not only brought together individuals from all social classes, they had also united individuals of all tastes—lovers of dance and painting, devotees of music and drama, proponents of philosophy, rhetoric, and the new religious cults—providing them all with a single, shared experience. Once Aeschylus had died, Greek art was reduced to scattered pursuits. Rather than inspiring all society at once, art became merely another trade, valued only by connoisseurs.

From his reading, Wagner had learned that, in the early history of tragedy, a wealthy individual was chosen each year to serve as *choregos*, the representative of the city who was taxed directly to defray the cost of dramatic festivals. By means of this limited tax, the aristocracy helped pay for the entertainment and edification of the masses. Nevertheless, with the growing disunity of the arts, the nobility turned their backs on civic duty, devoting their wealth, not to the commonweal, but to amassing private collections. "Each one of these dissevered arts, nursed and luxuriously tended for the entertainment of the rich, has filled the world to overflowing with its products; in each, great minds have brought forth marvels; but the one true Art has not been born again, either in or since the Renaissance. The perfect Art-work, the great united utterance of a free and lovely public life, the *Drama, Tragedy,*—howsoever great the poets who have here and there indited tragedies—is not yet born again: for reason that it cannot be *re-born*, but must be *born anew*."[58] Wagner believed that the artwork he could "bear anew" would be Aeschylean in that it would contain once again a perfect blending of all the arts. In addition, it would be Aristophanic in that it would seek to edify the populace rather than merely entertain them. And it would be Platonic because it would contain a perfect harmony between the themes expressed in the artwork and the beauty of the *form* through which these ideas were expressed.

The result is that there was a direct connection between Wagner's romantic classicism and his concept of the *Gesamtkunstwerk*, the "total work of art" that embodied all forms of artistic expression in a single poetic vision. Wagner believed that the *Gesamtkunstwerk*, like early tragedy, would unite society by appealing to individuals of widely varied cultural interests. As a result, he saw his reform of art as leading directly to a reform of society, much as the tragic festivals of the Athenians had, he imagined, influenced the relationships between citizens in other spheres of life. "As we marvel still to-day that 30,000 Greeks could once assemble to listen with the utmost interest to tragedies like those of Æschylus, I also asked what could have been the means of bringing forth effects so extraordinary; and I discovered that they lay precisely in the association of *all the arts* to form the one, the true great Artwork. . . . Thus my object was to shew the possibility of an artwork in which the highest and profoundest, that the human mind can grasp, should be imparted to purely human fellow-feeling in a way the most intelligible to its simplest faculties of reception, and so plainly and convincingly as to need no reflective Criticism to play the go-between. This work I called: '*the Artwork of the Future.*'"[59] *Der Ring des Nibelungen* was to be Wagner's first creation of this "Artwork of the Future." Inspired by his study of the classical past, Wagner chose a classical form to advance the highly romantic social goals of his own day.

✳ ✳ ✳

"The study of Greek civilization," the great baritone and scholar Dietrich Fischer-Dieskau once said, "which helped shape young Wagner and made him seem right for a career in classics, had a negligible effect on his life's work."[60] In light of Wagner's own writings, however, it now seems that both of Fischer-Dieskau's conclusions need to be reconsidered. While Wagner, like many others of his generation, was immersed in classical languages and literature as a young man—and while he continued to reread many authors in translation throughout his life—he never really seemed "right for a career in classics." Wagner's interest in classical literature was different in kind and focus from that of the classicists in his own day and from that of most classical scholars ever since. Unlike Wilamowitz—unlike even Nietzsche himself—Wagner never developed the vast array of linguistic, historical, textual, and literary skills that were the nineteenth-century philologist's stock-in-trade. What interested Wagner was not the origin and transmission of the classical texts themselves, but how these texts could serve as a model for the art, literature, and society of later periods.

In one sense, Wagner's interest in ancient literature and society was not what would nowadays be called a "classical" or "philological" approach at all, but rather a "great books" approach. Despite Wagner's early claims of linguistic mastery, virtually all the classical literature he read as an adult was read in translation. Nowhere in the many volumes of his prose works are there any passages to indicate that he retained more than a superficial acquaintance with the Greek language. He never cites long examples in Greek, demonstrates no particular knowledge of Greek grammar, and rarely uses the technical terms of Greek linguistic study. Wagner's youthful familiarity with the classical languages, unpracticed for many years, had simply ceased to be an active skill. All that remained from his years of early study were the *impressions* that the classical world had made on him.

Nevertheless, there is no reason to doubt that Wagner's lifelong affection for the classics was sincere and deep. By the 1850s, he was familiar with most major works of classical literature. References to the Greek gods, as well as to important authors and historical figures, appear on page after page of his essays. There is abundant evidence that his conversation frequently turned to classical literature and that even his most learned friends were impressed by the breadth of his knowledge. Wagner knew the classics because he, like many of his contemporaries, had been thoroughly immersed in them in school. Yet he retained this acquaintance, as many of his contemporaries did not, through repeated exposure to literature in translation, commentaries, and discussions of classical works by other authors.

In order to understand Wagner's classicism, therefore, it is not enough to illustrate the effect that classical literature had on the *plot* of the *Ring* or its depiction of the Norse gods. The real impact of the classics on Wagner must be found in the way that ancient literature caused him to see the relationship between form and meaning in drama. As we have noted, there is a straight line of development leading from Wagner's study of Greek literature to his discovery of the *Gesamtkunstwerk*. The "Artwork of the Future" was to be Wagner's first strike in a battle to create a new, more highly unified society. For this reason, the true impact of Wagner's classical background must be sought in the way the composer viewed the union of the arts in his dramas, the way in which he believed that a "total work of art" could advance a single, socially significant theme.

In the *Poetics* (1450 a 9), Aristotle stated that all dramas consist of six constituent elements: plot, character, speech, thought, spectacle, and song. If art were once again to become unified, Wagner's classical education taught him that these were the six elements that would have to be focused on the same thematic goal. Each of them would have to function identically, relate harmoniously to all the others, and combine to advance a single artistic goal. In order to find the true effect of Wagner's romantic classicism, we must seek it individually in each of Aristotle's six constituent elements of drama, looking for a single, common thread.

CHAPTER 2

Plot

Classical Form and Meaning in the
Structure of the *Ring*

*Best of all things is water; but gold, like a gleaming fire by
night, outshines all pride of wealth besides.*

—Pindar[61]

Aristotle introduces the *Poetics* with the words "Let us start our discussion following the model of nature herself: with first principles" (1447 a 1). For Aristotle, the first principles of dramatic construction involved a play's overall form, chiefly its plot. Plot (*mythos*) was defined by the philosopher as "the arrangement of incidents" (1450 a 8) and, as such, was the "greatest" and "most important" element of tragedy. "Tragedy," he contended, "does not serve to represent people but *action*" (1450 a 12). For this reason, it is possible to imagine a tragedy without character development—and certainly possible to imagine a tragedy without music, spectacle, or any other element of staging—but Aristotle regarded it as impossible for a work to be worthy of the name "tragedy" if it had no plot (1450 a 15).

Wagner intuitively agreed with Aristotle's theory of dramatic construction. Each of his completed music dramas (and several additional works that were planned but never developed) began with a sketch or prose outline of the work's plot. In 1848, when Wagner first conceived the work that would one day be known as *Der Ring des Nibelungen*, he began his sketch with an image of darkness.

The Womb of Night and Death once spawned a race that dwells in Nibelheim. There in gloomy clefts and caverns they are known as Nibelungen.[62]

This introduction to Wagner's mythic world—with its birth of Nibelheim from the night's primeval womb—still bears the traces of an important source for the *Ring*: the Icelandic myth of creation as retold by Snorri Sturluson in the *Prose Edda*.

In the beginning not anything existed, there was no sand nor sea nor cooling waves; earth was unknown and [in] heaven above only Open Gap was. . . . It was many æons before the earth was created that Niflheim was made. . . . [Far to the south, in Muspellheim,] it is light and hot and that region flames and burns so that those who do not belong to it and whose native land it is not, cannot endure it.[63]

At least on one level, therefore, Wagner saw this prose sketch as a way of providing dramatic form to Sturluson's poetic image. At the same time, he felt himself free to modify that image as much as he liked, making it reflect more completely the romantic sensibilities of his nineteenth-century audience. The *Prose Edda's* Open Gap was thus transformed into an image suggestive of both the beginning of life (the womb) and its end (night and death). This vivid tableau would have been a memorable way for Wagner's proposed drama to begin. But four years later, when the composer's original plan was rewritten to become the libretto for *Das Rheingold*, all reference to the Womb of Night and Death vanished. In its place, Wagner described the world as emerging from a faint and eerie glow.

At the bottom of the Rhine. A greenish twilight [*Dämmerung*], brighter at the top, darker towards the bottom. Near the surface, waters surge restlessly from right to left. Further down, waves dissolve into increasingly fine mist. At the bottom, for the distance of about a man's height, there does not appear to be any water at all but rather a thin fog like that which spreads upon the ground at night.[64]

In this stage description, every bit of Wagner's connection to his Scandinavian sources has been removed. Rather than arising out of a yawning void, the world has been created out of light, mist, and extraordinary colors. The composer, it is clear, had begun to rethink the opening to his dramatic cycle.

As Wagner turned from text to music, he moved even further from the images of his original prose sketch. Even in the libretto for *Das Rheingold*, for instance, aside from locating the opening scene at the bottom of the Rhine, Wagner had given no indication that both the origin and the ultimate destruction of the world were to be found in *water*. In fact, a close reading of the text gives one the impression that the world was created out of *light*. Nor, apart from the barest hint provided by Woglinde's initial utterance, is there any indication of a "primal substance," a mysterious element from which matter will arise at the beginning of *Das Rheingold* and to which it will return at the end of *Götterdämmerung*. The question must be asked, therefore: When did Wagner first incorporate these ideas into the *Ring*? More importantly, why did he find it necessary to do so, taking his work in such a fundamentally different direction from both the legend as it was presented in Norse mythology and his original plan for the drama?

The Vision of La Spezia

Wagner's own answer to these questions is well known. In a famous passage of *Mein Leben*, he suggests that the opening to *Das Rheingold* arose from a moment of almost mystical inspiration. Wagner says that in 1853, frustrated by the failure of others to appreciate his artistic plans, he sought refuge in a trip to Italy. There, in the coastal town of La Spezia, on the evening of September 5th, Wagner claims to have had a vision. The "vision of La Spezia," according to most biographers, inspired Wagner to give *Das Rheingold* the prelude that it has today.

After a sleepless and feverish night, I forced myself to undertake a long walk the following day . . . . Returning that afternoon, I stretched out dead-tired on a hard couch, awaiting the long-desired onset of sleep. It did not come; instead, I sank into a kind of somnambulistic state, in which I suddenly had the feeling of being immersed in rapidly flowing water. Its rushing soon resolved itself for me into the musical sound of the chord of E flat major, resounding in persistent broken chords; these in turn transformed themselves into melodic figurations of increasing motion, yet the E flat major triad never changed, and seemed by its continuance to impart infinite significance to the element in which I was sinking. I awoke in sudden terror from this trance, feeling as though the waves were crashing high above my head. I recognized at once that the orchestral prelude to *Das Rheingold*, long dormant within me but up to that moment inchoate, had at last been revealed; and I also saw immediately precisely how it was with me: the vital flood would come from within me, and not from without. I immediately decided to return to Zürich and begin setting my vast poem to music.[65]

The problem with "the vision of La Spezia" is that it simply may not have happened. At least, it may not have happened exactly as Wagner has presented it. Like so much else in *Mein Leben*, this vision appears to be at best an imaginative reconstruction of the truth. "Wagner's letters immediately after [the journey to La Spezia] make no mention of the experience."[66] The composer's earliest reference to his "vision" occurs in a letter written to Emilie Ritter *more than a year later*, on December 29th, 1854.[67] Moreover, the first musical sketch of the prelude—dated November 1st, 1853, nearly two months *after* the journey to La Spezia[68]—contains neither the familiar opening note of E^b nor the two horn motives that arise out of the E^b triad.[69] These important elements were added only gradually as Wagner began reshaping his isolated sketches of various scenes into the first continuous draft of *Das Rheingold* between November 1st, 1853 and January 1st, 1854.

Wagner continued to make changes (many of them substantial) in the prelude to *Das Rheingold* until the very moment when he completed its final score in September, 1854. Two examples of late modifications to the prelude are Wagner's introduction of the so-called "nature motive" (Example 1) to replace a series of runs in the strings, a figure that had been present ever since the first musical sketch and then his extension of this motive from E♭ to G in mm. 17-20.[70] According to Curt von Westernhagen[71] and John Deathridge,[72] Wagner incorporated the nature motive into the beginning of *Das Rheingold* only sometime early in 1854 when he composed it for the appearance of Erda in scene 4. The extension of the horn motive may be dated even later. It first appears as a correction in pencil to the instrumentation draft written between February 1st and May 28th, 1854.[73] Because of these and other late changes, the "vision of La Spezia," if indeed it actually occurred, must have contributed little to the opening of the prelude. The factors that *did* affect the beginning of *Das Rheingold* and that caused it to move in such a radically different direction from Wagner's initial plan for the drama must be traced to another source.

The Classical Structure of Plot in the *Ring*

Throughout the early 1850s, Wagner slowly realized that his drama needed to be reworked extensively in order to be understood by its intended audience. In 1848, he read the text of *The Death of Siegfried*—the play that, after many revisions, was to become *Götterdämmerung*—to the actor Eduard Devrient. At that time, Devrient was serving as a producer in Dresden, and Wagner regarded him as "my sole partner in discussions about art and the theater."[74] While Wagner later said that Devrient generally admired *The Death of Siegfried*, the actor's praise included at least one major criticism. He felt that Wagner was expecting his audience to know "too much" and that viewers, unlikely to be as familiar with mediæval epics as was Wagner himself, would be unable to follow the plot of the drama. In particular, Devrient told Wagner that the audience would need some additional information about the relationship between Siegfried and Brünnhilde in order to understand the first act of the play.[75] According to Wagner, Devrient "saw that I was headed away from any prospect of contact with the world of the modern theater, and naturally he did not approve of this. He tried, however, to take a positive view of my work as something that would not necessarily be too alien in the end, and might even be practicable in the theater."[76]

Over the next six years, Wagner's response to Devrient's criticism was twofold. He expanded his tragedy of Siegfried from a single work to a cycle of four dramas. (Wagner believed that this larger structure would give him enough scope to provide all the background information that his audience needed.) He also adopted as a plan for his cycle, not the loose and sprawling forms of the German poems that had first inspired him, but the tightly controlled order of classical Greek poetry and drama. (These familiar genres, he believed, would help his audience assimilate the work's unusual content.) The result is that, once again, the *Ring* combines Romantic ideas with a Classical structure, a mixture of innovative and traditional elements that gives the cycle its unique form.

Not all critics have accepted the notion that the *Ring*'s structure is derived from classical forms of literature. John Deathridge and Carl Dahlhaus, for instance, concluded that "[i]n terms of dramatic structure, *Der Ring des Nibelungen* can lay no claim to 'classical art-form', for all its grecianization of Germanic myths."[77] But such a conclusion is overstated, to say the least. The "classical art-form" of the *Ring* is clearly visible in its division into three major works and one minor work, a structure that Wagner specifically modeled on Aeschylus' *Oresteia*. Ancient tragic cycles like the *Oresteia* generally consisted of three tragedies (which formed the trilogy proper) and a final work known as a "satyr play," shorter and lighter in tone than the tragedies preceding it. In the fifth century B.C. when Aeschylus, Sophocles, and Euripides set the standards for classical tragedy, all dramatic authors tended to follow this structure. Aeschylus, however, was of particular interest to Wagner because he, almost alone among his contemporaries, elected to connect all four works of his cycle through a single story.[78] By tracing an individual legend through several generations, Aeschylus appeared to Wagner to have treated themes that were grander or more momentous than those of other authors. Nevertheless, for his own cycle, Wagner chose to reverse the position of the short "satyr play" from epilogue to "introductory evening" (*Vorabend*). This allowed him to end his entire cycle on a note of tragic grandeur, an experience that was made all the more poignant by its contrast to the cycle's initial comedy.

The structure of the *Ring* is thus a perfect example of how Wagner fused Classical and Romantic elements into a single form. Taking the four-drama structure of ancient tragedy and then rearranging the parts meant that Wagner's work contained the *elements* of a tragic cycle but the *emotional rhythm* of a romantic symphony. A quick and lively first movement (*Das Rheingold*) is followed by a slower, more lyrical second movement (*Die Walküre*), a joyous third movement (*Siegfried*), and a majestic, climactic final movement (*Götterdämmerung*). The result was Wagner's long-sought "Artwork of the Future," a new type of creation combining the intellectual weight of Aeschylus and the emotional depth of a Beethoven symphony.

Moreover, there was another reason why Wagner preferred to deviate from the traditional structure of a Greek tragic cycle. Ending his series with *Götterdämmerung* allowed him to recapitulate the form of his entire cycle in the plot of his last drama. Alone of the four operas, *Götterdämmerung* is composed of a prologue and four acts, just as the cycle itself consists of a preliminary evening and three dramas. To reinforce this similarity, *Götterdämmerung* begins with the appearance of the three Norns, goddesses charged with tending the World Ash, just as the cycle itself had begun with the appearance of the three Rhinemaidens, goddesses charged with tending the gold of their father. Entrusted with guarding their father's gold, the Rhinemaidens are (somewhat surprisingly) later identified by Brünnhilde as "wise" (*weise*: *Götterdämmerung* 3.3).[79] In a similar way, the Norns are described as embodying Erda's wisdom.[80] By basing the *Ring* on a Classical structure but reorganizing it along Romantic lines, Wagner was able to combine the symmetry and clarity of ancient tragedy with the intense emotional depth of the music and literature most familiar to members of his audience.

Furthermore, Wagner's *Ring* reveals its indebtedness to "classical art-forms" by borrowing a structure known (either ironically or appropriately) as "ring composition" (*Ringkomposition*). In ring composition, each individual poem or cycle of poems ends on the same idea, image, or theme with which it began. The result is that the work comes "full circle," providing an example of classical symmetry and completeness.[81] At times, a classical author's desire for balance will be taken to great extremes, and the two halves of a poem will become mirror images of one another, presenting the same themes or images first in one order, then in its reverse. The most famous examples of ring composition occurred in works that Wagner knew well. The *Oresteia* begins and ends on an image of light, as does another major poem of the same period, Pindar's *First Olympian Ode*, the opening to which serves as the epigraph to this chapter. The themes of the *First Olympian Ode*—water, gold, night, pride, wealth, and heroic excellence—parallel exactly the themes of Wagner's *Ring*, a coincidence that would not have been lost on a composer who, as we have already seen, had the works of Aeschylus and Pindar in both of the libraries he assembled.[82]

By reshaping *The Death of Siegfried* into a cycle of four dramas with a classical ring structure and the emotional rhythms of a romantic symphony, Wagner created a work with a form that would have been instantly recognizable by his contemporaries. More importantly perhaps, this was a form associated by them with works of great seriousness and deep emotional power. To intensify the parallel between his cycle and ancient tragedy, Wagner filled the *Ring* with classical story patterns, archetypical characters, and traditional literary images. The building of Valhalla became based upon the building of Troy.[83] The death of Fafner became based upon the deaths of Patroclus and Hector in the *Iliad*.[84] The ring of Alberich took on elements of Plato's ring of Gyges.[85] Siegfried's struggle with Wotan seems based on the selection of Greco-Roman priest kings, like that of Diana Nemorensis made famous by Sir James Frazer in *The Golden Bough*.[86] And similar occurrences may be found in nearly every episode of the dramas. Like the cycle's form, these elements of plot helped link Wagner's creation to Greek epic, lyric poetry, tragedy, and philosophical dialogues, genres that the composer's audience both knew and respected for their intellectual content. By contrast, the *Nibelungenlied* and the *Volsunga Saga*, while still supplying central figures and incidents to the drama, contained much that struck Wagner as quaint or even barbaric. His solution was to modify many of the elements found in the northern sagas, incorporating details of plot and character from such poems as the *Iliad* and *Prometheus Bound*, works that, since the time of Goethe, most educated Germans had read in school.[87]

That classical literature had an influence on the *Ring* was suggested as early as the beginning of the twentieth century by such scholars as Robert Petsch,[88] Georg Wrassiwanopulos-Braschowanoff,[89] and Pearl Cleveland Wilson.[90] All three of these authors cited parallels between the tragedies of Aeschylus and Wagnerian music drama. The obvious Aeschylean parallels to Wagner's work—the curse that extends over many generations, the blending of theater with theology, the similarity of Prometheus' theft of fire to Alberich's theft of the Rhinegold or Wotan's theft of the bough from the World Ash, and the double bind that ensnares nearly all of the central characters—were among the factors that first encouraged Nietzsche, himself trained as a classical philologist, to view Wagner as a literary successor to the Greek dramatists.[91]

In "Wagner and the Greeks," a landmark essay by Hugh Lloyd-Jones first published in 1976, a number of other parallels between Greek legend and the *Ring* were identified.[92] Lloyd-Jones traced important similarities between the characters of Prometheus in Aeschylus' *Prometheus Bound* and Loge in *Das Rheingold*, both fire gods who find themselves isolated from other deities, and between Athena and Brünnhilde, both spear-bearing warrior-goddesses who are the favorite offspring of a supreme deity. Most revealing of all, Lloyd-Jones notes that Norse mythology did not have a prophetic earth-mother goddess: Wagner's Erda is simply an adaptation of the Greek goddess Gaea, whose name also means "earth" and who is often depicted on Greek vases as half-rising from the ground just as does Erda in *Das Rheingold* and *Siegfried*.[93]

Michael Ewans has suggested that Wagner incorporated these classical elements into the *Ring* because so much of his Icelandic source material would have seemed unfamiliar, crude—even incomprehensible, as Devrient had suggested—to his original audience.[94] The popularity of the Norse myths in Germany was, we must remember, largely the *result* of Wagner's success with the *Ring*; it did not predate it. On the other hand, Germans of the nineteenth century *were* likely to be familiar with classical Greek legends. This, Ewans argued, helps to explain why Wagner made the Norse gods seem more "Olympian" by ignoring their traditional division into Vanir, an older race of fertility gods that included Frey and Freyja (Wagner's Froh and Freia), and Aesir, a younger race of warrior gods who lived in Asgard. Moreover, by transferring the quarrels of Zeus and Hera from the *Iliad* to Odin and Frigga (Wagner's Wotan and Fricka) in Norse mythology, Wagner made these figures resemble what an audience of his time would expect of a mythical high god and his consort.[95]

This same process may also help explain Wagner's frequent revisions in the prelude to *Das Rheingold*. The pseudo-Icelandic birth of the universe from "the womb of Night and Death" that Wagner had preserved in his original prose sketch was eventually replaced by a more classical, "Greek" beginning: a creation of matter from a primal substance that is soon associated with water. This primal substance, and Wagner's use of it as a plot element, can ultimately be traced to Greek philosophy.

Presocratic Philosophy and the Romantics

The works of all Greek philosophers before Plato survive only in limited fragments. As a result, what educated Germans in the nineteenth century knew about the presocratics tended to be derived from a few, identifiable sources. For the professional scholar or serious reader, there were the analyses of ancient Greek philosophical texts by such authors as Christian August Brandis,[96] the philosopher Hegel,[97]

Heinrich Ritter, and Ludwig Preller.[98] These surveys began to appear during the 1830s and greatly influenced German notions about presocratic thought before the publication of Hermann Diels' *Die Fragmente der Vorsokratiker* in 1903.[99]

It must not be assumed, however, that knowledge of presocratic philosophy was confined to academic circles. Nearly all educated Germans had at least some acquaintance with presocratic thought. Most readers in the nineteenth century first encountered the speculations of early philosophers in the widely read school texts of Plato, Aristotle, Plutarch, and Cicero.[100] Prominent among these texts, Aristotle's *Metaphysics* was commonly studied in German universities throughout the Romantic Period and exposed many of Wagner's contemporaries to ancient theories about the origin of the universe.

> That element from which all things arise—the first matter
> from which everything emerges and the last matter into
> which it is destroyed—this the early philosophers call "the
> primal substance" and "the first principle of all things." . . .
> Thales, who originated this type of philosophy, says that
> this primal substance is water.
>
> Aristotle *Metaphysics* 983 b 6[101]

Wagner almost certainly knew this passage of the *Metaphysics*. Hegel, whose works Wagner began reading in the late 1840s,[102] had translated and analyzed Aristotle's discussion of Thales at some length in the *Geschichte der Philosophie*.[103] Moreover, as early as 1831, during Wagner's brief stay at Leipzig University, he attended several lectures on philosophy given by one Professor Weiss who, as he himself says, "had just translated Aristotle's *Metaphysics*" into German and with whom he had become acquainted through his uncle Adolf.[104]

Certainly, *Nietzsche* seems to been aware of similarities between the opening of *Das Rheingold* and the views of ancient philosophers like Thales. In the brief essay entitled "Philosophy in the Tragic Age of the Greeks" (1873)—that same essay that helped precipitate the philosopher's final break with Wagner[105]—Nietzsche described the origins of presocratic philosophy in terms that appear to be a parody of the *Ring*. "Greek philosophy seems to begin with an absurd notion, with [Thales'] proposition that *water* is the primal origin and the womb of all things."[106] In this passage, Nietzsche ridicules both the view that matter was somehow born out of a primeval womb (the idea that Wagner had experimented with as the "Womb of Night and Death") and the metaphysical notion that the universe was created out of water (the image that Wagner finally adopted for *Das Rheingold*).

In a striking parallel between the *Ring* and presocratic philosophy, Nietzsche's essay includes a discussion of a theory first proposed by the philosopher Anaximander: the origin and the end of the universe are inevitably the same. "Anaximander says upon one occasion, 'Where the source of things is, to that place they must also pass away, according to necessity, for they must pay penance and be judged for their injustices, in accordance with the ordinance of time.'"[107] In other words, the creation of the universe was a distortion, an act of "injustice" that will lead to its inevitable doom. When time began, all that existed was a primal substance that, since it contained all qualities equally, ultimately contained no qualities at all. Hot was perfectly balanced by cold, wet by dry, light by dark, good by evil, and so on. Anaximander believed that, in order for the world to be created and for reality to become perceptible, this original balance had to be removed. The result was an "injustice" that must one day be repaid.[108]

Anaximander's theory had a profound impact on Wagner's structure of plot in the *Ring*. It lies behind the words of Erda to Wotan in *Das Rheingold* 4 where she says that she is "the world's eternal and primeval mother" (*der ew'gen Welt Ur-Wala*). Erda proclaims that "Everything in existence must someday fade away. The gods' dark dawn is coming."[109] Anaximander's theory also gave rise to the composer's portrayal of the gods as doomed inevitably by the very treaties that gave them power. Wotan's spear, carved from a bough torn from the World Ash, was the source of the high god's dominion. The very act of stealing that bough, however, was an injustice that will lead inexorably to the downfall of the gods "in accordance with the ordinance of time," to use Anaximander's phrase. Without the spear, Wotan would never have attained his stature as lord of the gods; with the spear, Wotan, for all his divine power, is doomed to failure. As Anaximander suggested, creation entails destruction. In his music, Wagner suggests this same idea. As Deathridge and Dahlhaus have observed, in "the *Ring*, rising movement means evolution, falling means decline ..."[110] This is why the motive of Wotan's spear has a relentlessly *descending* melody. (Example 2) The god's rule is founded on instability; Wotan is predestined to fail.

Later in the nineteenth century, Nietzsche would argue that the views of Anaximander were superseded "by a divine stroke of lightning" in the person of Heraclitus.[111] The philosophy of Heraclitus, with its theory of continual change and the illusion of permanence, greatly appealed to Nietzsche. He called Heraclitus one of "my ancestors"[112] and said that in the "proximity [of Heraclitus] I feel altogether warmer and better than anywhere else."[113] The similarity of the Heraclitean universe to that described by Wagner in the *Ring* was one of the factors that attracted Nietzsche to the composer at their first meeting in the autumn of 1868. Heraclitus believed, as did Wagner, that essential contradictions existed, not only in the primal substance (as Anaximander had argued), but in *everything*, especially in God.

> God is day-night, winter-summer, war-peace, plenty-famine. He changes in the same way that fire, when it is mixed with incense, is named according to each new scent.
>
> Heraclitus, fragment 67

To Heraclitus, the supreme deity, the purest and most divine form of reality, contained no opposite qualities. So, too, in the world imagined by Wagner: the struggle between Alberich and Wotan (or "Licht-Alberich," as he calls himself in *Siegfried* 1.2) is a struggle between forces so diametrically different that they end up being the *same*. Both Alberich and Wotan desire supreme power. Both of them are guilty of stealing the Rhinegold. Both of them are willing to sacrifice love for power. Both of them act through intermediaries (Hagen and Siegfried) to accomplish what they themselves could not do. As Wagner reveals in his cycle, the conflict between Alberich and Wotan is not really a conflict of evil against good. It is, rather, a struggle between two figures who represent different aspects of the same basic desire.

For Heraclitus, the fire that serves as his metaphor for God also represents a type of paradox that is inherent in all things. Fire symbolizes continuity since it remains unchanged no matter what type of incense is cast into it. Yet fire also represents change. Its flickering flames endlessly assume new forms and colors; its very substance is always in motion. This paradoxical ability of fire to remain unchanged even while constantly changing so fascinated Heraclitus that he sought several other images in order to explain it. Not surprisingly, nearly every image Heraclitus used to describe the paradox of unchanging change—fire, gold, water, rivers—plays an important role in the *Ring*. In one passage, for instance, the philosopher spoke of fire as an "elemental currency," saying that it serves the same function as gold in trade.

> All things may be changed into fire and fire may be changed into all things, just as goods may be exchanged for gold and gold for goods.[114]

In the *Ring*, too, the images of fire and gold—or, at least, the *leitmotivs* for fire and gold—work in precisely the way that Heraclitus describes. They are frequently transformed yet always present, always a factor in the work's musical structure. Variations of the fire motive are used in each of the dramas to suggest Loge's symbolic presence even when the god himself does not appear on stage. The bond uniting Alberich and Wotan is indicated through the motives for their two emblems of power, the ring (Example 3) and Valhalla (Example 4), both of which are ultimately derived from the motive of the gold (Example 5).

In the most famous passage of Heraclitus—a brief statement in Plato's *Cratylus* (402 a 8-10)—eternal change and transformation are described as being like a river.

> Heraclitus says somewhere that everything flows and noth-
> ing remains; comparing matter to the stream of a river, he
> says you cannot step into the same river twice.

Though fire and water seem so different in other ways, Heraclitus saw
them both as fitting symbols of nature's paradox. Since the river continually flows, it is always different. Since the river is always recognizable, it never really changes at all. In his summary of Heraclitus' philosophy, Plato thus recorded an appropriate image both for the world
as it appears in the *Ring* and for Wagner's own approach to music.
"The art of composition," Wagner said, "is the art of transition."[115] In
the *Ring* itself, the transition from one musical motive to another, like
the transition from a youthful version of a character to a more mature
version of that same character, depends upon an audience's ability to
recognize *both* persistence *and* change. By the end of the cycle, Wagner's
very world of gods and heroes has both persisted and changed. In the
final measures of *Götterdämmerung*, the universe returns first to
Heraclitus' river, then to Thales' water, and finally to the same primeval
element from which it arose in the prelude to *Das Rheingold*. But how
the audience perceives this universe—why it was created, why the
events that occurred in it were important, what it tells us about life and
its ultimate meaning—has been changed immeasurably by the story
that unfolds during each of the four music dramas.

The belief shared by Heraclitus and other early philosophers that
the world arose from a single primal substance, that this substance
persists even while being altered in form, that (according to Thales, at
least) the primal substance was water, and that (according to
Anaximander, at least) the act of creation made the eventual destruction of the universe inevitable . . . all of this helps explain the revisions
made by Wagner to the prelude of *Das Rheingold*. Those adaptations
gave the *Ring* a philosophical basis that the composer did not find in
his northern sources. At the same time, the echoes of classical thought
that Wagner included in his cycle made this highly innovative work
more accessible to an audience that was educated in the classics and

that equated ancient Greek ideas with *all* early speculation about the origins of the universe.

An Additional Source for Classical Elements in the Plot of the *Ring*

Shortly after the final notes of *Das Rheingold* were written,[116] the German poet Georg Herwegh reintroduced Wagner to the philosophy of Arthur Schopenhauer.[117] The works of Schopenhauer articulated for the composer many of the ideas he had been struggling without success to express in the *Ring*.

> I looked at my Nibelung poems and recognized to my amazement that the very things I now found so unpalatable in [my first reading of Schopenhauer's] theory were already long familiar to me in my own poetic conception. Only now did I understand my own Wotan myself and, greatly shaken, I went on to a closer study of Schopenhauer's book.[118]

The pessimistic philosophy of Schopenhauer, with its view that suffering is an inevitable aspect of human life and that redemption may only be found by annihilating the self and the will, was perfectly suited to Wagner's outlook on life at this stage in his career. As Wagner struggled with several different forms of his cycle's ending, he knew that, whichever version he chose, his vast work must not permit any possibility of hope . . . not even for the gods . . . not even for Wotan.

Wagner continued studying Schopenhauer's philosophy in Zürich from late 1854 through mid-1857 as he composed the music for *Die Walküre* and the first two acts of *Siegfried*. During this same period, he became increasingly dissatisfied with the text that would end his cycle. Everything that Wagner was reading and studying in this period seemed to reinforce the echoes of classical Greek literature that had given him the basic structure of the *Ring*'s plot. What is more, his reading probably suggested to Wagner the metaphor (or perhaps we should say "the myth") of how the beginning of his cycle had been inspired in the first place. It is Schopenhauer's theories about the relationship between creativity and dreams, present in both *The World as Will and Idea* (1819) and *Parerga and Paralipomena* (1851), that appear to lie behind "the vision of La Spezia." In a major section of *Parerga and Paralipomena*, the "Essay on Spirit Seeing and everything connected therewith,"[119] Schopenhauer discusses dreams and the intermediary stage between wakefulness and sleep. During this half-drowsing state, Schopenhauer argues, the dreamer may confuse metaphysical truths perceived by the mind with actual experiences perceived by the senses.[120] This is precisely the experience that Wagner claimed to have had at La Spezia in 1853. His later descriptions of the event in the letter to Emilie Ritter and in *Mein Leben* are thus important, not because they relate an actual experience from his Italian journey, but because they are closely modeled on Schopenhauer's description of how such inspiration *should* occur.[121]

Parerga and Paralipomena was published during the very period that Wagner was writing the libretto for *Das Rheingold*. Nevertheless, Wagner did not begin reading these essays until 1855.[122] Once he did so, however, he encountered still more support for his revised, more "presocratic" opening to *Das Rheingold* and for its parallel at the end of *Götterdämmerung*. In the second essay of *Parerga and Paralipomena*, a work titled simply "Fragments for the History of Philosophy,"[123] Schopenhauer provides a brief synopsis of presocratic thought about the origins of the universe. In particular, he discusses the views of the early philosophers Anaxagoras and Empedocles that matter emerged from a primeval, chaotic mass, developed into one or more basic elements, and would eventually return to the same primal substance from which it arose.

Schopenhauer also discussed Empedocles' view that the four classical elements, once emerging from the primal substance, either developed new combinations through attraction or split off into new creations through repulsion. This eternal opposition between the elemental forces of attraction, love, or *philia* on the one hand and repulsion, hatred, or *neikos* on the other—almost identical to Wagner's own opposition of love and power in the *Ring*—was seen by Empedocles as a basic principle that governed the creation of the world. Since these two forces were perfectly balanced, however, the eventual destruction of the universe was assured from the very moment of its creation. Neither attraction nor repulsion could ever dominate the other, and the world would eventually collapse into the same chaos from which it began.

Wagner's reading of Schopenhauer exposed him to a philosophical justification of his own pessimism. That fatalistic philosophy was described by Schopenhauer himself as continuing an unbroken line of thought that extended from classical antiquity until his own day. Though Wagner originally claimed that he "didn't want to abandon the so-called 'cheerful' Greek view of the world which had provided my vantage point for surveying my 'Art-work of the Future',"[124] he now realized that he did not have to do so. Schopenhauer's essays showed him that the classical Greek outlook on life was, even in philosophical works, essentially tragic. Classicism and pessimism seemed to go together. Moreover, his lifelong enthusiasm for ancient literature intensified his conviction that his artistic vision and Schopenhauer's philosophy of the will were ultimately derived from the same intellectual source.

* * *

Wagner's study of classical literature thus did appear to have a significant effect on both the form and content of the *Ring*. While it is undeniable that most of the cycle's characters were taken from the *Nibelungenlied*, the *Volsunga Saga*, and the *Prose Edda*,[125] Wagner's sources were not limited to these texts. Were we to remove from the *Ring* every detail found in the German and Scandinavian epics, a major portion of Wagner's plot would remain unchanged. The *Nibelungenlied*, as M. Owen Lee[126] observed, "contains no gold stolen from water nymphs, no scenes in Valhalla, no earth-flooding, heaven-firing catastrophe, and no redemption of the world by love." Nor, according to Norse mythology, was the onset of Ragnarök brought about by Brünnhilde, Alberich's theft of the Rhinegold, or Wotan's

(Odin's) removal of the bough from Yggdrasill. The Norse peoples did not believe that the universe was either created out of or that it would inevitably return to water. Love was not set in eternal opposition to either hatred or power. The existence of matter was not regarded as an "injustice" that could only be redeemed by the obliteration of every trace of life, thought, and matter. These ideas were derived, either wholly or in part, from Wagner's fascination with classical Greek literature. By combining the Classical with the Romantic, therefore, the composer reinterpreted Germanic legend. The details that so fascinated him in the northern epics were rewritten into a plot structured along classical lines. All the revisions Wagner made to the prelude of *Das Rheingold* should be viewed against this background, as an element in the composer's attempt to merge the worlds of Norse mythology and Greek philosophy, imparting what his audience would view as a familiar structure to the unfamiliar body of Icelandic legends.

CHAPTER 3

Music

Wagner's Thematic Form of Composition

"A dominant strain of Romantic aesthetics, led by E.T.A. Hoffman and Schopenhauer, had maintained that music of the highest sort was necessarily 'pure' instrumental music, that its transcendental qualities were dimmed by an association with texts or literary counterparts. The philosophy of Hegel and the Hegelians, . . . in the ascendant [by the middle of the nineteenth century], held otherwise."[127] With these words, Leon Plantinga reviewed the battle lines of what many regard as the great musical conflict of the Romantic Age: the rivalry between Absolute Music and Program Music. Those who favored Absolute Music believed that a work's structure itself was important, not its ability to evoke extra-musical associations; this is the type of music usually identified with Brahms, Bruckner, and their supporters. Defenders of Program Music, on the other hand, believed that the highest form of music was that which expressed some specific story, image, or setting; this is the type of music associated most of all with Berlioz, Liszt, and Wagner.

With hindsight, it now seems obvious that much of this supposed "conflict" was never waged beyond the essays of Eduard Hanslick and a few of his contemporaries. "Bülow did not turn against Wagner's music when he began to champion Brahms. Richter conducted the premiere of Brahms' Second Symphony a little more than a year after conducting the *Ring*, and Levi was a personal friend of Brahms as well as a musical protagonist. The greatest performers, like most audiences, saw no reason to choose one to the exclusion of the other."[128] It was thus not at all uncommon for Absolute Music and Program Music to appear side by side at the same concert, performed by the same conductor and orchestra, even at times written by the same composer.

Nevertheless, what Hanslick and others saw as the difference between Absolute Music and Program Music did lead to one of Wagner's few serious departures from his philosophical mentor, Arthur Schopenhauer.[129] Schopenhauer ridiculed all forms of Program Music and said that music, as it is properly understood, "speaks not of things, but simply of weal and woe as being for the *will* the sole realities. It therefore says so much to the heart, whereas to the head it has nothing *direct* to say; and it is an improper use if this is required of it, as happens in all *descriptive* music. Such music should, therefore, be rejected once for all . . . . For to express passions is one thing and to paint objects another."[130] The irony of this passage, with Schopenhauer's emphasis on the heart over the head, is that it defends the central premise of the Romantic Movement while exalting a style of composition that most people today would associate with the Classical Period. Perhaps with equal irony, Wagner, who spent his life celebrating the literature and values of the classical world, composed in a style that is now regarded as the very essence of Romantic composition. Why was it, then, that Wagner and Schopenhauer, so frequently in agreement with one another in other matters, ended up diverging so sharply on this particular issue? Why was it that, while Wagner adored Schopenhauer's philosophy, Schopenhauer could not abide Wagner's music? Most importantly of all perhaps, why was it that both of these figures defended a style of music so seemingly opposed to their values elsewhere?

In pursuing the answers to these questions, it is important to realize that, while Schopenhauer sought to condemn all "descriptive" music, he reserved his fiercest barbs for *opera*, a type of music that he regarded as an illegitimate hybrid of song and drama.

> Music . . ., as the most powerful of the arts, is by itself alone capable of completely occupying the mind that is susceptible to it. Indeed, to be properly interpreted and

enjoyed, the highest productions of music demand the wholly undivided and undistracted attention of the mind so that it may surrender itself to, and become absorbed in, them in order thoroughly to understand its incredibly profound and intimate language. Instead of this, the mind during a piece of highly complicated opera music is at the same time acted on by means of the most variegated display and magnificence, the most fantastic pictures and images, and the most vivid impressions of light and colour; moreover, it is occupied with the plot of the piece. Through all this it is diverted, distracted, deadened, and thus rendered as little susceptible as possible to the sacred, mysterious, and profound language of tones; and so such things are directly opposed to an attainment of the musical purpose.[131]

As this passage makes clear, Schopenhauer's fundamental objection to opera may be traced to his Romantic sensibilities. Music, Schopenhauer believed, was something to be *felt* rather than to be *understood*. The problem with opera was that it did not permit a purely emotional response. Opera stimulated the mind with details of plot, distracted the eyes with color and spectacle, and confused the ears by mingling words with "pure tone." "The words [of a song] are and remain for the music a foreign extra of secondary value, as the effect of tones is incomparably more powerful, more infallible, and more rapid than that of the words."[132]

Schopenhauer's Romantic values led him, by the sheer force of his logic, to prefer music written *before* the Romantic Period. In the classical symphonies of Haydn, Mozart, and Beethoven, Schopenhauer could find instrumental works that, he believed, did not attempt to tell a story or interpret a text. These works were all about tone and structure, he concluded, with the result that the will and emotion of the composer were communicated directly to the audience. Even operatic compositions, Schopenhauer suggested, would be much improved if they were performed in concert settings, with all the words, actors, and staging removed. "The music of an opera, as presented in the score, has a wholly independent, separate, and as it were abstract existence by itself, to which the incidents and characters of the piece are foreign, and which follows its own unchangeable rules; it can therefore be completely effective without the text."[133]

To Wagner, the creator of the *Gesamtkunstwerk*, this was heresy. "Nothing is less absolute (as to its appearance in Life, of course) than Music, and the champions of an Absolute Music evidently don't know what they're talking about . . . ."[134] At the very least, Wagner believed, music contained an "extra-musical reference" by imitating the rhythms of speech and movement. The origin of music itself, Wagner reasoned, was in song and dance, not in the rarified environment of the concert hall. The problem with contemporary music was, therefore, not that it was insufficiently pure and "absolute," but that it had become *too far separated* from the perfect union of all the arts that had been found in the tragic cycles of Aeschylus. To restore this classic ideal of unity, Wagner believed, the artwork of the future had to move away from such aberrations as early symphonic "tunes" and embark upon a bold new direction.[135] Thus, in order to be true to his classical values, Wagner felt that he had to create something that was, for his age, utterly new.

What Wagner hoped to create was a type of music that was not isolated from the audience's mental images, memories, and ideas, as Schopenhauer had suggested. Rather, Wagner's artwork of the future would be a perfect combination of those experiences. Musical sound would be enhanced by relying upon the vast array of sensory impressions already known to the audience. While a relatively uncommon idea for its time, this concept of music was, like so many of Wagner's other ideas, ultimately classical in origin. From his reading in Aristotle, Wagner knew that the Greeks believed all music consisted of impressions taken from the physical world. Even "most flute- and harp-playing," Aristotle says in the *Poetics*, are among the "representative arts" (*mimêseis*: 1447 a 2). Instrumental music was "representative" either because it imitated nature directly (evoking such sounds as the chirping of birds or the crash of thunder) or because it conjured up emotions associated with particular memories (causing marches to be "stir-

ring" because they are associated with battle or lullabies to be "sooth-
ing" because they mimic the singsong patterns of a mother's voice).
Plato, too, suggested to Wagner that it is ridiculous to "divorce rhythm
and figure from melody, by giving metrical form to bare discourse
[i.e., creating poems that are not songs], and melody and rhythm from
words [i.e., creating songs that are not poems], by employment of
cithara and flute without vocal accompaniment, though it is the hard-
est of tasks to discover what such wordless rhythm and tune signify,
not subordinated to the control of dance or song for the display and
virtuosity; . . . the use of either as an independent instrument is no
better than unmusical legerdemain."[136]

Wagner thus concluded that, to argue as Schopenhauer did and
believe opera could be "improved" by reducing it to a symphonic work
was a complete misunderstanding of what music was. Words were
never an unwelcome intrusion into a piece of music. They were, rather,
an essential ingredient in a total work of art. What is more, in the type
of artwork that Wagner envisioned, it would be *impossible* to separate
the words from the melody. Both would be created solely for the existence of the other, and neither could be understood in isolation. A
perfectly written libretto, Wagner believed, would have one and only
one score. Any other combination of melody and words would distort
the natural rhythms of the text and ignore the thematic associations
that were essential to the author's ideas.

At root, therefore, Wagner and Schopenhauer saw music in completely different ways. Despite his own classical training (which, it
must be remembered, was significantly more complete than Wagner's),
Schopenhauer approached music from an essentially modern perspective. He saw it as a series of sounds given shape by patterns of tone,
harmony, rhythm, dynamics, and timbre. Wagner, on the other hand,
was always aware of the *etymological* root of the word "music" as "any
art over which the Muses presided."[137] As a development of his own
"romantic classicism," Wagner mentioned frequently in his writings
that ancient Greek *mousikê* [*technê*] involved philosophy as well as poetry, history as well as song, drama as well as melody. "We have accus-
tomed ourselves," he said, "to limiting our idea of 'music' to the mere

art, and now at last to the mere artifice, of *Tone*. That it is an arbitrary restriction, we know very well; for *that* people which invented the name of '*Music*,' connoted by it not only *the arts of poetry and tone*, but each several artistic manifestation of the inner man, insofar as to the senses he conveyed his feelings and beholdings, in ultimate persuasiveness, through the organ of ringing speech."[138]

Wagner might have been directing these words to Schopenhauer himself. Eliminate the language from opera, he was saying, and you eliminate the very reason for composing an opera. Wagner even saw the *Gesamtkunstwerk*, not as a way of forcing song to be more like "pure" instrumental music, but as a way of making music itself more like a *language*. Wagner wanted music to communicate with an audience as effectively as did words when a poet spoke in measured syllables or when an author recorded letters on a page. To make his music more potent as a medium, therefore, Wagner believed that he had to treat the tones and chords of his compositions just as though they were the sounds of a language or the characters of an alphabet. He had to group them into patterns that were both complex and recognizable and then he had to imbue those patterns with thematic associations. This process of thematic composition meant that Wagner needed to erect his music dramas "from the ground up," using those short building blocks of melody that are commonly known as *leitmotivs*.

More has been written about Wagner's use of leitmotivs than about any other aspect of his music dramas. Wagnerian leitmotivs, especially those in the *Ring*, have been studied, analyzed, and catalogued in elaborate detail. As a result, it would be unnecessary (even if it were possible) to provide an exhaustive catalog of all the *Ring*'s motives or to describe all the ways in which Wagner used these themes.[139] Nevertheless, in a study of the *Ring*'s classical form and meaning, it would be inappropriate to ignore them completely. Leitmotivs were yet another formal element that Wagner adopted in his effort to create a perfectly unified work of art such as he believed that Aeschylus' tetralogies had been. Leitmotivs gave the *Ring* a focus in much the same way that, in Wagner's view, Aeschylus' repeated images of light, blood, and lions provided thematic unity to the *Oresteia*. For this reason, no study of the *Ring*'s classical structure would be complete without a survey of at least several of the major ways in which leitmotivs function as structural elements in Wagner's cycle.

To Reinforce an Idea

Leitmotivs, as Wagner uses them, should be regarded as a type of image or thematic device. That is to say, like metaphors, synecdoche, and the other types of *literary* images that Wagner adopted, leitmotivs helped the composer juxtapose contrasting ideas. Even more specifically, they helped Wagner tie musical ideas to visual ones. Like literary images, the composer's leitmotivs frequently create an association between two dissimilar ideas in such a way that they bring about a renewed understanding of both of them.

At its simplest level, a leitmotif occurs whenever a specific musical theme is attached to a specific person, object, setting, emotion, or idea. This type of musical reference is not at all unusual and numerous examples of it may be found both before and after Wagner. For instance, one well-known leitmotif appears as the clarinet theme associated with the figure of the cat in Sergei Prokofiev's *Peter and the Wolf*. That particular theme evokes stealth and cunning, and whenever it is heard, any member of the audience instantly understands what is signified, regardless of whether the narrator has specifically mentioned the cat. In a similar way, Wagner causes individual themes to be associated with characters at many points in the *Ring*. As but one example, Hagen, the evil half-brother of Gunther and Gutrune in *Götterdämmerung*, is associated with a suitably dark and menacing theme (Example 6) during the last work of the cycle.

Wagner was rarely content with squandering his "musical vocabulary" on such simplistic ideas as "Here is Hagen" or "This is fire." He wanted to create a "musical language" that had all the complexity and nuances of any spoken or written language. He thus avoided the very term *Leitmotif* ("leading theme"), already familiar in his day, and preferred such expressions as *Gedächtnismotiv* ("theme of memory or association") and other terms that he himself coined. "Wagner ..., as we know, did not speak of *Leitmotiven*, but employed a variety of other terms and circumlocutions to describe the thing we now know by that name: *melodische Momenten, Themen, Melodien, Grundthemen, Hauptthemen, Grundmotiven, plastische Natur-Motiven, musikalische Motiven*, or simply *Motiven*."[140] The reason for this vast number of expressions was that Wagner did not want his themes to be reduced to the "musical calling cards" or "signature tunes" that many of his later critics accused them of being.[141] Wagner's *Gedächtnismotiven* were thus intended to be, not obvious musical cues, but the thematic building blocks of an entirely new approach to composition. Each theme in the *Ring* was conceived as representing an image drawn from nature or memory,[142] the origins that Aristotle had said all music should have. Most important of all was that each theme as Wagner imagined it was capable of being formed into larger and more complex units (essentially, "musical sentences" and "musical paragraphs") so as to convey the composer's meaning in a manner that, he believed, could not be misunderstood.[143]

Wagner's resistance to using leitmotivs in their most obvious way did not mean, however, that he *never* introduced a melodic phrase primarily to reinforce an image on stage. It merely means that he rarely *stopped* there. For instance, near the end of *Das Rheingold*, the lightning god Donner summons a storm that will cleanse the "sultry haze" filling the air with "turbid pressure" (*Schwüles Gedünst . . . trübe Druck*). As these words are spoken, a theme is heard in the orchestra that immediately becomes associated with Donner and his power (Example 7). So effective is this single thematic association of melody and visual image that, although Donner never again appears on stage, the recurrence of his theme in any succeeding drama will always remind the audience of the god's invisible presence. For example, during the "storm music" that introduces *Die Walküre*, the Donner theme is heard, evoking memories that suggest both the severity of the storm itself and the role of the gods in what is about to occur.

As we saw earlier, one of the chief benefits to using leitmotivs in the *Ring* was that they helped Wagner maintain a high degree of unity throughout his drama. For instance, the "dragon motive" (Example 8), first encountered in *Das Rheingold* 3, links a number of episodes that might otherwise appear to be unrelated. At the first appearance of the dragon theme, the melody reinforces the visual image of Alberich who has just assumed the shape of a dragon by means of the Tarnhelm. The low, lumbering melody of this theme evokes the awkward movements of a huge, reptilian creature. Later in the cycle when a second dragon appears—this time it is the giant Fafner in *Siegfried* 2.2 who has been transformed by the Tarnhelm—the same theme is heard. This repetition of the theme establishes a close connection between the two scenes. Visually as well as musically, Wagner has established a parallel that reminds his audience of earlier events in the cycle. As we shall see in our discussion of character, Wagner had specific reasons for making history repeat itself here: he wanted to draw a comparison between the reactions of Wotan and of Siegfried when they were faced with a similar situation.

Moreover, like the Donner motive, the dragon theme is used by Wagner to evoke the image of a character even when that figure is not visible to the audience. Near the beginning of *Siegfried* 1.1, for instance, as Mime recalls Fafner's presence in a dank forest lair (*Fafner, der wilde Wurm, lagert im finstren Wald*), the dragon motive emerges in the orchestra. The sounding of this theme reinforces the dragon's "symbolic presence" in Mime's words. In much the same way, in *Siegfried* 1.2 while the Wanderer is posing a riddle to Mime, the dragon motive reinforces a reference to Fafner in the text. Again, in *Die Walküre* 3.1, Schwertleite informs Brünnhilde that Fafner keeps watch over Alberich's ring in a cave; at this point, the dragon motive is heard once more. As the Valkyrie says that the giant has now been transformed into a dragon (*Wurmesgestalt schuf sich der Wilde*), the "presence" of this creature in her words is suggested by the presence of his theme in the music. Text and score combine in a manner that Schopenhauer, with his dismissal of words as an "unnecessary" element of opera, would never have completely understood.

To Undermine an Idea

A second way in which Wagner used leitmotivs in the *Ring* initially seems antithetical to the use we have just seen. This function occurs whenever Wagner adopts leitmotivs to contrast with, undermine, or contradict the action that is occurring on stage. Leitmotivs, Wagner knew, provided an effective source of dramatic irony, the situation that occurs when an audience understands more than do the characters in the drama. For instance, in *Siegfried* 1.3, the Wanderer asks Mime a question that the dwarf cannot answer: "Who will weld the mighty fragments of the sword Notung?" (*Wer wird aus den starcken Stücken Notung, das Schwert, wohl schweißen?*). The Wanderer's phrasing of this question, however, suggests its answer. It is sung to the motive of Siegfried the Hero (Example 9), the first appearance of which the audience will recall from *Die Walküre* 3.1. Mime's inability to answer Wotan's question is thus made poignant by an ironic tension between score and libretto. His deafness to the truth means that Mime cannot hear an answer which seems so simple, so apparent to any member of the audience.

A similar use of dramatic irony occurs in *Die Walküre* 1.2 when Siegmund relates his life story to Hunding and Sieglinde. Siegmund notes that, as a young man, he one day became separated from his father. He never saw his father again, later finding only a wolfskin in the forest. As Siegmund says the words "I never found my father" (*den Vater fand ich nicht*), the Valhalla theme is heard in the orchestra. (Example 4) Through this device, Wagner both reminds his audience who Siegmund's father was and informs them where he has gone.[144] Siegmund, however, did not know that his father was Wotan. He knew him only as "Wolf" (*Wolfe*), and thus the score provides the audience with information that a character on stage does not have.

One striking instance of how Wagner can use leitmotivs to undermine ideas in his text may be found in the very first line of *Götterdämmerung* 1.2. In that passage, Hagen greets Siegfried as he approaches the Gibichungs' castle. As Hagen says "Hail, Siegfried, dear hero!" his outward heartiness is undermined by Wagner's score.

These words are sung to the theme of Alberich's curse (Example 10). With only a few notes, therefore, Wagner reminds his audience of Hagen's ancestry, characterizes him as a hypocrite, foreshadows Siegfried's fate, and identifies the ring as the instrument of that fate. With pure dramatic irony, the audience is aware of all these underlying issues while the pure-hearted Siegfried hears only the false warmth conveyed by his enemy's greeting

This love of contrast between text and music has a number of parallels elsewhere in Wagner's theatrical method. He displays a great fondness for puns and word play that create a similar form of dramatic irony. For instance, in *Das Rheingold* 2, as Loge explains why his search revealed that nothing in the world is as rich and desirable as love, he uses the expression "nothing in the entire *circuit* of the world" (*in der Welten Ring nichts*), adopting the very term that has such a different connotation elsewhere in the cycle. Wagner uses this play on words to highlight the conflict between love and power long before Alberich's ring is ever actually *seen* by the audience. Again, in *Götterdämmerung* 3.1 as Siegfried explains to the Rhinemaidens why he will not surrender the ring, he says that he would not care even if the ring were to win him all the wealth of the world (*Der Welt Erbe gewänne* ...). This is a verbal echo that the audience was certain to remember. At the end of *Das Rheingold* 1, when Alberich was musing about what he might gain from the world's wealth (*Der Welt Erbe gewänn'* ...), he used the very same words. Siegfried and Alberich, perhaps the two most antithetical figures in the cycle, ironically adopt precisely the same patterns of speech. Nevertheless, Siegfried would gladly exchange wealth and power for the love of a woman, while Alberich makes the completely opposite choice. Although both figures respond thoroughly in character, it is an example of Wagner's fondness for irony that both of them chose identical words to do so.

Foreshadowing

A third major use of leitmotivs in the *Ring* occurs when Wagner introduces a specific musical theme, not to reinforce or undermine an idea already presented to the audience, but to *anticipate* something that the audience will eventually see. This use of leitmotivs provides Wagner with a musical equivalent to the literary device of foreshadowing. For instance, in the prelude to the second act of *Siegfried*, the dragon motive (Example 8) is used in such a way that the audience begins thinking about this creature long before it actually appears on stage. The use of this particular theme sets the mood for the events that follow, heightening the level of suspense and increasing the audience's degree of anticipation.

As might be expected, the use of leitmotivs to foreshadow events is particularly common in the *Ring*'s preludes. Nevertheless, it appears in other sections of the drama as well. One frequent use of anticipatory leitmotivs occurs when Wagner introduces them to "outline" a character's speech or sequence of thought in a lengthy monologue. This device is noticeable, for instance, during Wotan's speech to Brünnhilde in *Die Walküre* 2.2 where a number of leitmotivs are introduced just prior to their thematic associations in the text. Thus, after Wotan says *maßlose Macht* (the "unlimited power" that Alberich has gained by placing his curse on love), the ring motive (Example 3) is heard in the orchestra. Only *after* this motive is complete does Wotan proceed to speak about the ring. What Wagner has done is to reverse his usual compositional practice. His more customary approach is to sound a leitmotif either simultaneously with or immediately *after* its thematic association in the text. By reversing this practice in Wotan's speech, the composer creates a strong contrast to the first appearance of the ring motive in *Das Rheingold*. There Wellgunde had said, "The world's wealth was to be won by forging a ring from the gold of the Rhine." With these words, an embryonic form of the ring motive was heard in the woodwinds, *followed* by a reference to "unlimited power" (*maßlose Macht*). With a complete reversal of this structure in *Die Walküre* 2.2, words and music come together to make a clear, though distinctly different, parallel to the earlier scene. Wotan and Alberich, the major figures in the two episodes, are both very different from one another and very much alike. Moreover, the verbal and musical echoes that appear in *Die Walküre* 2.2 help to clarify the sequence of Wotan's thoughts. His reflections on power remind him of the ring, an idea that seems to produce an abrupt change of subject. By introducing the ring motive, therefore, Wagner provides a thematic bridge between Wotan's reference to the curse and his thoughts about the ring. He reminds us that, were it not for Alberich's curse, the dwarf could never have created the ring in the first place.

A similar use of leitmotivs occurs only a few lines later. Wotan is speaking about Valhalla when suddenly, in a manner seemingly unrelated to the subject at hand, Erda's theme (Example 11) is heard in the orchestra. Only after this motive is complete does Wotan then shift his attention to the earth goddess. Once again, the composer uses music to provide a transition that would have seemed abrupt from Wotan's words alone. Moreover, the timing of this motive has special significance for the audience. It reminds them that the first time the gods ever entered Valhalla (the very subject Wotan was discussing) came shortly after the first appearance of Erda in *Das Rheingold.* Like Wagner's use of the ring motive, therefore, Erda's theme in the current passage advances Wotan's narrative from one subject to the next. At the same time, it reminds the audience that Erda's wisdom was a vital source of the god's plan.

Among the most interesting of Wagner's "anticipatory leitmotivs" are those that will be understood by an audience only upon repeated exposure to the *Ring.* For instance, in *Die Walküre* 1.1 as Sieglinde gives Siegmund a refreshing drink, a distinctive melody is heard. To a person seeing the *Ring* for the first time, this particular theme has no special significance. Yet, two scenes later, this very theme provides the basis for "Du bist der Lenz" (Example 12), one of the most important love themes of the cycle. Only when a member of the audience sees the *Ring* a second time, therefore, will the eventual role of this theme become clear. Appropriately, the form that "Du bist der Lenz" assumes in *Die Walküre* 1.1 is merely a rudimentary version of the theme. It achieves its most complete form only when the love of Siegmund and Sieglinde matures from an incipient first attraction to a fully developed passion.

The imagery of "Du bist der Lenz,"—the revival of life in spring, the melting warmth that restores the world after an extended frost, the intensity of a lover's glance at the first sight of one's beloved, the instant flash of recognition that occurs when a passion is truly fated—is appropriate, not only to the moment of Sieglinde's aria when we actually hear it, but also to the earlier arrival of Siegmund at Hunding's cottage when the initial form of the theme is introduced. As Sieglinde will later say, Siegmund *is* the "spring" that arrived on the breezes after a winter's storm. He provides the emotional warmth that was denied her throughout her icy marriage to Hunding. Siegmund's eyes sparkle, supplying the first light she has ever seen in her husband's gloomy cabin. Only upon our second acquaintance with the *Ring*, therefore, do we realize how appropriate all this later symbolism was to the moment of the lovers' initial meeting when the theme is first heard.

Perhaps the two most important instances of anticipatory leitmotivs in the *Ring* are those in which Wagner introduces the themes usually known as "the sword" (Example 13) and "Siegfried the Hero" (Example 9). Like the appearance of "Du bist der Lenz" in *Die Walküre* 1.1, these two motives are first encountered in a manner that does not reveal their true significance. Only after further acquaintance with the cycle will an audience understand the full implication of both themes. The "sword motive," for example, is first heard near the end of *Das Rheingold* as Wotan wonders how he might rule Valhalla in perfect safety. Wagner's stage directions describe the god at this point as suddenly possessed by a great idea (*Wie von einem grossen Gedanken ergriffen, sehr entschlossen*) and, as soon as the inspiration strikes him, the sword motive is heard in the orchestra.[145] Wotan's "great idea," as the audience learns only later, is to create a hero who can accomplish what he himself cannot do: recover the ring. Wotan's oaths prevent him from taking the ring by force; a hero, acting on his own volition and for his own ends, would be under no such restriction. Only in *Die Walküre* 1.3, when the sword motive appears a second time, will an audience truly understand it. Sieglinde tells Siegmund that a mysterious stranger once fixed a sword in the ash tree standing in Hunding's hall. As the motive of the sword sounds once again in the orchestra, the audience will recall Wotan's moment of inspiration from *Das Rheingold* and finally understand something of the high god's plan. For the rest of the cycle, this triple association—Wotan's "great idea," the hero, and the sacred weapon—remain inextricably bound to this theme.

Through this anticipatory use of the sword motive in *Das Rheingold*, Wagner treats the *theme* of the sword precisely as Wotan treats the sword itself: he "embeds" it in full view where it will be reserved for later use. Only when Wotan's "great idea" advances to the point where the hero's sword can be useful—only when the plot of the cycle itself advances to the point where the sword motive can be fully understood—is each reintroduced and permitted to fill its intended role. As we have seen before and shall continue to see, Wagner approaches score and libretto in precisely the same way, handling thematic patterns in a single consistent fashion.

Later in the cycle, the theme of "Siegfried the Hero" (Example 9) is also introduced in an anticipatory manner. In *Die Walküre* 3.1, just after Brünnhilde announces to Sieglinde that her womb carries "the noblest hero in the world," the Valkyrie adds one further observation about this future champion: "He will forge the very sword that will lead him to triumph. So, let me grant him his name: 'Siegfried,' the hero for whom victory is joy." The motive to which Brünnhilde sings these words is Siegfried's heroic theme. Although its introduction is anticipatory in the sense that Siegfried has not yet appeared onstage, at least part of its meaning is made clear by Brünnhilde's words. Introducing Siegfried's theme now establishes a level of anticipation that will be resolved only later in the cycle. Moreover, Brünnhilde's indication that Siegfried will restore Siegmund's sword associates the hero, even at this early point in his story, with the full range of that weapon's thematic associations. Wotan's "great idea," the hero's messianic mission, the providential role of the gods, and Siegfried himself . . . all these become fused with the image of Notung, the divinely ordained weapon of the hero.

To Associate Two or More Ideas

Just as Wagner intensifies the significance of both "the hero" and "the sword" by associating these two themes with one another from the very beginning, so does he associate other ideas in the cycle through his extensive use of leitmotivs. Even within the musical theme of the sword itself (Example 13), there is a pattern that ties this particular motive with another theme. Between the second and third notes of the sword motive there appears a characteristic octave leap downward. This octave leap, which in one sense is merely part of the larger sword motive, also develops its own individual "meaning" in the cycle. This is clear from *Die Walküre* 1.3 where Siegmund first retrieves and names the sword that Wotan has left for him. As he does so, he introduces the sword's name with this same octave leap downward: Notung. That two-note pattern, a subset of the sword motive, becomes the leitmotif for this particular sword (Example 14). Wagner's association of these two ideas is thus made in an almost Aristotelian fashion. Just as Notung is a specific example drawn from the larger category of swords, so is Notung's leitmotif merely a "subset" taken from the larger *leitmotif* of the sword.

Wagner used this type of musical, thematic relationship to associate many other ideas in the *Ring*. Shortly before Sieglinde reveals the sword to Siegmund, the hero is reminded of the sacred weapon that his father, "Wälse," once promised him in the hour of his deepest need. That hour, Siegmund concludes, has now arrived. As he utters the words, "Wälse! Wälse, where is your sword?" the name Wälse is sung to the very octave leap that will soon be associated with Notung itself. Wagner, we recall, had wanted to draw a strong connection among three ideas—the hero's sword, Notung as a particular manifestation of that sword, and Wälse (Wotan), the figure who created the sword—and he does so here through the use of a single musical pattern.

A similar thematic association is made between the Rhinemaidens' ecstatic cry of "Rhinegold!" (Example 15) and Alberich's mournful cry of "Woe!" (*Wehe!*) (Example 16), both of which appear in *Das Rheingold* 1. Each of these themes consists of a single downward step. Joy and grief, Wagner seems to be suggesting, are two sides of the same coin. It is a person's response to what happens, not the power of destiny itself, that determines whether a person is happy. With this idea, Wagner has returned to the outlook of Heraclitus. All opposites are ultimately the same. Nature has a deeper unity than we sometimes imagine. Day/night, war/peace, summer/winter, happiness/grief . . . all of these are not names for reality itself; they are simply names that human beings *impose* upon reality.

In a larger sense, there is also a relationship in the *Ring* among *all* the two-note patterns we have seen, both those involving single steps and those involving octave leaps. All of the ideas represented by these themes—the hero, Wotan, his "great idea," Notung, happiness, and grief—are continually interwoven throughout the cycle. For instance, we shall see in the next chapter how the symbolism with which Wagner surrounds Notung is intentionally ambiguous. When this weapon first appears, it is unclear whether it will ultimately be an instrument of joy (the "Rheingold!" pattern) or of sorrow (the "Wehe!" pattern). All that its initial two-note theme suggests is a boundless range of possibility. Only as the *Ring* unfolds does the composer's final (and, as shall see, very complex) answer emerge.

The way in which Wagner links the sword and the hero also suggests a second way in which music may be used to associate several ideas. Characters in the *Ring* are frequently identified with particular objects, elements, or places and, as a result, the themes of these characters become almost interchangeable with those of these objects, elements, or places. Wotan becomes associated with both Valhalla and the spear, Alberich with the ring, Loge with fire, Freia with love, and Mime with Nibelheim.[146] In Wagner's musical vocabulary, distinctions between these characters and their objects frequently do not matter. The object is the emblem of its owner. The owner is the master of the object. In an almost heraldic fashion, Wagner approached his score with the idea that the person and his symbol were, in terms of larger thematic purposes, largely one and the same.

To Transform One Idea into Another

In addition to linking two or more ideas through similar themes, Wagner sometimes modifies a single theme so that it develops into a second affiliated pattern. In its most developed form, this approach results in entire "families" of related themes. This concept, usually referred to as melodic or thematic transformation, did not originate with Wagner. It may already be seen in the *idée fixe* found in Berlioz's *Symphonie Fantastique* (1831) and the elaborate thematic transformations found in Liszt's *Faust Symphony* (1857) and other works. In all three of these composers, a single melodic pattern could be developed through changes in key, rhythm, orchestration, expansion or contraction, and other devices until it becomes a different, but still recognizable, melodic pattern. Like Heraclitus' river, the altered melody is both the same and different simultaneously.

Since Wagner's own time, scholars have tried to link all the themes of the *Ring* to just a few major families. Some have even attempted to link these patterns to a single all-encompassing family. For instance, we have already seen how the themes of both the ring (Example 3) and Valhalla (Example 4) are derived from the theme of the gold (Example 5). Deryck Cooke, who was perhaps the most creative scholar to analyze the *Ring*'s musical structure, demonstrated that the basic theme of nature (Example 1) served, through simple thematic transformation, to create such diverse leitmotivs as the sword (Example 13), Erda (Example 11), the Twilight of the Gods (Example 18), the symphonic melody known as "Forest Murmurs," and even the gold itself (Example 5).[147] It is true, of course, that in order for most members of the audience to observe these relationships, they would need highly perceptive ears, substantial knowledge of chordal structures, and perhaps even access to the score itself. Nevertheless, other relationships among Wagner's leitmotivs are more easily perceived, even upon an initial encounter with the *Ring*. For instance, the motive sometimes known as "the mature Siegfried" (Example 19) is a relatively simple development of the theme we have called "Siegfried the Hero" (Example 9). To indicate that the hero has grown in both stature and importance, Wagner merely expands his earlier melody, making it grander and more majestic. As W.J. Henderson says, "The change is chiefly one of rhythm. Siegfried, the youth, is depicted musically in six-eight measure, a rhythm buoyant and piquant. For Siegfried the mature hero, the melodic sequence is preserved, but the rhythm is changed to a dual one. The change is one founded on the nature of the music, for the dual rhythm is firm, square, and solid."[148] In a similar way, Brünnhilde's theme when it appears late in the cycle, a pattern sometimes known as "Brünnhilde the Woman" (Example 20), is derived melodically from an earlier theme in the cycle, "Brünnhilde the Valkyrie" (Example 21).

Perhaps the clearest example of melodic transformation Wagner uses in the *Ring* is a theme we might call "Fafner the Dragon" (Example 22). This pattern contains an obvious connection to the giant theme (Example 17), first heard in *Das Rheingold*. Both motives consist of awkward, lumbering melodies performed on the tympani. Yet the giant theme is characterized by the downward leap of a fourth, while "Fafner the Dragon" replaces this interval with a plunging fifth. The motive of "Fafner the Dragon" thus retains the same essential rhythm as the giant theme, but with a slight difference in melody and a tempo that is considerably slowed. The result suggests the ponderous, slithering motions of a dragon, while reminding the audience that Fafner was equally as clumsy as a giant. The similarity of these two themes thus serves to underscore a relationship that is not immediately visible to the audience. Transformed into a dragon, Fafner looks completely different in *Siegfried* 2.2 from his last appearance in *Das Rheingold* 4. Nevertheless, by constructing this character's new theme as a minor variant of the old, Wagner reinforces musically what has transpired in the plot of his drama. Fafner's internal nature has remained the same, much as the basic rhythm and orchestration of his motive have remained the same. It is merely Fafner's outer appearance that has been altered, just as there has been a slight change in his theme's melody and tempo.

Other examples of thematic transformation in the *Ring* illustrate how Wagner uses slight variants to establish connections among groups of ideas. The motive usually known as "Brünnhilde's Love for the

Volsungs" (Example 23) results from a minor elaboration of the spear
motive (Example 2). Whereas the spear motive consists of a straight
progression down the scale, "Brünnhilde's Love for the Volsungs" periodically interrupts that pattern with an octave leap upward. Brünnhilde's
love for Wotan's family is thus tied thematically to the high god's un-
breakable oaths. One is not possible without the other. As the personification of her father's will, Brünnhilde embodies a love that manifests
his will directly. Yet while the relentless downward motion of the spear
motive suggests that Wotan's power, built upon his oaths, is doomed
irrevocably, the power of Brünnhilde's love offers some small hope of
evading that doom, illustrated by the orchestra's periodic leaps.

In much the same way, the song of the forest bird (Example 24)
bears a strong thematic relationship to Woglinde's cry of "Weia! Waga!"
(Example 25) from the opening of *Das Rheingold*. The Rhinemaidens'
"rising and falling pentatonic theme," Deryck Cooke said, "is slightly
transformed and speeded up" to become the initial theme of the forest
bird.[149] "Evidently," according to Cooke, the forest bird "is first cousin
to the Rhinemaidens." A more likely explanation is, however, that
Wagner saw an inherent, logical connection between these two primeval voices of nature. The songs of both the Rhinemaidens and the
forest bird convey wisdom masked by childlike innocence. Moreover,
it should be remembered that the forest bird guides Siegfried to the
Rhinemaidens' hoard of gold and then to Brünnhilde just as Woglinde's
song had once lured Alberich to the Rhinemaidens and the gold. By
associating these two scenes in this way, therefore, Wagner draws a
thematic parallel that could never have been apparent through plot and
staging alone.

One final example of Wagner's use of leitmotivs to transform one
idea into another may be seen in his so-called "composite motives."
These are themes in which two or more themes, already clearly established as independent units, become "fused" or repeatedly performed
in sequence. Perhaps the most famous of the composite leitmotivs in
the *Ring* is the theme known as "The Need of the Gods" (Example 26)
which is first heard in the second act of *Die Walküre*. "The Need of the
Gods" consists of three separate themes in rapid succession. Two of

these themes—Erda (Example 11) and the Twilight of the Gods (Example 18)—we have already encountered and are simple inverses of one another. The third theme, Wotan's frustration (Example 27), is introduced throughout the *Ring* whenever Wotan's desires are thwarted either by Fricka's infallible logic or by the power of his own oaths. By grouping these three themes into a single composite motive, Wagner begins building his musical "vocabulary" into a consistent, easily recognized "phrase." As a unit, the new theme reminds the audience that it was Erda who first predicted the gods' downfall. Her prediction caused Wotan to embark on his great plan of salvation, each aspect of which has been thwarted, resulting in the gods' continuing need.

To someone as familiar with classical literature as was Wagner, this building of musical phrases into longer and more complex units must have seemed quite similar to the use of poetic "formulae" found in such works as the *Iliad* and the *Odyssey*. The repetitions of epic poetry—starting with epithets ("swift-footed Achilles," "Hector of the shining helm," "rosy-fingered dawn," and the like) and stock phrases ("So answering him, he spoke," "He addressed him using winged words," "He fell and his armor clattered upon him") and continuing to complete arming scenes, heroic exchanges, and descriptions of sacrifice—served many of the same functions for literature as Wagner's leitmotivs served his music. They gave the work a stylistic integrity that might otherwise have been difficult to attain.[150] They remind their audience of similar incidents and characters encountered earlier. And they fill a vital role in their works' thematic structure. For instance, epithets may be little more than ritualistic titles or they may be introduced thematically to provide emphasis, irony, or subtle humor. They even appear in sometimes unexpected combinations as the author manipulates them among the colors of his poetic palette. In much the same way, Wagner's leitmotivs may *occasionally* reiterate what the audience has already seen on the stage, but far more frequently they associate, combine, or develop ideas. Approaching music as though it *were* poetry, Wagner combined and recombined his leitmotivs until they became increasingly complex units. He filled both his text and his music alike with meaningful "words," "phrases," and "sentences," creating one of the most richly leveled of all artistic works.

Non-Musical Leitmotivs in the *Ring*

Leitmotivs are thus used for many different purposes in the *Ring*. They give Wagner's cycle a melodic unity that such a long and complex work might not otherwise have had. They incorporate recognizable melodies into Wagner's drama without resorting to the independent arias and recitatives of a "numbers opera." Most importantly of all, however, they provided Wagner with his central thematic principle of composition. Leitmotivs were the elements he relied on to establish relationships among characters, events, and ideas. They served much the same purpose as does imagery in poetry, highlighting unexpected similarities among people or ideas. In this way, Wagner used leitmotivs to make the *Ring* the most "programmatic" of all program music. Nearly every phrase in the cycle was imbued with *some* meaning, and the score was intended both to communicate (part of its classical heritage) and to make its audience feel the emotions of the characters (its romantic heritage).

Nevertheless, if Wagner sought to make his score more of a "text," it is equally true that he sought to make his text more of a "score" through the musicality of his words and ideas. This interrelationship between text and music may be seen in a number of different ways throughout the *Ring*. For instance, if one of the purposes of leitmotivs was to provide melodic unity throughout the cycle, Wagner also approached the plot and structure of his drama in much the same fashion. There are at a number of points in the *Ring* repeated patterns of narrative that can only be regarded as "plot leitmotivs." When Mime is first encountered in *Das Rheingold* 3, Alberich is abusing him for (supposedly) not completing a task assigned to him; when Mime is next seen in *Siegfried* 1.1, the hero of that drama abuses him for precisely the same reason. In *Die Walküre* 1.2 as Siegmund is relating his history to Hunding, we learn that the house in which Siegmund grew up has been burnt and its massive oak tree cut down;[151] by the end of the drama, Siegmund's father, Wotan, will again see his great hall consumed by flames and the World Ash felled for kindling. The poignant farewell that the Rhinemaidens bid Siegfried (*Leb wohl!*) is an explicit parallel to Wotan's last words to Brünnhilde. Two of the four dramas, *Die Walküre* and *Götterdämmerung*, end with spectacular images of fire; the remaining two dramas, *Das Rheingold* and *Siegfried*, end with a celebration shortly after a prophecy of the world's destruction has been made. The entire structure of *Götterdämmerung* is, as we have seen, a microcosm of all that has gone before. This drama has a brief prologue followed by three longer acts, just as the *Ring* itself consists of a "preliminary evening" (*Vorabend*) followed by three longer dramas. Both the cycle as a whole and *Götterdämmerung* in particular begin with three goddesses charged with protecting a sacred object. The "symphonic" structure and emotional progression of the cycle's dramas—a quick and lively "first movement" (*Das Rheingold*), a slower, more lyrical "second movement" (*Die Walküre*), a joyous "third movement scherzo" (*Siegfried*), and a majestic "final movement" (*Götterdämmerung*)—are all reproduced in exactly this order during the four sections of the *Ring*'s final work.

These repeated elements of plot and structure are not coincidental. Wagner used them to achieve many of the same goals that he achieved through musical leitmotivs. By creating easily perceived patterns of either plot or melody, he reminds his audience of incidents that occurred earlier in his cycle. By drawing comparisons among the many events and characters of the *Ring*, he maintains a remarkable sense of unity in a story that spans generations. By suggesting that events do not occur randomly or in isolation, he gives his story a sense of "epic significance." Every incident that occurs, we feel, relates in at least some small way to the will of Wotan, just as every incident in Homer relates in at least some small way to the *boulê* of Zeus (*Iliad* 1.5).

It must be asked, however, whether the "non-musical leitmotivs" of the *Ring* share any of the *thematic* functions of Wagner's musical phrases? Did Wagner, for instance, attach specific "meanings" to the "theme" of Mime being beaten or of three goddesses protecting a sacred object? Did he, in short, apply a thematic method of composition to anything *beyond* his score, to the text, characters, and staging of his work? The answer to these questions is that Wagner most certainly did. Yet, in order to understand how Wagner's thematic method of composition was applied to other aspects of his drama, it will be necessary to explore individually the other components that Aristotle regarded as necessary for tragedy: speech, thought, character, and spectacle.

CHAPTER 4

Speech

The Thematic Role of Stabreim in the *Ring*

*Thought and language are to the artist instruments of an
art. . . . From the point of view of form, the type of all the
arts is the art of the musician.*

—Oscar Wilde[152]

The libretto of the *Ring* is characterized by an alliterative style of poetry known as Stabreim. In *A History of the German Language*, John T. Waterman notes that this type of "alliteration . . . was the formal principle of versification in the early period of all the Germanic languages."[153] Speakers of English, if they are familiar with Stabreim at all, will perhaps recognize it from *Beowulf*, *Sir Gawain and the Green Knight*,[154] or William Langland's *Piers Plowman*.[155] In Germany itself, alliterative poetry had a long oral tradition, resulting at the start of the ninth century in such poems as the *Hildesbrandslied* and *Heliand*. In Scandinavia, the *Poetic* (or *Earlier*) *Edda* is a late mediæval collection of alliterative poems—composed originally during the ninth through twelfth centuries—that retold the legends of the Norse gods and heroes. Though today the word "Stabreim" may be applied to any of these mediæval works, it was coined as a technical term only during the Romantic Age.[156] In the sixteenth century, speakers of German referred to poetry with repeated initial consonants by adopting the Latin word "*alliteratio.*" Only in the nineteenth century, when nationalists objected to using a Latin word for such a characteristically German form of verse, was a new term developed.[157] The nationalistic scholars of the period recognized that the Old Norse expression for a sound or written character, "stafr," shared a linguistic root with its German counterpart, "Buchstabe."[158] The word "Stabreim" was thus intended both to suggest "Buchstabreim" ("letter rhyme") and to sound archaic in imitation of its Norse predecessor.

Wagner had several reasons for adopting Stabreim as he wrote the text of the *Ring*.

- His story was based at least in part on legends found in the *Poetic Edda*. Just as the scholars of his day had coined the term "Stabreim" because of its archaic sound, Wagner was attracted to the archaic sound of the verse itself. Stabreim, Wagner believed, made his libretto immediately reminiscent of the historic or mythic period of his story.[159]
- Since Stabreim avoided both end-rhyme and a rigid metrical scheme, it allowed Wagner to set aside the artificial poetry of grand opera in favor of a flexible rhythm more similar to that of ordinary speech.[160]
- Wagner found the repetition of initial consonants to be itself highly musical. With Stabreim, he could create both linguistic harmonies[161] and dissonances[162] at will and thus use his text to reinforce the orchestral line.
- Wagner saw in Stabreim support for his view that vowels or "tone speech" (*Tonsprache*) developed historically before consonants. For this reason, Wagner argued, the vowels that were characteristic of end-rhyme affected the listener on a primitive or emotional level. On the other hand, the consonants that were the distinctive feature of Stabreim had a more rational or intellectual function.[163]
- As a refinement of this theory, Wagner sought to associate specific consonants with specific themes or ideas. He thus regarded Stabreim as a sort of "phonetic leitmotif," a linguistic equivalent to the musical phrases that he associated with characters or ideas throughout the *Ring*.

Of these five functions of Stabreim, the first four have been discussed at length since the composer's own day.[164] The *thematic* role of Stabreim has, however, largely been ignored.[165] This is a major oversight since Wagner himself regarded the connection between themes and sound as vitally important. For instance, in *Opera and Drama* he described how "in *Stabreim* . . . kindred speech-roots are fitted to one another in such a way, that, just as they sound alike to the physical ear, they also knit like objects into one collective image."[166] Later in the same treatise, he provided examples of how this process might be applied to the libretto of a music drama. Stabreim, Wagner said, could be used to reinforce the similarity of words having equivalent emotional content (as in the verse *Liebe giebt Lust zum Leben*, "Love gives delight to living") or to provide an ironic contrast between words of opposing emotional effect (as in the verse *Die Liebe bringt Lust und Leid*, "Love brings delight and sorrow").[167] These two examples of Stabreim have direct parallels to the first two uses of musical leitmotivs that we saw in the last chapter: to reinforce an idea and to undermine an idea.

That Wagner intended Stabreim to function thematically in the *Ring* is apparent from his use of phrases almost identical to these examples at several points in the cycle. For instance, in *Die Walküre* 2.4, Siegmund tells Brünnhilde *Wo Sieglinde lebt in Lust und Leid, da will Siegmund auch säumen* ("Wherever Sieglinde lives in joy or grief, there shall Siegmund also remain"). Again, in *Siegfried* 2.3, the Forest Bird declares *Lustig im Leid sing' ich von Liebe* ("Glad in the midst of grief I sing of love"). There are many similar passages throughout the *Ring*. Since Wagner was completing the text of his cycle at the same time that he was publishing his theoretical works, he used the *Ring* as a way of putting the theories of *Opera and Drama* into practice. For this reason, the text of the *Ring* provides numerous instances of specific alliterations linked to specific ideas. Examining them reveals that the composer treated Stabreim in his text in a manner almost identical to the way in which he treated musical leitmotivs in his score.

"W": The Theme of Nature

The first thematic use of Stabreim in the *Ring* appears at the very
opening of the cycle.

> *Weia! Waga! Woge, du Welle! Walle zur Wiege! Wagalaweia!*
> *Wallala weiala weia! Weia! Waga!*
> [Weia! Waga! Billow, you waves! Waft to the cradle!
> Wagalaweia! Wallala weiala weia!]

As these words suggest, the *Ring* begins not so much with sense as with
sound. Woglinde's first utterances are not really speech at all. They are
merely the rudiments of speech, a seemingly pointless repetition of
syllables beginning in "w" that assume meaning only gradually in the
words that follow.

> Wellgunde: *Woglinde, wachst du allein?*
> [Woglinde, are you watching alone?]
> Woglinde: *Mit Wellgunde wär' ich zu zwei.*
> [With you, Wellgunde, we'd be two.]
> Wellgunde: *Lass sehn, wie du wachst.*
> [Let's see how you watch.]
> Woglinde: *Sicher vor dir.*
> [Safe from you.]
> Flosshilde: *Heiaha weia! Wildes Geschwister!*
> [Heiaha weia! Unruly sisters!]

As one might expect in a *Gesamtkunstwerk*, the sounds that these characters utter have a close parallel to the music heard in the opening bars
of the prelude, the spectacle seen as the drama begins, and the story
that unfolds in the course of *Das Rheingold*. In the music, a single, low
E^b (Example 28) becomes the basis for a broken chord (the E^b triad).
This chord, when heard in isolation, is often regarded as the "theme of
nature" in the *Ring*. (Example 1) With slightly more elaboration, that
same theme then becomes associated with the River Rhine. (Example
29) In the music, therefore, a single note, a "primal substance," takes
shape to become a general theme; that general theme is then developed
into the leitmotif of one particular river.

There are a number of parallels to this pattern of development at
the beginning of the cycle.

THE CREATION OF THE UNIVERSE

PATTERN:	non-existence ⇨	existence	⇨	chaos	⇨	order
SOUND:	$E^\flat$ ⇨	$E^\flat$ triad	⇨	nature motive	⇨	Rhine motive
SIGHT:	darkness ⇨	light	⇨	motion	⇨	Rhinemaidens
THOUGHT:	nothing ⇨	primal substance ⇨		water	⇨	Rhine
SPEECH:	silence ⇨	"w"	⇨	"w"-nonsense	⇨	"w"-sense

Parallel Developments at the Beginning of *Das Rheingold*

On stage, the initial darkness of the theater slowly yields to light, then to motion, and then to the appearance of the Rhinemaidens. In the realm of ideas, the audience witnesses a scene of creation: as in the music, a shapeless "primal substance" takes form as water and then water takes the form of a river. To each of the audience's senses, therefore, Wagner illustrates the same process of creation: a progression from a single, formless jumble to a meaningful substance of great complexity. That is precisely the way in which Wagner uses the repetition of "w" in the opening lines of the work. Meaningless sounds beginning with "w" become meaningful words beginning with "w" as the action of the drama proceeds.

The complex set of associations that Wagner establishes in this opening scene returns a number of times in the cycle. Whenever the audience hears an alliteration in "w" or an arpeggiated E^b chord, whenever it sees light arising out of the darkness or stillness gradually becoming motion, it will be reminded of this opening scene. Slightly later in *Das Rheingold* 1, for example, Woglinde notes that the "waking sun" (*Die Weckerin*) is smiling upon the sleeping gold, rousing it from its slumbers. All three of the Rhinemaidens bid the gold to awaken and play with them (*Wache, Freunde, wache froh! Wonnige Spiele spenden wir dir.*) Wagner's return to alliteration in "w" is intended to draw a parallel between the awakening of the gold in this scene and the awakening of creation that had occurred at the beginning of the cycle. Wellgunde asks Alberich whether he does not know of the gold that wakes and sleeps in turn (*Nicht weiss der Alp von des Goldes Auge, das wechselnd wacht und schläft?*). At the moment these lines are spoken, Alberich must confess his ignorance. But Wellgunde's revelation that the gold has power sets forces into motion that will ultimately lead to the *Ring*'s conclusion.

Wagner's use of "w" to suggest the awakening of nature continues in *Das Rheingold* 2. The goddess Fricka awakens Wotan with these words:

> *Wotan! Gemahl! erwache!*...
>
> *Erwache, Mann, und erwäge!*
>
> [Wotan, my spouse, awake! ...
>
> Awake, husband, and think!]

Still later in *Das Rheingold* when Erda warns Wotan of the danger he is facing, she too awakens, half rising from the ground with the words

> *Weiche, Wotan, weiche!* ...
>
> *Wie alles war, weiss ich;*
>
> *wie alles wird, wie alles sein wird,*
>
> *seh' ich auch:*
>
> *der ew'gen Welt Ur-Wala.*
>
> [Yield, Wotan, yield! ...
>
> I know whatever was.
>
> I also see whatever is and
>
> whatever will be: I,
>
> the primal mother of the eternal world.]

Just as Erda's *musical* leitmotif (Example 11) is an adaptation in duple meter of the nature motive (first heard in triple meter; Example 1), so is the Stabreim of her speech a reflection of the sounds that were heard at the opening of the drama. Erda embodies the force of natural wisdom[168] and, as such, she is always represented on stage as though she

were still half-immersed in nature itself.[169] It is perhaps for this reason
that both the melody of her leitmotif and the sound of her own words
suggest themes that Wagner has associated with nature.

In *Die Walküre* there is a yet another parallel between Wagner's
thematic use of Stabreim and his musical leitmotivs. As we saw in the
last chapter, a musical theme will sometimes be introduced for the
sake of dramatic irony, to alert the audience to something that a character on stage does not yet know. One example of this was Wagner's
use of the "Valhalla theme" (Example 4) in *Die Walküre* 1.2 when he
wanted to remind his audience of something that Siegmund did not know:
the identity of his father. In a similar manner, Wagner provides a clue to
the identity of Siegmund's father in the alliteration of his text. Siegmund
mentions that his father was known as "Wolf" (*Wolfe*) and that

Wehrlich und stark war Wolfe . . .
Lange Jahre lebt die Junge
mit Wolfe in wilden Wald.
[Wolf was strong and warlike . . .
For long years as a young man
I lived with Wolf in the wild woods.]

Later, Sieglinde reveals that, years before at her wedding, a stranger
had thrust a sword into an ash tree. That tree still stands in the very hall
where Siegmund has come for refuge. At first, Sieglinde did not recognize the stranger but she soon knew it to be her father, Wälse, in
disguise. She tells Siegmund of her discovery with the words *Da wusst'
ich, wer der war* ("Then I knew who he was"). Similarly, in *Siegfried*
1.2, Mime asks the Wanderer who he is. The very way in which Mime
phrases this question suggests its own answer: the Wanderer is Wotan
in disguise, though Mime does not recognize him.

Wer ist's, der im wilden Walde mich sucht?
[Who is it that searches for me in the wild woods?]

Wotan, Wolfe, Wälse, der Wanderer: all the names that the supreme
god assumes in the *Ring* bind him inexorably to the forces of nature.
Though Wotan may try to deceive these forces through his plans to
regain the ring, he is doomed to failure. The central lesson that Wotan
must learn in the cycle is that not even his will can be set in opposition

to nature's law. By continually surrounding Wotan with words and titles
that suggest the nature theme, Wagner reveals to his audience the type
of wisdom that Wotan must gain. Not incidentally, that same use of
Stabreim also links _W_otan's name to that of _W_agner. Confirming what
he had once said in a famous letter to August Röckel,[170] Wagner believed that Wotan stood for himself and for all of us, that "Wotan
resembles us to a hair." The truths the god must learn are those that
face the entire world as well.

Siegmund's own link to Wotan and his heritage is revealed by the
name that _he_ assumes when tells his story to Hunding: _Wehwalt_ ("Woeful").[171] Like father, like son: both reveal their lineage through the titles
they invent for themselves. In a similar fashion, Brünnhilde suggests
through alliteration that she is also a member of this family. In _Die
Walküre_ 2.2, Brünnhilde says

> _Zu _W_otans _W_illen sprichst du,_
> _sagst du mir, _w_as du _w_illst;_
> _wer bin ich, _w_är' ich dein _W_ille nicht?_
> [You are speaking _to_ Wotan's will
> when you tell me what you want.
> Who am I if not your will?[172]]

Later in the same scene, Wotan refers to Erda—not only "Mother
Nature" but _Brünnhilde's_ mother, it must be remembered—as "the
world's wisest woman" (_der _W_elt _w_eisestes _W_eib_). Finally, to remind the
audience that Siegfried will also be a member of this family, his arrival
is foreshadowed in the last scene of _Die Walküre_ with the words

> _W_er so die _W_ehrlose _w_eckt,_
> _dem, er_w_acht, sie zum _W_eib!_
> [Defenseless, you will be the
> wife of whoever wakes you!]

The association between nature and the descendants of Wotan returns
in _Siegfried_ 1.2 where Mime retells the history of that family.

> _Die _W_älsungen sind das _W_unschgeschlecht,_
> _das _W_otan zeugte und zärtlich liebte._
> [The Wälsungs are the chosen race
> whom Wotan sired and dearly loved.]

The result of all these passages is to make "w" something of a "monogram" for the Wälsungs. It is the first letter of their name and it indicates that they are *all* bound to the forces of nature. Wagner was particularly fond of the device, already found in his German sources, that linked families through the alliteration of their names or titles.[173] At times, the composer intentionally chose a variant of a character's name so as to reinforce this type of alliteration. As a result, the *Ring* is filled with such groups as: Freia, Froh, and Fricka; Fasolt and Fafner; Gunther and Gutrune, the Gibichungs; and Siegmund, Sieglinde, and Siegfried. The underlying principle in each case is that the sound of these characters' names somehow expresses a deeper sort of family resemblance.[174]

Another device that Wagner adopted repeatedly in the *Ring* was to use Stabreim to remind his audience of earlier events that have a bearing on later scenes. Once again, this function of Stabreim parallels one of the uses of musical leitmotivs that we have seen. For instance, at the beginning of *Siegfried* 3.1, Wotan invokes the goddess Erda with the words

> *Wache, Wala! Wala! Erwach!* . . .
> *Erda! Erda! Ewiges Weib!*
> [Awake, mother! Mother! Awake! . . .
> Erda! Erda! Eternal woman!]

The alliteration of this passage reminds the audience of two earlier scenes: the first appearances of both Wotan (*Wotan! Gemahl! erwache!*) and Erda (*Weiche, Wotan, weiche!*). Wagner's intention in this scene was to associate these two characters in the minds of his audience. His reflection of those earlier passages suggests not only the sexual union of Wotan and Erda but also their interlocked fates. Moreover, Wotan and Erda are endowed with a wisdom that Wagner, once again echoing Schopenhauer,[175] linked to the intuition of dreams. By representing his characters as awakening to words that contain the "theme of nature," Wagner indicates that their dreamlike visions are derived from their (at times subconscious) proximity to nature. In order to reinforce this point, Wagner assigns Wotan a lengthy passage of Stabreim.

> *Der Weckrufer bin ich, und Weisen üb' ich,*
> *dass weithin wache, was fester Schlaf*

verschliesst. Die W*elt durchzog ich,*
w*anderte viel, Kunde zu* w*erben,*
*ur*w*eisen Rat zu ge*w*innen.*
[I am the one who has awakened you,
and I used charms
to wake from afar what sleep held fast.
The world I have roamed.
I have wandered far to win knowledge
and gain possession of primeval lore.]

What Wotan believes he has learned from his travels has led him to rely on Siegfried in his efforts to win back the ring. Nevertheless, Wagner also makes it clear that Siegfried will be bound by fate no less than were Wotan and Erda. The Rhinemaidens address Siegfried with these words in *Götterdämmerung* 3.1:

Siegfried! Siegfried!
W*ir* w*eissen dich* w*ahr.*
W*eiche,* w*eiche den Fluch!*
[Siegfried! Siegfried!
We warn you truly.
Beware! Beware the curse!]

The close parallel between these words and Erda's earlier warning to Wotan helps to reinforce the cycle's classical structure by bringing the *Ring* full circle. With what we might now call a "plot leitmotif," the same pattern appears at both the beginning and the end of the cycle: male figures are warned by wise women[176] that they should yield. On the level of both sound and ideas, therefore, the *Ring* ends as it began, with the world returning to a pure and formless state of "nature."

"SCH": The Theme of Sleep

If the "theme of nature" has an antithesis in the *Ring*, it is to be found in Wagner's frequent repetition of "sch." Building upon such pairs of words as *wachen* and *schlafen*, *weiss* and *schwarz*, Wagner uses Stabreim to establish a fundamental contrast between "w" [v] and "sch" [ʃ]. While "w" is the sound that the audience comes to associate with *Wotan*,

Walhall and *Wille*, "sch" proves to be associated with *schlecht*, *Schmerz* and *Schaden*. An early example of this contrast appears in Flosshilde's reference to the "sleeping" gold just before it "awakens" (accompanied by those alliterations of "w" mentioned earlier).

> *Des Goldes <u>Sch</u>laf hütet ihr <u>sch</u>lect;*
> *besser bewacht des <u>Sch</u>lummernden Bett,*
> *sonst büsst ihr beide das <u>Sp</u>iel!*[177]
> [Badly you guard the sleeping gold.
> You'd better watch the sleeper's bed
> or you'll both pay for this game!]

In a later passage, when Wellgunde notices that the light of dawn is about to wake the gold, the same sound appears.

> *Durch den grünen <u>Sch</u>wall*
> *den wonnigen <u>Sch</u>läfer sie grüsst. . . .*
> *<u>Sch</u>aut, es lächnet in lichten <u>Sch</u>ein.*
> [Through the green spume
> (the sun) greets the blissful sleeper . . . .
> Look, he smiles in the shining light!]

This pattern of alliteration appears consistently throughout *Das Rheingold* whenever there are passages that deal with sleep. Thus, when Fasolt notes in *Das Rheingold* 2 that he and Fafner completed Valhalla while the gods were asleep, the audience is reminded of the Rhinemaidens' earlier description of the sleeping gold.

> *Sanft <u>sch</u>loss <u>Sch</u>laf dein Aug':*
> *wir beide bauten <u>Sch</u>lummers bar die Burg . . .*
> *<u>St</u>eiler Turm, Tür und Tor*
> *deckt und <u>sch</u>liesst im <u>sch</u>lanken*
> *<u>Sch</u>loss den Saal . . . .*
> *<u>Sch</u>immernd hell be<u>sch</u>eint's der Tag.*
> [Gently sleep closed your eyes.
> The two of us, sleepless, built the castle . . .
> A steep tower, door and gate
> seal and close the hall
> in the fine fortress . . .

Brightly shining it gleams in the day.]

A similar passage appears in *Das Rheingold* 3 when Alberich boasts that, deep in the caverns of the Nibelungs, the dark night will conceal his crimes and permit his evil to go unpunished.

Schätze zu schaffen und Schätze zu bergen,
nütze mir Nibelheims nacht.

[To make treasure and to hide treasure
the darkness of Nibelheim serves me.]

In *Die Walküre*, a hint of alliteration in "sch" occurs in Wotan's pronouncement that the penalty for Brünnhilde's disobedience will be a deep sleep (*In festen Schlaf verschliess ich dich*). A clearer statement of the theme may be found in Brünnhilde's plea that Wotan construct a wall of fire to guard her while she is helpless (*Die Schlafende schütze mit scheuchendem Schrecken*). In *Siegfried* 1.1, the theme of sleep is heard when the hero says that he would loathe Mime even if the dwarf were to bring him a fine cushion to sleep on.

Schaffst du ein leichtes Lager zum Schlaf,
der Schlummer wird mir da schwer.

[Bring me a soft couch to sleep on
and slumber will still come hard to me.]

Later, in *Siegfried* 2.1, Wagner intensifies Fafner's demand that Wotan merely let him sleep (*Lasst mich schlafen!*) by introducing the sound of "sch" repeatedly in Wotan's bemused reply.

Nun, Alberich, das schlug fehl.
Doch schilt mich nicht mehr Schelm!

[Well, Alberich, we failed that time.
But at least you can't say that I'm cheating you!]

Even Alberich adopts this theme in *Siegfried* 2.3 when he rejects Mime's offer to let him keep the ring in exchange for the Tarnhelm.

Wie schlau du bist!
Sicher schlief' ich
niemals vor deinen Schlingen!

[How cunning you are!
I'd never sleep safe
from your snares!]

By the end of *Siegfried*, alliteration in "sch" to suggest sleep has become a well-established pattern. Wotan uses it as he dismisses Erda to endless sleep (*Siegfried* 3.1), . . .

> Drum *sch*lafe nun da, *sch*liesse dein Auge:
> träumend er*sch*au mein Ende!
> [So sleep on. Close your eyes:
> as you dream, behold my destruction!]

. . . and Siegfried uses it one final time as he catches sight of the sleeping Grane (*Siegfried* 2.3).

> Was ruht dort *sch*lummernd
> im *sch*attingen Tann?
> Ein Ross ist's, rastend in tiefen *Sch*laf!
> [What rests there,
> sleeping in that shady glen?
> It is a steed, deep in sleep!]

In *Götterdämmerung*, however, alliteration in "sch" becomes far less common. Even so, a hint of this phonetic pattern is preserved at the beginning of the second act when Alberich appears to Hagen in a dream.

> Alberich: *Sch*läfst du, Hagen, mein Sohn?
> Du *sch*läfst und hörst mich nicht,
> den Ruh' und *Sch*laf verriet?
> [Are you asleep, Hagen my son?
> You're asleep and you don't hear me,
> I who was betrayed by rest and sleep?]
> Hagen: Ich höre dich, *sch*limmer Albe:
> was hast du meinem *Sch*laf zu sagen?
> [I hear you, wicked elf:
> what do you have to say to me in my sleep?]

A similar hint of this theme may also be found at the beginning of Brünnhilde's immolation scene. In this climactic passage, Brünnhilde bids eternal rest to Wotan (*Ruhe, ruhe, du Gott!*: recall Wotan's final words to Erda) and to the whole world.

> *St*arke *Sch*eite *sch*ichtet mir dort
> am Rande des Rheins zuhauf!

> [Pile up stout logs for me there
> on the shore of the Rhine!]

Wagner uses Brünnhilde's words at the end of the cycle to reinforce an image of which the audience has gradually become aware: sleep in the *Ring* is symbolic of death. It is for this reason that, in *Die Walküre* 2.5, the phonetic "theme of sleep" resounds in Siegmund's final words before he is killed.

> *Deines Hauses heimischem Stamm*
> *entzog ich zaglos das Schwert;*
> *seine Schneide schmecke jetzt du!*
> [From the trunk of the tree that grows in your house
> I fearlessly drew the sword.
> Now taste its edge!]

Just as Wagner had expanded his use of "w" to suggest not only nature but also the apparent awakening of nature that is seen in the act of creation, so does he use repeated patterns of "sch" to suggest both sleep itself and the eternal sleep of death.

Moreover, since Wagner associated "w" with positive phenomena such as light, life, and creation, he often introduced "sch" when he desired to create an effect that was more negative or sinister. For instance, Stabreim is used to suggest delight when Siegfried refers to the "joyfully surging wave" (*die wonnig wogende Welle*) after Brünnhilde has been awakened. Contrast the effect achieved through alliteration in Alberich's angry denunciation of Wotan (*Schmäliche Tücke, schändlicher Trug! Wirfst du Schächer die Schuld mir vor?*) in *Das Rheingold* 4. In fact, the hissing or sneering sound of "sch"—especially when it takes the form "schw"—is particularly appropriate whenever Wagner wishes to imply that a character is criticizing or condemning someone. Examples of this type of alliteration include:

> *Das Rheingold*—
>> *1: Wellgunde expresses disgust of Alberich*
>> *Schwarzes, schwieliges Schwefelgezwerg!*
>> [Black, calloused, sulfurous gnome!]

2: Fricka explains her contempt for Loge
Viel <u>Sch</u>limmes <u>sch</u>uf er uns <u>sch</u>on.
[Much evil has he done to us already.]

3: Alberich upbraids Mime
Mime, zu mir, <u>sch</u>äbiger <u>Sch</u>uft!
<u>Sch</u>watzest du gar mit dem <u>sch</u>weifenden Paar?
[Mime! Come here, you mangy rogue!
Are you gossiping with these two idlers?]

4: Alberich condemns Wotan
<u>Sch</u>ändlicher <u>Sch</u>ächer! Du <u>Sch</u>alk! Du <u>Sch</u>elm!
[Disgraceful thief! Rogue! Knave!]

Die Walküre—
> *1.3: Sieglinde recounts her sufferings to Siegmund*
> . . . was je mich ge<u>sch</u>merz
> in <u>Sch</u>ande und <u>Sch</u>mach . . .
> [. . . whatever I suffered
> in shame and disgrace . . .]
>
> *3.2: Wotan condemns Brünnhilde before the Valkyries*
> Aus eurer <u>Sch</u>ar ist die treulose
> <u>Sch</u>wester ge<u>sch</u>ieden.
> [Your faithless sister is henceforth banished
> from your company.]

Siegfried—
> *1.1: Siegfried rejects the sword that Mime has made*
> Den <u>sch</u>wachen <u>St</u>ift nennst du ein <u>Sch</u>wert?
> Da hast du die <u>St</u>ücken, <u>sch</u>ändlicher <u>St</u>ümper:
> hätt' ich am <u>Sch</u>ädel dir sie zer<u>sch</u>lagen!
> [You call this feeble pin a sword?
> Take these pieces, you disgraceful bungler!

I should have broken them on your skull!]

1.3: Mime describes the sensation of fear
Sch̲wellend Sch̲wirren zu Leib dir sch̲webt.
[A swelling buzz hovers near you.]

2.3: Siegfried kills Mime
Sch̲meck du mein Sch̲wert, ekliger Sch̲wätzer!
[Taste my sword, you disgusting babbler!]

Götterdämmerung—
>   *1.4: Brünnhilde blames the gods for her suffering*
>   *Sch̲uft ihr mir Sch̲mach,*
>   *wie nie sie gesch̲merzt?*
>   [Did you create a shame for me
>   that no one has ever suffered before?]

In a *Gesamtkunstwerk*, we remember, every element of the drama should
support every other element. Alliteration, with its patterns repeated in
exactly the same way as Wagner's musical leitmotivs, reinforces the
score. Yet alliteration also plays an important role in reinforcing *char-
acterization* in the dramas. For instance, the same contrast between
"w" and "sch" may be seen in the struggle that exists between the forces
of light (W̲otan and the W̲älsungs) on the one hand and Alberich's
"army of the night" (Sch̲warz-Alberich and that *Sch̲uft* ["rogue"], Mime)
on the other. In the realm of ideas, a similar contrast exists between
the awakening of nature (*wachen*) with which the cycle begins and the
twilight of the gods (*schlafen*) with which it ends.

Perhaps nowhere in the *Ring* does this type of opposition become
more important than when Wagner wishes to suggest the possibility
that a single person or object has a dual nature, potentially good but
also potentially evil. The most fully developed instance of this idea may
be seen in Notung, the sword that Siegmund discovers and that Siegfried
later repairs from its fragments. Unlike the ring (which Alberich has
cursed and thus is wholly evil) or Wotan's spear (which bears the runes

of the law and thus was intended to be wholly good), Notung is, quite literally, a "double-edged sword." That it may be used for good is clear when Wotan leaves Notung behind to aid Siegmund in the hour of his greatest need, when Siegfried performs countless acts of heroism with this sword, and when it helps Siegfried preserve his pledge of loyalty to Gunther. Yet Notung also has a more destructive nature as may be seen when Wotan causes the death of Siegmund by shattering the sword, when Notung fulfills the ring's curse by slaying Fafner, when Siegfried uses it to splinter Wotan's spear, and when the young hero foolishly boasts that his sword could sever even the Norns' eternal rope of primeval law.[178] The very name of the sword, Notung ("Needful"), suggests the dual nature of this weapon: by itself, need can be called neither good nor evil; only when need is directed towards some particular object does it become a force of creation or destruction.

In the score of the *Ring*, Wagner reinforced the sword's paradoxical nature by assigning Notung a two-note leitmotif, reminiscent of both joy (the "Rheingold!" pattern) and grief (the "Wehe!" pattern). In his text, Wagner used Stabreim to accomplish this same purpose. Notung is, after all, both a "*Waffe*" (weapon) and a "*Schwert*" (sword). Before Wotan shatters Notung in Siegmund's hands, the images that surround the sword are consistently positive. This may be seen in Siegmund's cry in *Die Walküre* 1.3 . . .

> *Wälse! Wälse! Wo is dein Schwert?*
> [Wälse! Wälse! Where is your sword?]

. . . and in the way that Sieglinde reveals the sword later in the same scene.

> *Eine Waffe lass mich dir weisen:*
> *o wenn du sie gewännst!*
> [Let me show you a sword.
> Oh, if only you could attain it!]

Once Notung is shattered, however, and Wotan has failed in his plans to regain the ring through Siegmund, the destructive nature of the sword becomes more prominent in the text. Throughout Mime's opening tirade in *Siegfried*, for instance, the smith sputters imprecations against both Siegfried and the sword. Line after line is filled with such words as _Schwert_ (sword), _geschweisst_ (welded), _geschmiedet_ (forged), _schmäliche_ (shameful), _schmeisst_ (threw), _schüf_ (made), _Kindergeschmeid_ (trinket), _zerschwänge_ (shatter) and _Schmach_ (shame). In the following scene, during Mime's lengthy exchange with the Wanderer, the dwarf becomes distraught upon discovering that he cannot answer the final question posed to him.

> _Wer schweisst nun das Schwert,_
> _schaff' ich es nicht?_
> [Who shall make Notung whole again?
> Who shall weld the sword if I cannot do it?]

Most ironically of all, this same motive appears in Siegfried's triumphant conclusion to _Siegfried_ 1 when he has finally succeeded in repairing the sword.

> _Zeige den Schächern nun deinen Schein!_
> _Schlage den Falschen, fälle den Schelm!_
> _Schau, Mime, du Schmied:_
> _So schneidet Siegfrieds Schwert!_
> [Now, Notung, show the wretches your shine!
> Smite the false! Smash the base!
> Look, Mime, you smith:
> this is how Siegfried's sword can cut!]

In the hero's moment of victory, Wagner provides a hint of foreboding. Siegfried's sword will guide him to his greatest adventures but it will also lead him to his doom. Since Siegfried's death also entails the destruction of the world, the recasting of Notung should be seen as a melancholy victory at best.

* * *

While Wagner does assign a thematic role to several other alliterative patterns—most notably, "n" to suggest the theme of envy,[179] "f" for the theme of the curse,[180] and "h" for the theme of Hunding and his clan[181]— none of these other instances becomes as prominent as the alliterations in "w" and "sch." In all other cases, Wagner's thematic use of Stabreim tends to be limited to a few scenes and, at times, to a single dramatic passage.[182] Nevertheless, it is clear that the composer saw alliteration as having a potential similar to that of his musical leitmotivs. By associating specific ideas with specific sounds—whether in the text or in the score—Wagner was able to reinforce the images that his audience was seeing on the stage and the ideas he wished to convey through his words. Though the composer did not use alliteration with perfect consistency, it must be remembered that a similar inconsistency is seen in his use of musical leitmotivs as well. Admittedly, there are lines of alliteration in "sch" that have little to do with either sleep or death; in much the same way, the leitmotif associated with a particular character or idea is sometimes heard in the *Ring* for reasons known only to the composer himself. In text as in music, Wagner never permitted a minor inconsistency to detract from the overall effect he was trying to create.

As a type of "phonetic leitmotif," therefore, Wagner's use of Stabreim makes it clear that his thematic approach to composition extended far beyond the score of his cycle. The text reinforces what is occurring in the music. The music reinforces what is occurring on stage. The actions of the drama reinforce what is occurring on the level of ideas. So, if the theme of sleep and awakening plays such an important role in the *sound* of Wagner's text, it may be expected to have a parallel on the level of ideas or what Aristotle called the thought of the drama.

CHAPTER 5

Thought

Sleep in the *Ring*

Death is the cool night.
Life is the sultry day.
Darkness comes and I am getting sleepy.
The day has made me tired.

—Heinrich Heine[183]

In its thought and in its imagery, Wagner's *Ring* moves, quite literally, from cradle to grave. It begins with Woglinde's famous reference to the cradle (*Wiege*) where the gold, sleeping peacefully,[184] wakes to the light of a new day. It ends with the funeral pyre of Siegfried, a blaze that encompasses first Brünnhilde, then the gods, and finally the entire world. The structure of the *Ring* thus mirrors the structure of life itself. Progressing from birth to death, it leaves unanswered the question of whether death is a final, everlasting sleep or the soul's awakening to the dawn of a new life.

These twin images—life and death, wakefulness and sleep—form one of the most important symbolic patterns of the *Ring*. As Schopenhauer wrote in *Parerga und Paralipomena.*

Each day is a little life for which our waking up is the birth and which is brought to an end by sleep as death. Thus going to sleep is a daily death and every waking up a new birth. In fact to complete the simile, we could regard the discomfort and difficulty of getting up as labour pains.[185]

These same ideas were repeated, virtually word for word, in several of

Schopenhauer's other essays[186] and they became quite familiar to Wagner himself. In 1854, in a letter to Franz Liszt, the composer spoke of death as a type of sleep[187] and in 1858, while writing to Mathilde Wesendonck, he wished that death would come to him as gently as had sleep the night before.[188]

In addition to Schopenhauer, Wagner also drew the image of sleep as death from ancient Greek literature. In Homer's *Iliad* (16.672, 682, and elsewhere), which Wagner once considered adapting into an opera or dramatic poem,[189] Sleep and Death are described as twin brothers. In the *Odyssey*, the eventual death of Odysseus is foreshadowed several times by the hero's sudden surrender to an overpowering sleep.[190] Hesiod in the *Theogony* (211-212) said that the gods Fate, Doom, Dreams, Sleep, and Death were born to the goddess Night in a single generation.[191]

For Wagner, these images of Greek poetry provided a framework of thought to which he would return repeatedly. Building upon a theme that appears several times in the gospels,[192] he included this image near the beginning of his prose sketch *Jesus of Nazareth*. There, the daughter of the publican Levi is restored to life with the words "Bury the dead, not the living: she sleepeth."[193] The girl's father then exclaims, "My child liveth; thou hast awakened it from death." To this Jesus replies, "What lived, I have preserved to life: open thou thine heart, that *thee* I may awake from death!"

Sleep As Death, Awakening As Birth in
Das Rheingold

In the *Ring* itself, Wagner's first association of awakening with life and birth appears at the very beginning of *Das Rheingold*. We saw in the last chapter that Wagner uses the prelude of the cycle to depict the creation of the universe. He begins with a motive we have called "the Primal Element" (Example 28), builds this single note into an arpeggiated chord that serves as the theme of "Nature" (Example 1), and then develops this motive even further into a flowing theme that symbolizes water (Example 30). Within a few moments, this theme too is developed, doubling in tempo to become the agitated melody of the river Rhine (Example 29). The effect is that of an entire musical universe being created out of a single note. At least on one level, therefore, the first words heard in the drama, "*Weia! Waga!*", might be taken as a cry of "labor pains" accompanying the birth of this new world.[194] Such an idea is implicit in the words themselves. Wagner drew the expression "*Weia!*" from roots that appear in the German words for birth pangs (*Wehen*), consecration (*Weihe*),[195] and "woe!" (*weh*); "*Waga!*" is simply the word for water itself (*Wasser*) in a rudimentary or embryonic form. In his 1872 letter to Friedrich Nietzsche, Wagner claimed that the expression "*Weia! Waga!*" was connected to the term "*Weihwasser*," "holy water."[196]

Wagner tied these words to one of those two-note musical patterns that have great symbolic importance throughout the *Ring*. (Example 25) The melody of "*Weia! Waga!*" inspires the ecstatic "*Rheingold!*" theme (Example 15), its mournful "*Wehe!*" antithesis (Example 16), and a whole series of related motives.[197] In its first appearance, however, Woglinde's sing-song melody expresses neither the joy of "*Rheingold!*" nor the sorrow of "*Wehe!*". It contains, rather, the possibility of both. Like the moment of birth itself, the initial form of this melody embodies great happiness and great suffering simultaneously. Perhaps for this reason, critical reactions to the opening of the cycle have varied considerably. M. Owen Lee, for instance, borrowed a phrase from Wagner himself and described the beginning of *Das Rheingold* as "a cradle song for a new world evolving."[198] Robert Donington, however, detected something far more ominous. The opening of the *Ring*, he says, presents an image of humanity on the verge of its fall from a state of "pristine innocence."[199]

The imagery of awakening and birth that appears in the prelude to *Das Rheingold* and in Woglinde's opening words is developed throughout the entire first scene of the drama. Flosshilde warns her sisters to watch over the sleeping gold (*Des Goldes Schlaf*) as they guard the slumberer's bed (*des Schlummernden Bett*). When the rays of the sun begin to pierce the waters of the Rhine, Woglinde calls this light "the awakener," *die Weckerin*, a feminine form of the word for "alarm clock."

Together the three Rhinemaidens urge the gold to "Wake, friend! Wake joyfully!" (*Wache, Freunde, wache froh!*) and once again refer to the gold's bed (*dein Bett*). Alberich asks the Rhinemaidens why they are fascinated by this glittering trifle. Such ignorance astounds Wellgunde. She cannot believe that Alberich knows nothing of the gold that wakes and sleeps in turn (*das wechselnd wacht und schläft*). As we have already seen, these passages are filled with alliteration of "w," a pattern that Wagner used as a "phonetic leitmotif" for the birth of nature. The sound of the composer's text and the images of his narrative thus work together to produce a single, imposing effect. For this reason, we might regard the thematic pattern in the *Ring* that occurs when someone (or, in this case, some*thing*) awakens as having a "leitmotivic function," precisely as do certain musical themes, bits of plot, and patterns of Stabreim. As an element of thought or imagery, this repeated pattern serves to unite disparate incidents in the composer's cycle and relates them thematically. The symbol of awakening is an "image leitmotif" that Wagner will return to at a number of critical moments in the *Ring*.

For example, the second scene of *Das Rheingold* begins, like the first, with a scene of awakening. Wotan, deep in sleep before his newly completed castle of Valhalla, is awakened by his wife, Fricka, with yet another cry. Her words, "*Wotan! Gemahl! erwache!*" ("Wotan! Husband! Wake up!") and "*Erwache, Mann, und erwäge!*" ("Wake up, man, and think!") contain that same alliterative pattern that is found in Woglinde's opening words. By representing Wotan in a manner reminiscent of nature coming to life at the beginning of the drama, Wagner draws a parallel between his central character and the forces of creation that surround him. Moreover, this scene serves to foreshadow the lesson that Wotan must learn in the *Ring*. Like Odysseus, Wotan must be brought to recognize the inevitability of his own death. And so, like Odysseus, Wotan symbolically surrenders to death in the form of sleep. The wisdom that will be revealed to Wotan only gradually and painfully as the cycle continues is represented to the audience in the god's very first appearance on stage.

Dreams As Wisdom

Wotan, however, is not merely asleep as the second act of *Das Rheingold* opens. He is also dreaming. By introducing his audience to the veiled, poetic language of dreams, Wagner passes to a *second* level of imagery that he will use repeatedly in the *Ring*. Sleep, the composer suggests, is not only a symbol for death; it can also be a source of great wisdom. In reality, these two aspects of sleep are closely related. As Wagner knew from his reading of Homeric epic, it was widely believed in ancient Greece that, during the moments before death, one could be endowed with wisdom or prophecy.[200] Since sleep was regarded as a way of passing between the worlds of life and death, many believed that sleep itself exposed the dreamer to truth in a highly pure form.

Wagner adopted this idea in his libretto for the *Ring*. In *Das Rheingold* 4, the earth goddess, Erda, tells Wotan that he nightly sees the same truth that is revealed to her in prophetic visions. An additional source for this idea may be found once again in Wagner's reading of Schopenhauer. In the essay entitled "On Spirit Seeing and Everything Connected Therewith,"[201] Schopenhauer argued that, during sleep, the spirit could grasp intuitively what the rational mind could not perceive while awake. In his essay on Beethoven, Wagner admitted borrowing this notion from Schopenhauer.

> As the Dream-organ cannot be roused into action by outer impressions, against which the brain is now fast locked, this must take place through happenings in the inner organism that our waking consciousness merely feels as vague sensations. But it is this inner life through which we are directly allied with the whole of Nature, and thus are brought into a relation with the essence of things that eludes the forms of outer knowledge, Time and Space; whereby Schopenhauer so convincingly explains the genesis of prophetic or telepathic (*das Fernste wahrnehmbar*), fatidical dreams, ay, in rare and extreme cases the occurrence of somnabulistic clairvoyance.[202]

We recall, too, Wagner's "vision of La Spezia" where that moment of inspiration was said to have been preceded by "a sleepless and feverish night" that led to a "somnambulistic state." Sleep, Wagner knew both from Schopenhauer and his reading of classical literature, was the condition that permitted divine wisdom to be revealed to mortals. Wagner was strongly attracted to this idea, incorporating it both into the myths that he created about his own life and into the dramas that he created for the stage.

Dreams in the *Ring* are often presented as sources of great wisdom. Though Fricka may say that Wotan's dreams about Valhalla are but "delightful illusions" (*aus der Träume wonnigem Trug!*), his visions are actually more insightful than she realizes. In his sleep, Wotan had mentioned the gate and door (*Tür und Tor*) of the sacred hall that stand in clear view of the audience, though he himself has not yet seen them. Moreover, the "eternal fame" that he attributes to Valhalla in his dream is an accurate prediction of the future. Fricka's complaints, on the other hand, are short-sighted. In her anxiety, she is unable to rise above her present troubles. To indicate the gulf that separates Wotan's wisdom from Fricka's mundane rationalism, Wagner assigns the high god an ironic twist on her earlier words *Träume* and *Trug*: Wotan says that his first glimpse of Valhalla is just as he had imagined it in his dreams (*Wie im Traum ich ihn trug*).

Wagner continued to combine these two images of sleep—the unconscious state that symbolizes death and the dream-filled state that conveys great wisdom—throughout the second half of the *Das Rheingold*. When Fasolt arrives to claim Freia, for instance, only the first of these two images appears. Fasolt speaks of the soft sleep that seals the eyes of the gods (*Sanft schloss Schlaf dein Aug'*) and contrasts it to his own wakefulness in building Wotan's majestic castle. Once again, the image of sleep is used in this passage to foreshadow the doom of the gods. At the same time, however, Wagner provides a subtle reminder of his *other* symbolic use of sleep. In Fasolt's boasting of Valhalla's might, the giant devotes special pride to the castle's door and gate (*Tür und Tor*), the very features that Wotan had foreseen in his dream.[203]

Sleep in *Die Walküre*

We recall that, near the end of *Das Rheingold*, Wotan suddenly develops a plan that will permit him to achieve what he himself is forbidden to do. The hero who represents the central part of this "great idea" is Siegmund, the first character whom the audience sees in *Die Walküre*. Siegmund will fail, however, in his efforts to live up to Wotan's expectations. The inevitability of Siegmund's failure is suggested by Wagner through this character's first appearance on-stage. At the opening of *Die Walküre*, Siegmund bursts through the door, takes a few steps, and instantly falls asleep. As he himself later says in describing this scene, "night descended over [his] eyes." The audience's first impression of this hero is, therefore, very similar to its first impression of Wotan himself. Both figures are seen as vulnerable to sleep and so, on a symbolic level, vulnerable to death.

The entire first act of *Die Walküre* is filled with references to Siegmund's sleep. Later in the first scene, Siegmund says that he has "rested and slept sweetly." Sieglinde's first words to her husband, Hunding, are that she found this stranger "exhausted" on their hearth. As Sieglinde exits to prepare her husband for sleep, Siegmund says repeatedly that the darkness of night had sealed his eyes (*Nächtiges Dunkel deckte mein Aug*) in the days before he met Sieglinde. When Sieglinde returns, her very first words to Siegmund are "Are you sleeping, my guest?" (*Schläfst du, Gast?*).

All of these references underscore Siegmund's mortality. Siegmund, Wagner wants the audience to understand, is doomed. But if it is true that Siegmund cannot escape his fate, then it is all the more true that a similar disaster is awaiting Hunding. The destiny of Hunding is suggested by the deep sleep (*tiefem Schlaf: Die Walküre* 1.3; *hartem Schlaf:* 2.3) into which he falls midway through the first act of the drama. Though one critic regards Hunding's sleeping potion as "a less than significant plot device that seems to appear in every synopsis but mine,"[204] the night drink is actually a powerful image in the drama. Through its ability to make Hunding sleep, it suggests that his fate is sealed. Hunding's deep sleep binds him to all of the other doomed figures in the *Ring*. Like Fafner in *Siegfried*, for instance, Hunding in *Die Walküre* cannot rouse himself from sleep even as his fate is being decided around him.

Most importantly of all, Hunding's night drink is the first example of one particular "image leitmotif" that is rather similar to those surrounding awakening and sleep that we have already examined. This new thematic device is that of the "magic potion" which threatens sleep and death. Wagner returns to this plot element several times in the cycle. The fatal potion that Mime brews for Siegfried,[205] Gutrune's drink that clouds Siegfried's memory, the cup offered by Hagen moments before he kills Siegfried are all, like Hunding's night drink, potential sources of death. They stand in stark contrast to other beverages—including the vessel of pure water that Sieglinde offers Siegmund and the mead of love they later share—capable of *reviving* those who drink them. The potions of life and love and their direct opposites, the potions of sleep and death, are an important corollary to the sleep imagery that is found throughout the *Ring*.

In *Die Walküre* 2.3, Hunding wakes up (*Hunding erwachte aus hartem Schlaf!*) and Sieglinde falls asleep. But Hunding's unconscious, death-like sleep is far different from the prophetic, dream-filled sleep of Sieglinde. In a vision, Sieglinde foresees Siegmund's doom. Dogs (*Hunde*), Hunding's namesakes, tear at the hero's flesh and kill him. Siegmund's sword shatters. The trunk of an ash tree, symbolic both of the Wälsung family[206] and of the Norns' primeval World-Ash, falls to the ground. Siegmund himself understands little of these images. To him, Sieglinde's sleep seems reminiscent only of death. He remarks that his sister appears lifeless in sleep although she is still alive (*Leblos scheint sie, die dennoch lebt*) and he hopes that she may sleep peacefully during the impending battle. Almost immediately after this hope is uttered, however, it proves to be vain. With a start, Sieglinde awakes just in time to see her brother killed and her nightmares fulfilled.

Each act of *Die Walküre* presents a different character overcome by sleep. The sleep of both Siegmund in Act 1 and Sieglinde in Act 2 continue the symbolic association of sleep with death that Wagner had introduced in *Das Rheingold*. But for neither of these characters is sleep so *literally* tied to mortality as it is for the Valkyrie Brünnhilde in the third act of the drama. As punishment for defying Wotan's command to kill Siegmund, the high god condemns Brünnhilde to deep, defenseless sleep (*in wehrlosen Schlaf: Die Walküre* 3.2; compare *in festen Schlaf:* 3.3). Immediately, Brünnhilde's sisters equate this sleep with death. Is Brünnhilde, they ask, really going to fade away and die (*verblühn und verbleichen*)? Wotan then explains what he had earlier suggested only in veiled terms. Brünnhilde will awaken from her sleep a mere mortal, a wife to the man who finds her, and a partner in all his toil and labor. For Brünnhilde, sleep and mortality are inextricably linked. The child, whose similarity to her father is noted throughout the drama, is at this moment more closely identified with him than either father or daughter will ever realize.

The mournful descending scale that accompanies Wotan's words as he pronounces Brünnhilde's fate is a motive that is usually known simply as "Sleep." (Example 31) The source for this theme can be traced to the series of first inversion chords moving down the chromatic scale in the descending segment of the motive customarily called "Loge's Fire."[207] (Example 32) This motive is heard repeatedly in *Das Rheingold* and will soon reappear near the end of *Die Walküre*. In this way, the connection that will soon be made between Brünnhilde's magic sleep and the ring of fire with which Loge surrounds her is already implicit in Wotan's words. Once again, Wagner is tying sleep to one of the elements of nature and, by extension, to nature itself. As in *Das Rheingold* where waking was shown to be as natural as water, in *Die Walküre* sleep is portrayed as natural as fire.

As Wotan continues to explain the full extent of Brünnhilde's punishment, a second theme of sleep—usually referred to as "Brünnhilde's Sleep"—begins to be heard repeatedly. (Example 33) As Deryck Cooke has demonstrated,[208] this motive is actually a rhythmic variant of Woglinde's opening words, that cry of birth and *awakening* with which the cycle had begun. (Example 25). Both of these melodies may ultimately be traced to the nature motive (Example 1), the first theme heard in the *Ring* and the genesis of all (or nearly all) of the drama's subsequent motives. Cooke explains this relationship by noting that

"Brünnhilde . . . may not be a voice of nature, but she is a latent, inspiring *force* of nature."[209] A more plausible explanation, however, may be that in this passage Wagner is relating the awakening of the universe with which *Das Rheingold* began to the magic sleep of Brünnhilde with which *Die Walküre* ends. The composer's central idea continues to be that life and death, sleep and awakening are all essential parts of nature. By tying the theme of the sleeping Brünnhilde to the motive of creation or nature, Wagner is saying that sleep—as well as the death that it symbolizes—are inescapable because they are natural. What is *un*natural is the quest for unending power that is represented by Wotan and Alberich.

Sleep in *Siegfried*

The hero Siegfried's first appearance in the *Ring* contrasts sharply to those of his father and grandfather. While Wotan was encountered asleep on stage and Siegmund collapsed soon after bursting into the hall of Hunding, Siegfried appears before the audience in a state of high excitement. Three times it is repeated that Mime had made the young hero "a soft couch to sleep on" (*dein Lager schuf ich, daß leicht du schliefst*), but Siegfried was still unable to sleep (*der Schlummer wird mir da schwer*). So intense is Siegfried's energy, in fact, that he revives what others had long given up as dead. In a climactic moment at the end of *Siegfried* 1, the hero says that he has "wakened to life" (*zum Leben weckt' ich*) the sword Notung. This is the weapon that had "lain dead in fragments," far beyond the skill of Mime to repair.

Siegfried's awakening of Notung establishes a new pattern that will be important in this drama of the cycle. Just as each act of *Die Walküre* presented one of its three major characters falling asleep, each act of *Siegfried* focuses on a moment when its central character *awakens* someone or something. In the *Siegfried* 2, for instance, the character whom Siegfried awakens is Fafner, the giant who has assumed the form of a dragon through the magic of the Tarnhelm. As an appropriate introduction to this image, *Siegfried* 2 had begun with dawn, a *false* dawn that had quickly receded into night. The light that had been believed to herald the morning was actually that of Wotan who is often represented as a "shining deity" in Norse literature. Wotan, who has disguised himself as "the Wanderer" in his travels about the world, then encounters an equally potent force of darkness, Alberich or "*Schwarz*-Alberich" or "*Nacht*-Alberich" as he is called several times in the cycle. (See, for instance, Loge's first long speech in *Das Rheingold* 2). The god of light proposes that the two of them join forces, awakening Fafner and offering to save his life in return for the ring. But, although first Wotan (*Erwache, Wurm!*) and then Alberich (*Wache, Fafner! Wache, du Wurm!*) try their best to awaken him, Fafner prefers to sleep (*lasst mich schlafen!*). This episode is filled with irony: in *Das Rheingold*, Fafner's own brother had contrasted the energy of the giants to the sleep of the gods. Now, on the very day of his death, Fafner himself has chosen a sleep that will lead to his doom.

Almost immediately after this scene, Siegfried and Mime appear. Foreshadowing an episode that will include the deaths of two major characters, *Siegfried* 2.3 is filled with references to sleep, rest, and lying down. Mime portends his own fate by choosing to rest by the spring while Siegfried faces the dragon alone. Wagner then makes an explicit reference to the relationship between sleep and death: disgusted by his lazy companion, Siegfried threatens to have Fafner kill Mime. He advises the dwarf *not* to rest by the spring (*raste nicht dort am Quell*) if he values his life, but Mime does not listen. Through the imagery of Mime's rest at the spring, Wagner suggests that this character will soon die.

In Mime's absence, Siegfried succeeds at waking Fafner where Wotan and Alberich had so recently failed. With a new motive—a rapid composite of "the Sword" and Siegfried's horn call that Deryck Cooke dubbed "Siegfried's Indomitable Vitality"[210] (Example 34)—the young hero wakens Fafner in his lair. This musical theme, symbolizing the energy of Siegfried, rouses the sleeping dragon. Following an exchange that seems surprisingly short after such a prolonged introduction, Siegfried quickly pierces Fafner through the heart. As the dragon dies, he warns Siegfried to keep an alert watch over himself: Mime is plotting his doom.

Fafner's advice proves to be timely. No sooner has Siegfried killed Fafner and taken possession of the ring than Mime decides once and for all to close his enemy's eyes in eternal sleep (*zum ew'gen Schlaf schliess' ich dir die Augen bald!*). Nevertheless, Mime has not reckoned with Siegfried's "indomitable vitality" or with his newly acquired ability to see beyond deceptive schemes. Siegfried cries out in astonishment, asking Mime whether he intends to slay him while he sleeps (*Im Schlafe willst du mich morden?*). After receiving proof of the dwarf's murderous intentions, Siegfried takes his vengeance on him. He kills Mime, lays the bodies of his two victims together in the cave, and utters the sarcastic wish that both of them may now find eternal rest (*so fandet beide ihr nun Ruh!*).

In this way, *Siegfried* 2 presents the deaths of two major characters, each of them foreshadowed by that character's sleep. To balance these events, *Siegfried* 3 focuses on two important awakenings, those of Erda and of Brünnhilde. The first awakening occurs when Wotan, seeking a wisdom even greater than his own, descends to the earth in an effort to rouse Brünnhilde's mother from her long rest (*aus langen Schlaf*). His words as he calls to her—*Wache, Wala! Wala! Erwach!* and *Wache, erwache, du Wala! Erwache!*—once again unite "w" (the phonetic leitmotif for awakening) with the image of a character being roused from a deep sleep. As we have seen before, the composer's thematic approach to composition is operating here on several levels simultaneously.

It is also important to recognize that, as *Siegfried* 3 begins, Wotan is awakening the Earth Mother from *prophetic* dreams. He identifies himself as the "awakener" (*Der Weckrufer bin ich*) who has come to sing a "waking song" (*Dein Wecklied sing' ich*). This song, Wotan believes, may rouse the slumberer (*Schlummernde*) from the depths of her sleep (*fester Schlaf*, a phrase intentionally reminiscent of the words *in festen Schlaf* that Wotan had used when the "Sleep" motive was first introduced). Numerous phrases that appear during this scene make it clear that Wagner viewed Erda's rest as far different from the dreamless sleep of death that has just overtaken Mime and Fafner. For instance, Wotan says that, for Erda, sleep has been filled with reflection (*sinnendem*

Schlafe). The goddess herself says that it was a sleep of wisdom (*wissendem Schlaf*). And, in what is perhaps the most remarkable passage of all, Wagner recalls Schopenhauer's theories of dreams and intuition by having Erda say

> *Mein Schlaf ist Träumen,*
> *mein Träumen Sinnen,*
> *mein Sinnen Walten des Wissens.*
> [My sleep is dreaming,
> my dreaming reflection,
> my reflection the mastery of wisdom.]

These words contain Wagner's most complete summation of Schopenhauer's notion that dreams express a wisdom beyond rational thought. The goddess' dreams, like those of Wotan at the beginning of *Das Rheingold* 2,[211] are visions of a natural order. For this reason, they reveal truth at its most profound level. Erda's sleep seems more "real," more "natural" than the world of everyday life. The goddess is thus a unique figure in the cycle. Wagner's text suggests that most characters who awaken in the *Ring* are symbolically "reborn" to a richer, more challenging life. Erda, on the other hand, awakens to a world that seems less real and more confusing than the one she had seen in her dreams (*wild und kraus kreist die Welt!*). As Erda herself says, if the world has been so inverted that Brünnhilde is now imprisoned by sleep while she herself was not awake to protect her, then may sleep lock away her wisdom forever (*Schlaf verschliesse mein Wissen!*).

Shortly after the goddess speaks these words, Wotan demonstrates the first tentative signs that he has gained insight from what has occurred. He says that he will tell Erda a truth which will allow her to sleep in peace for all eternity (*daß sorglos ewig du nun schläfst!*). Wotan's secret is that he no longer fears the end of the gods. In fact, he has begun to *desire* it. During Erda's first appearance in *Das Rheingold*, she had alluded to what Wotan would learn when she said that "Everything that exists must someday fade away" (*Alles was ist, endet!*). What Wotan has now begun to realize is that destruction is natural, even for the gods. To indicate this, he dismisses Erda to eternal sleep (*zu ew'gem Schlaf!*), using the very words that Mime, one act earlier, had used to describe the eternal sleep of death. In the orchestra, a hint of the motive known as "Brünnhilde's Sleep" (Example 33) is heard. Wagner slows the tempo to such a degree that the effect is one of time eternally suspended.

The second major awakening that occurs in *Siegfried* 3 appears in the final scene of the drama during the hero's climactic encounter with Brünnhilde. The entire plot of *Siegfried* had been moving towards this moment, as may be seen from the frequent allusions to it in earlier scenes. At the end of *Siegfried* 2, for instance, the Forest Bird had told Siegfried of a marvelous bride who was sleeping on a lofty cliff. Whoever woke this woman, the Forest Bird said, would be able to marry her. Siegfried had wondered whether he would be the one to awaken Brünnhilde (*Kann ich erwecken die Braut?*). Told that no coward could ever rouse her (*Brünnhild' erweckt ein Feiger nie*), but only one who had never known fear, Siegfried became convinced that this was his destiny.

Later, in his dramatic confrontation with the Wanderer in *Siegfried* 3.2, the hero had referred impatiently to the sleeping girl (*dort schläft ein Weib, daß ich wecken will . . . führt es zur schlafenden Frau*) whom he was eager to find. Now, as Siegfried finally arrives at the summit of this lonely rock, he seems to be surrounded by symbols of sleep. There is a horse slumbering (*schlummernd*), resting in a deep sleep (*rastend in tiefem Schlaf*). Far more important, perhaps, there is what appears to be a warrior, reclining in brilliant armor.

When Siegfried at long last realizes that this is no warrior but a woman, his senses reel. He is filled with a sensation that he has never known before and, on the brink of falling unconscious, Siegfried's words become filled with the sound "sch," the alliterative pattern that Wagner has consistently tied to images of sleep.

> *Mir schwankt und schwindelt der Sinn!* . . .
> *Mir schwebt und schwankt und schwirrt es umher!*
> [My senses spin and reel! . . .
> Everything swims and spins and buzzes around me!]

Though Siegfried fears the woman who lies before him, he knows that he must awaken her before *he himself* can ever be fully awake (*Daß ich selbst erwache, muß die Maid ich erwecken!).* Ironically, this phrase contains an echo of what Mime had told the hero earlier (*Siegfried* 2.3). If Siegfried every *really* woke up, Mime had said, then he himself would never be safe from him. Now, however, Siegfried does wake up by attempting to rouse Brünnhilde. He begins by adopting an expression similar to those used to awaken Wotan and Erda earlier in the cycle (*Erwache! Erwache! Heiliges Weib!).* In Brünnhilde's case, these words have no effect. Unable to disturb the woman's sleep by calling to her, Siegfried follows the example of the sun which had kissed the gold awake in the first scene of *Das Rheingold.* Just as Wotan once kissed away Brünnhilde's immortality, so now does Siegfried awaken Brünnhilde with a kiss. To do so, Siegfried bends over the sleeping figure, according to Wagner's original stage directions, "as if swooning in death."

The awakening of Brünnhilde is accompanied by yet another new motive, one that will assume increasing importance during the final scenes of the *Ring.* (Example 35) This motive, commonly called "Awakening," begins with a blocked chord. The triad used here is a simple variant of the nature motive (an *arpeggiated* triad) with which the cycle had begun. (Example 1) Traces of this motive may also be seen in the chords played by the orchestra when the light of the sun began to awaken the Rhinemaidens' gold. (Example 36) As so often occurs in the *Ring,* Wagner in this passage is using the musical line to associate both sleep and awakening with nature. Just as Wotan had learned earlier that death is an inevitable part of nature, so does the final episode of *Siegfried* indicate that *awakening* is natural. Life and death, birth and dying, all of which Wagner has associated with wakefulness and sleep, are simply two aspects of the same phenomenon.

Siegfried's words as he calls to Brünnhilde remind the audience of Wotan's words as he once tried to awaken Erda. To extend this parallel, Wagner then assigns Brünnhilde and Erda almost the same words as they open their eyes. Erda, for instance, had said that she awoke from her sleep of wisdom (*Ich bin erwacht aus wissendem Schlaf: Siegfried* 3.1). In a similar way, Brünnhilde, upon awakening, greets the sun, greets Siegfried, and says that, though her sleep was long, she is now fully awake: *Lang war mein Schlaf; ich bin erwacht* (*Siegfried* 3.3). Throughout the remainder of this passage, the two sights first beheld by Brünnhilde—the light of the sun and the face of Siegfried—are continually merged. Both the sun and Siegfried have woken Brünnhilde, both perform their awakening with kisses, both fill her vision as she opens her eyes, and both are recipients of her most rapturous greetings. She says that Siegfried has awoken her to life, that he is her victorious light (*Du Wecker des Lebens, siegendes Licht!*).

Returning for a moment to the association of sleep with death, Wagner then presents Siegfried as wondering whether his mother's death might have been nothing more than Brünnhilde's deep sleep. Brünnhilde immediately replies that, unfortunately, this was far from the case. But Wagner continues to interweave the images of sleep and death throughout the rest of this drama. Because they have not yet been joined in love, Siegfried says that, to him, Brünnhilde remains the dreaming woman that he found alone on her rock. Though she may be awake, he has not yet shattered her sleep *completely*. This, however, is what he intends to do, what he *will* have done if Brünnhilde "awakens" to become his lover.

> *Noch bist du mir die träumende Maid:*
> *Brünnhildes Schlaf brach ich noch nicht.*
> *Erwache, sei mir ein Weib!* . . .
> *Erwache, Brünnhilde! Wache, du Maid!*
> [In my eyes, you are *still* dreaming.
> I haven't yet broken Brünnhilde's sleep.
> Wake up! Be my wife! . . .
> Wake up, Brünnhilde. Awaken, maid.]

Brünnhilde knows that surrender to Siegfried will mean her death and the end of the gods' reign in Valhalla. Nevertheless, like Wotan whose creation she was, Brünnhilde has learned to long for the death that awaits her. She embraces her mortality—once a punishment, now a joy—and laughingly anticipates the doom of the gods.

> *Leb wohl, prangende Götterpracht*
> *End in Wonne, du ewig Geschlecht!*
> *Zerreisst, ihr Nornen, das Runenseil!*

Götterdämm'rung, dunkle herauf!
[Farewell, shining splendor of the gods!
Rest in peace, undying race!
Rip, you Norns, your rope of runes!
Twilight of the gods! Darkness descends!]
As Brünnhilde says these words, Siegfried stands in awe of her. He cannot believe that she is awake and alive (*Sie wacht, sie lebt*). As the curtain falls on the drama, the lovers call one another their gleaming light and laughing death (*leuchtende Liebe, lachender Tod!*), joyful that they have been able, for a time, to dispel eternal sleep.

Sleep in *Götterdämmerung*

The motive of "Awakening" (Example 35) is repeated three times as the prelude to *Götterdämmerung* begins. Barely audible beneath this motive is a soft restatement of the "Primal Substance" (Example 28) and "Nature" (Example 1) themes in their original form. Then, at the very end of this passage, Wagner introduces the motive of "Fate." (Example 37) The composer's organizational scheme for *Götterdämmerung* is thus made clear at the start. As we saw in our discussion of "plot leitmotivs," the drama that had once inspired the entire *Ring* will now be a reprise of the complete cycle. Just as the *Ring* itself had begun with a combined image of dawn, awakening, and birth that had soon given way to parallel symbols of twilight, sleep, and death, so does *Götterdämmerung* follow this same progression. "What light is shining there? Is the day dawning?" (*Welch' Licht leuchtet dort? Dämmert der Tag?*), the first Norn asks in the opening words of the drama that is destined to end with the twilight of the gods. *Das Rheingold* had begun with the three Rhinemaidens teasing and questioning one another at the bottom of a river; *Götterdämmerung* begins with the three Norns exchanging questions at the foot of a massive tree. Just as the entire cycle moves from the world's first awakening to the gods' eternal sleep, so does the plot of *Götterdämmerung* move in this same direction. By restating his central patterns in this way, Wagner is able to reinforce themes that had been important throughout the *Ring*, developing them into what will be their fullest and most devastating form. Once again he does this by using repeated images and symbols in such a way that they become "thought leitmotivs." When the audience encounters Brünnhilde in *Götterdämmerung*, she has already been stripped of her immortality. The former Valkyrie remembers, as though it had happened long ago, the deep sleep (*tiefem Schlaf*) in which Siegfried had found her. The hero, too, shares her delight as he recalls his journey to this remote place intending to awaken Brünnhilde from her death-like sleep. Further recollections of that sleep occur later in *Götterdämmerung* 1 when the Valkyrie Waltraute visits her sister, now alone on her rock, and greets her by asking whether she is awake or asleep.

That same question appears several times at the beginning of *Götterdämmerung* 2.1. This time, however, it is Alberich who poses the question and his son, Hagen, who replies. Three times Alberich wonders whether Hagen is asleep (*Schläfst du, Hagen, mein Sohn?*) and says that he is the one whom rest and sleep betrayed (*den Ruh' und Schlaf verrieth*). Although this scene is sometimes staged as though Hagen is merely pretending to be asleep,[212] it is clear both from the stage directions (*Hagen . . . sitzt schlafend*) and the question that he asks his father (*was hast du meinem Schlaf zu zagen?*) that this sleep is genuine, an anticipation of his own impending death.

In fact, it seems particularly appropriate, as Wagner's world nears its apocalypse, that character after character is described as though they found sleep all but irresistible. For example, one of Siegfried's first questions after his return from Brünnhilde's rock, is whether Gutrune has yet woken. For her part, Gutrune wonders whether Siegfried needs to rest (*Rastest du, schlimmer Held?*) after his heroic labors. Finally, when Brünnhilde swoons upon seeing Siegfried about to marry Gutrune, the hero attempts to revive her using words reminiscent of those he had adopted when she was sleeping on her rock: *Erwache, Frau!*

All of these references to sleep serve to anticipate the two great images of sleep that appear as the cycle ends: the eternal rest of Siegfried and, shortly thereafter, that of the entire world. Siegfried's own death is foreshadowed during his encounter with the Rhinemaidens in

Götterdämmerung 3.1. Warning Siegfried of the ring's curse, the Rhinemaidens use an expression that recalls Erda's words to Wotan in *Das Rheingold* 4: *Weiche, weiche dem Fluch!* Even more remarkable, however, is the imagery of sleep and awakening that surrounds Siegfried's death itself. Shortly after Hagen treacherously stabs Siegfried in the back, it is neither the motive of "Fate" nor "the Annunciation of Death" that is heard, but the theme of "*Awakening.*" What Wagner suggests here is that Siegfried, in his final moments on earth, recalls his first encounter with Brünnhilde, the occasion when this motive was introduced. Moreover, through this musical theme, Wagner presents Siegfried's death as a great awakening. In death, Siegfried leaves behind the world of falsehood and illusion that the Rhinemaidens had described in the last words of *Das Rheingold* (*falsch und feig ist was dort oben sich freut!*) and is awakened or reborn into a world greater than the one he had known before.

On a linguistic level, both of these notions are reflected in the words of Siegfried that he sings to a variation of "*Heil dir, Sonne!*" (Example 38).

> *Brünnhilde, heilige Braut!*
> *Wach auf! Öffne dein Auge!*
> *Wer verschloss dich wieder in Schlaf?*
> *Wer band dich in Schlummer so bang?*
> *Der Wecker kam; er küsst dich wach . . .*
> *Ach! Dieses Auge, ewig nun offnen!*
> [Brünnhilde, holy bride!
> Wake up! Open your eyes!
> Who bound you once again in sleep?
> Who has wrapped you in such restless slumber?
> The one who woke you has come.
> He kissed you awake . . .
> Ah! Those eyes! Now forever open!]

Wagner did not intend Siegfried's words to be mere irony. They establish an important relationship that the composer wished his audience to understand before the climactic last scene of his cycle. For, though death may be an eternal sleep, it may also be seen as an eternal awakening, a departure from the world of falsehood, torment, and troubling dreams. To cling firmly to life is to cling to an illusion. To accept death—to accept life's impermanence—is the first step towards appreciating life's value.

Wagner develops this notion in the following scene when Gutrune says that that her sleep has been troubled by bad dreams. While the dying Siegfried had imagined hearing Brünnhilde's laughter (*da lacht ihm Brünnhildes Lust!*), Gutrune has *awoken* to the sound of Brünnhilde laughing. While the dying Siegfried had believed that he saw an image of Brünnhilde eternally awake, Gutrune wonders whether perhaps Brünnhilde is now asleep. Hagen, too, shares this image as he returns to the hall, shouting in an effort to awaken everyone (*Wacht auf! Wacht auf!*). Gradually, Wagner has brought into place all the images necessary for a great awakening and, simultaneously, for the eternal rest of the gods.

The body of Siegfried is then brought forward and Brünnhilde bends over it, greeting the hero for the last time. The tableau that results is a complete reversal of Siegfried's earlier encounter with the sleeping Brünnhilde. In that scene, Brünnhilde had greeted the sun after awakening from her long slumber. Now, she compares Siegfried once again to the light of the sun, and prepares both the world and herself for a lasting sleep. Wotan, too, can rest (*Ruhe, ruhe, du Gott!*): his daughter has done what he could not bring himself to do. As Wotan's representative, Brünnhilde has brought about the destruction that the supreme god had first feared and had then come to desire. At this point in one of the endings for the cycle that Wagner eventually discarded (the so-called "Schopenhauer ending"), Brünnhilde refers to herself as "the one who knows" (*die Wissende*) and says that sorrow has opened her eyes. In the words of L.J. Rather, "she is now . . . *one who is fully awake.*"[213] Fulfilling Erda's prophecy that everything must come to an end, Brünnhilde then lights the pyre that annihilates the world.

The opening image of the *Ring* in which the universe arises out of nothing is now played in reverse. The Rhine overflows its banks, reducing the world first to water, then to nature, and finally to the primal substance itself. The music collapses into a major chord: just as *Das*

Rheingold began with an E♭ triad, *Götterdämmerung* ends with a D♭ triad. Light fades into darkness. And the *Ring* ends, just as it had begun, with a cry. The last words of the drama, Hagen's shout of *Zurück vom Ring!* ("Keep away from the ring!"), are the only words *spoken* in the entire cycle. The *Ring*, which had begun with a cry that has no meaning, ends with a cry that has no music. The world has come full circle.

* * *

On January 25th, 1854, in a letter to his friend, August Röckel, Wagner spoke about what *he* saw as the meaning of the *Ring*.

> We must all learn to *die*, in fact to *die* in the most absolute sense of the word; the fear of the end is the source of all lovelessness and it arises only where love itself has already faded. How did it come about that mankind so lost touch with this bringer of the highest happiness to everything living that in the end everything they did, everything they understood and established, was done solely out of fear for that end? My poem shows how.[214]

Ten years later, Wagner returned to this theme. In a letter written to Ludwig II just before Wagner resumed composing the *Ring* after a break of twelve years, he related his ideas to the figure of Wotan.

> [*Siegfried* 3.1, at which point Wagner would resume composing the drama] is the most sublime of all scenes for the most tragic of all my heroes, Wotan, who is the all-powerful will-to-exist and who is resolved upon his own self-sacrifice; greater now in renunciation that he ever was when he coveted power, he now feels all-mighty, as he calls out to the earth's primeval wisdom, to Erda, the mother of nature, who had once taught him to fear for his end, telling her that dismay can no longer hold him in thrall since he now wills his own end with the selfsame will with which he had once desired to live.[215]

As Wagner makes clear in this passage, Wotan has learned to die.

And since we recall that Wagner, in his letter to Röckel, had described Wotan as "resembling us to a hair,"[216] we who form the audience of the *Ring* must learn to die as well.

Wagner suggests in these two letters that Wotan ultimately had no reason to fear his own destruction. Creation (the motive of "Erda": Example 11) and destruction (the motive of "the Twilight of the Gods": Example 18) are simply the same notes moving in opposite directions. As Heraclitus once said, the road up and the road down are one and the same. (Fragment 60.) One of the central themes of the *Ring* is the notion that Wagner had borrowed first from Greek philosophy and then from Schopenhauer: there can be no creation without destruction, no life without death, no dawn without twilight, no awakening without sleep. To long for one without the other is to desire something that can never be.

In the end, the symbol of sleep—whether one is examining Wagner's text, his music, or his plot—is a critically important image in the *Ring*. It reappears throughout the cycle like a recurrent pattern of nature. Through it, Wagner develops the central theme of his work, that the very impermanence of life is what makes it precious. The image of sleep underscores Wagner's pessimism because it suggests that death is inevitable. But it also underscores his optimism because the cycle shows that, if mankind were ever *really* given the choice, then we, like Wotan, would not want it to be any other way.

CHAPTER 6

Character

The Messianic Hero in the *Ring*

After completing his tragedy *Siegfried's Death* in 1848, Wagner drafted a prose sketch for possible use as an opera or drama.[217] The resulting work, *Jesus of Nazareth*, never advanced beyond the stage of a detailed outline. Even in this rough form, however, it is clear that Wagner saw the sketch as a means of exploring many of the same ideas to which he would later return in the *Ring*. Like the cycle, *Jesus of Nazareth* retells a familiar story freely altered and rearranged by the composer to reflect his own philosophy. For Wagner, Jesus was a social revolutionary who rose to become a leader of the Jews only when Barabbas—now also presented as a political activist—was arrested for sedition. Unfortunately, Wagner's Jesus does not adapt easily to the role that others impose on him. He fails to do what is expected of a political leader and, in the end, realizes that he can change society only through a perfect act of self-sacrifice. To fulfill his mission, Jesus becomes a willing participant in his own destruction. Near the end of the drama, the apostle Peter explains the significance of this voluntary death, teaching Judas and others "to understand the sacrificial death of Jesus" and saying that " . . . this death is his apotheosis . . . . "[218]

As Jean-Jacques Nattiez observed,[219] Wagner viewed Jesus as a figure not unlike the heroes of his later music dramas. Like Siegfried in the *Ring*, Jesus of Nazareth is a "natural man" who has no use for society and its vanities, who embraces love by renouncing power and the law, who bears a striking resemblance to his divine forebear, and who illustrates the path to redemption through his own innocence and death. These ideas were reinforced by Wagner in his late (and vehemently anti-Semitic) essay entitled "Heroism and Christianity."[220] In that work, Wagner describes the Christian saint as the historical successor to those mythological heroes whom centuries of legend had characterized as figures of suffering and natural honesty.[221] The importance of these ideas was acknowledged by Cosima Wagner who, shortly before her husband's death, said that he regarded "Heroism and Christianity" as the finest of all his essays.[222]

As an early embodiment of these thoughts, Jesus of Nazareth represents an intermediate stage between the pagan hero and the Christian saint. Wagner's prose sketch explores the nature of what might be termed "the messianic hero": a character who serves as God's representative on earth and who, through his own suffering and death, provides others with a model of redemption. Throughout the sketch, frequent reference is made to Jesus' descent from, and close resemblance to, his heavenly father. As Wagner has Jesus say in act 2, "God is the father and the son, begetting himself anew forever; in the father was the son, and in the son is the father."[223] (Cf. John 10:38.) One act later, Wagner has Jesus expand on this thought and say, "Ye know neither me, nor my father; if ye knew me, ye would know my Father also. . . . *I and the Father are one!*"[224] (John 10:30.)

This close connection between God and hero is precisely what makes the messianic role of Jesus possible. As Wagner says in his summary of act 3, "*Jesus* announces his true mission, his quality as son of God, the redemption of all peoples of the earth through him . . . " In act 4, Jesus continues, "I know that I am son of God, and therefore that ye all are my brothers: I serve you all, and go for you to sacrificial death: when ye shall know, like me, ye will also do like me."[225] The messianic role of Wagner's Jesus was thus the result of a willingness to serve as a model of self-sacrifice. *Jesus of Nazareth* was intended to teach people how to die (and thus, by extension, how to live), suggesting that those who cling to illusions of permanence gain only frustration and unhappiness.[226] The kinship that Jesus shares with God is Wagner's way of suggesting that the hero's insight is divine. When Jesus accepts his own mortality, renounces life, and frees himself from the vanity of hope, he approaches God. This is what Peter meant by referring to Jesus' self-sacrifice as his "apotheosis." In death, Jesus provides inspiration for all who witness his destruction. Moreover, to Wagner, Jesus also provided inspiration for something on a completely different level: he was the prototype of the composer's greatest creation, the figure of Wotan in the *Ring*.

The Messianic Hero as Wotan's "Great Idea"

Near the end of *Das Rheingold*, Wagner confronts Wotan with what appears to be an insoluble dilemma. In order to preserve his dominion and protect his new fortress of Valhalla, he must seize the ring that has just been acquired by the giant Fafner. That very act of treachery would, however, violate the oaths and treaties on which Wotan's rule depends.[227] As Alberich later describes this predicament, "You do not dare steal back from the giants the ransom that you paid them. If you do, you yourself would shatter the shaft of your spear. In your own hands the strong, lordly staff would crumble to dust!" (*Siegfried* 2.1) It is this dilemma that provides the basis for the dramatic tension of the *Ring*. If Wotan does not steal the ring of supreme power, the giants will gain ascendancy over the gods and Wotan's reign will end. Yet if Wotan *does* steal the ring, he will violate the treaties that are the basis of his power, and his reign will end anyway. As *Das Rheingold* draws to its conclusion, it looks as though there is nothing that Wotan can do to solve this problem and continue to rule forever.

As we have already seen, however, Wagner's unexpected solution appears shortly before the gods enter Valhalla. At that time, Wagner describes the god as struck by a "great idea," and the sword motive (Example 13) is heard for the first time in the cycle.[228] By the end of *Das Rheingold*, the audience receives no further information about the nature of this "great idea." Only in the god's long speech to Fricka in *Die Walküre* 2.1 does an explanation finally appear. "Necessity demands a hero who, since he is free from divine protection, is also free from divine law. Only he will be able to accomplish the deed that, though the gods need it done, a god is forbidden to do." A similar passage appears in *Die Walküre* 2.2 as Wotan speaks to his daughter Brünnhilde.

These are the bonds that bind me.
By the same treaties that made me lord,
I am now a slave.
Only one man can do what I cannot:
a hero whom I have never deigned to help.
A stranger to the god, free of his favor—
unaware, unaided—
from his own need and with his own arms . . .
only he can do the deed that I am forbidden,
that I never advised him,
even though it is all that I wish!

In a letter to Franz Liszt dated October 3rd, 1855,[229] Wagner calls this "the most important scene of all" in the *Ring*. It is easy to understand why. In it, Wotan elaborates on his "great idea": he will create a hero who can achieve what is forbidden to the god himself because of his oaths.[230] The hero will act as Wotan's surrogate in the world but, since he is not bound by the god's treaties, he will have greater freedom.[231] Unconstrained by law, this hero will be able to act of his own initiative.

The image of the hero's sword involves a mythic pattern that Wagner encountered during his study of Greek literature. Characteristic weapons or objects, like Wotan's spear, Brünnhilde's horse, and the hero's sword all serve as examples of the *external soul*, a traditional element in which a hero's strength or even his life was bound to some physical object. In ancient mythology, the theme of the external soul is extremely common. When Samson's hair is cut, for instance, his strength wanes, suggesting that his strength was somehow "tied to" or "contained in" his hair. Meleager, the son of Althaea, dies when a firebrand safeguarded by his mother is consumed. Pterelaus, the mythical king of the Teleboans, dies when his single golden hair is cut. In a similar way, Nisus, a king of Megara, is destroyed when his daughter trims his lock of purple hair. As Wagner was writing the poems that would become the *Ring*, he was mindful of these mythic predecessors and used them as models for the sacred weapons borne by the heroes of his cycle.

Moreover, on a more profound level, Wagner associates characters and objects in the *Ring* as a means of reinforcing the futility of Wotan's actions. Just as the declining melody of the spear motive (Example 2) indicates that Wotan's efforts are doomed to failure, so does the eventual shattering of this spear *visually* suggest the loss of the high god's power. Valhalla and all that it represents must pass away because the gods' dominion, like the parallel dominion of Alberich, is based on dishonesty. Alberich's dishonesty is clear: he stole the gold of the Rhinemaidens to forge the magic ring. But Wotan, too, has been guilty of a theft: he stole a bough from the World Ash to carve his spear. As the First Norn reveals in the prologue to *Götterdämmerung*, "From the World Ash Wotan broke a bough. He cut from the mighty trunk the shaft of his spear. Then, over the course of time, the wound gnawed at the woods. The leaves fell. The tree decayed. Sadly, the water of the spring went dry." Wotan's theft meant that he had violated his treaties before they were even recorded on the shaft of his spear. The moment that his reign began was the same moment that his world began to disintegrate. In recognition of this, Wagner has Alberich utter these words as he curses the ring in scene 3 of *Das Rheingold*: "May its magic bring death to whoever wears it!" In full view of the audience at the very moment these words are uttered, Wotan is associated with one particular object. As Alberich pronounces his curse, Wotan is wearing the ring.

Wotan's First Attempt at Creating a Hero

Though the audience may be aware that Wotan's plan will fail, the god himself ends *Das Rheingold* full of confidence in his new idea. As *Die Walküre* begins, Wotan's plan is already well under way. The first character who appears onstage in this drama is Wotan's fulfillment of the "great idea," the hero, his son Siegmund.

Reared in the wild, an outlaw free of oaths and treaties, Siegmund was at liberty to do what was forbidden to Wotan himself. To underscore Siegmund's role as the high god's surrogate, Wagner creates an elaborate connection between his hero and Wotan. Just as in the prose sketch to *Jesus of Nazareth*, Wagner drew frequent parallels between the deity who devised the plan and the hero whose role was to fulfill it.

1. There is a close physical bond between Siegmund and Wotan.[232] In *Die Walküre* 1.3, Sieglinde says that she sees the same "glow" in Siegmund's eyes that she had noticed years before in the eyes of Wotan. This statement continues an idea introduced one scene earlier where Hunding noticed a family resemblance between Siegmund and Sieglinde (*Die Walküre* 1.2). As Siegfried later tells Mime (*Siegfried* 1.1), children always resemble their parents.

2. In addition to being "gleaming-eyed," both Wotan and Siegmund are described, somewhat incongruously, as "blind." Wotan's partial blindness is indicated by the patch he wears over one eye. In the prologue to *Götterdämmerung*, the First Norn retells how the god forfeited this eye so that he might drink at the spring of eternal wisdom flowing beneath the World Ash. Yet shortly after mentioning the sword that his father had promised him, Siegmund too is suddenly "blinded" by a startling gleam of light (*Die Walküre* 1.3).

3. As we noted earlier, Siegmund is associated *phonetically* with his father. Wotan, who also calls himself Wolfe, Wälse, and Wanderer, is associated with the "theme of nature," the repeated sound of "w" in the *Ring*. Siegmund shares this connection by assuming the name Wehwalt ("Woeful") after his arrival at Hunding's cottage.

4. We have also observed scenic parallels between Wotan and Siegmund. For instance, at Wotan's first appearance in *Das Rheingold* 2, he is asleep. Immediately after Siegmund enters Hunding's hall at the beginning of *Die Walküre*, he too falls asleep.

5. Both Wotan and Siegmund arrive at Hunding's hall as strangers. In *Die Walküre* 1.3, Sieglinde describes Wotan merely as a stranger who had appeared at her wedding. She uses nearly the same words in speaking of Siegmund earlier in the act.

6. Both Wotan and Siegmund are bound by "sacred oaths" sworn on a weapon. Wotan's power stems from the sacred treaties carved on his spear. In *Die Walküre* 1.3, Siegmund likewise swears an oath on a weapon. Shortly before seizing Notung in the hall of Hunding, he declares that he is truly "Siegmund" (the Victor) as the sword he holds shall bear witness.

7. Both Wotan and Siegmund gain power through the agency of a magical weapon. For Wotan, the object involved is a spear; for Siegmund it is the sacred sword, Notung. The inevitable loss of this power is in each case suggested by the musical leitmotivs of the weapons, moving downward in indication of decline and failure. (Examples 2 and 14.)

8. Both Wotan and Siegmund arm themselves with a spear that shatters. As Siegmund tells Sieglinde in *Die Walküre* 1.1: "My spear and shield were shattered." In the next scene, he repeats this to Hunding, saying "My spear and shield were cut from me as I fled" (*Die Walküre* 1.2). Wotan's spear also shatters when he encounters the young hero in *Siegfried* 3.2.

9. The shattering of Wotan's and Siegmund's weapons leads to the destruction of both figures. In each case, a wise woman explains why this must occur. In *Die Walküre* 2.1, Fricka tells Wotan that Notung must be splintered and that Siegmund must die because the hero's will is not really free. In *Siegfried* 3.1, Erda suggests that Wotan's dominion must end because "he who upholds right and enforces vows has now banished right through his own perjury."

10. Finally, both Wotan and Siegmund are associated with a burning hall and the destruction of a massive tree. As Siegmund tells Hunding in *Die Walküre* 1.2, the "gleaming hall" that he shared with his father "was burned to ashes. The flourishing trunk of the oak tree was burned to a stump." This event foreshadows the conflagration that will engulf both Valhalla and the World Ash at the conclusion of the cycle.

These repeated parallels explain why Fricka says that in Siegmund she sees only Wotan (*Die Walküre* 2.1). Wagner wanted his audience to interpret Siegmund as "the new Wotan," the figure who will serve as the god's representative in his quest for the ring. Yet Wagner also had a second reason for establishing close parallels between Wotan and Siegmund. As we have seen, the lesson that Wotan must learn in the *Ring* is that everything has its limits. Even the gods must die.[233] By drawing a parallel between the god and his doomed son, Siegmund's own death foreshadows the death of Wotan himself.

Allowing a central character to "die by proxy" is a frequent theme in epic literature. In the *Iliad*, both Patroclus (the friend of Achilles) and Hector (the hero's enemy) die wearing Achilles' armor. Through this device, Achilles' own inevitable death is suggested twice during the course of the poem. In *The Epic of Gilgamesh*, translated at the British museum near the end of Wagner's life, the citizens of Uruk note a remarkable similarity between the hero and his companion, saying of the latter that "He is like Gilgamesh *to a hair!*"[234] When Gilgamesh's companion later dies in the poem, the hero fully understands the horror of death—it is as though he himself had died—and he begins his famous quest for eternal life. Wotan, as the central figure of the *Ring*, also undergoes this type of symbolic death when his representative "second self" perishes.

Wagner then enhances this traditional epic theme by suggesting that, when Siegmund dies, his death is not merely in spite of his connection to his heavenly father, but *because of it*. As Fricka points out in *Die Walküre* 2.1, Wotan's "great idea" was flawed all along. Despite the god's insistence that he had created a hero with free will, Siegmund was conceived specifically to accomplish the will of Wotan. The close resemblance of these two figures is an indication that Siegmund was never really "his own man" but merely an extension of Wotan. Siegmund's entire course of action, as well as the opportunities he was given to pursue those actions, was planned and executed by Wotan himself. Fricka concludes: "Through you alone he is brave. . . . You created this need for him just as you created his mighty sword. . . . It was for him that you thrust the sword into the tree. You *promised* him that weapon." Since he is not at all independent, Fricka calls Siegmund her husband's "slave."

Though Siegmund was intended by Wotan to be an epic hero, he proves in the end to be a messianic hero. Like Jesus of Nazareth, Siegmund serves as surrogate for a deity (who in both cases is the hero's father) and provides others with a model for redemption. Though Wotan does not realize it at the time, Siegmund's death foreshadows the only release from his suffering that the lord of Valhalla will ever know. Until Wotan himself "dies" to his illusions of eternal power, he will remain "the least free of all! . . . the saddest of all!" (*Die Walküre* 2.2).

An Anti-Messianic Hero

Siegmund's messianic heroism establishes a pattern that will be repeated twice more in the *Ring*. In this way, the messianic hero is a recursive pattern that functions on the level of character in much the same way that the theme of the spear (Example 2) operates on the level of music, the parallel between the Rhinemaidens and the Norns operates on the level of plot, the association of "w" with nature operates on the level of speech, or the image of sleep as death on the level of thought. Nor is the messianic hero the only instance of a "character leitmotif" in the cycle. A similar repeated pattern is established by two brothers who struggle for the ring and whose conflict results in violent death of one brother. This leitmotif of character first appears in the argument between Fasolt and Fafner in *Das Rheingold* 4 and later is reprised by Gunther and Hagen in *Götterdämmerung* 3.3.[235] A subtler example of a character leitmotif is the figure who screams in horror as someone else violently seizes the ring. This image, first established by Alberich when Wotan wrenches the ring from his finger in *Das Rheingold* 4, achieves its most memorable form when Brünnhilde is compelled to surrender the ring to Siegfried in *Götterdämmerung* 1.3.

We have noted that Wagner's musical leitmotivs are sometimes created in opposing pairs in order to highlight a contrast. The most famous example of such a pairing is the theme of the Twilight of the Gods (Example 18) which is merely Erda's theme (Example 11) played in reverse. In much the same way, Wagner also introduces into the *Ring* a character leitmotif that may be regarded as the messianic hero's antithesis, the complete opposite of Siegmund and the rest of the Wälsung race. This character is Hagen, the offspring of Alberich and the mortal woman Grimhild whom Alberich bribed and seduced. Hagen's background is revealed in a chilling passage more than *a drama and a half* before he actually appears on stage in *Götterdämmerung*. Speaking to Brünnhilde, Wotan reveals that Erda had predicted, "If the dark enemy of love ever conceives a son in anger, then the end of the Blissful Ones will soon come to pass." Wotan goes on to explain that Alberich "has suborned a wife. He seduced her with a gift of gold. That woman now carries the fruit of his hatred. The power of his envy stirs in her womb. Such is the monstrosity that has been sired by one who does not know love." (*Die Walküre* 2.2) Later in the cycle, Alberich, the father whom Wotan was describing to Brünnhilde, explains to his son, Hagen, that he was conceived so that he may keep his father "safe from heroes" (*Götterdämmerung* 2.1).

As might be expected, Wagner portrays Hagen as resembling Alberich in much the same way that Siegmund resembles Wotan. Like Alberich, Hagen is "old," unhappy, and filled with hatred. These are the very expressions that he uses to describe himself in *Götterdämmerung* 2.1. The word *"frühalt,"* literally meaning "old before my time" or "prematurely gray," suggests that Hagen's resemblance to his father transcends generational differences. Their physical appearance— wizened, stooped, and unhappy—stands in marked contrast to the youthful vigor of Wotan and the Wälsung race.

Throughout the *Ring*, there are a number of parallel tableaux involving first Alberich and then Hagen. Each of these characters is seen scrambling futilely in the Rhine. At the very beginning of the cycle Alberich vainly attempts to seize one Rhinemaiden after another.[236] Hagen unintentionally re-enacts this moment in the final scene of *Götterdämmerung* when he slips into the Rhine, struggling to recover the ring. Both Alberich and Hagen are heard to cry "Wehe! Wehe!" ["Woe!"] in the course of the drama. Alberich does so in *Das Rheingold* 1 when he realizes that the Rhinemaidens have alluded him. Hagen repeats his father's remark in *Götterdämmerung* 2.3 as he summons the Gibichungs' vassals to Gunther's wedding. Although both Alberich and Hagen are grim and unlikable individuals—and although the "Wehe!" theme (Example 16) is introduced in a serious form elsewhere in the drama—each of these scenes occurs during a moment of uncharacteristic comedy.

What is more, Alberich's relationship with Hagen bears a striking similarity to Wotan's relationship with his own children. In *Götterdämmerung* 2.1, Alberich calls Hagen a "hero," the same word that Wotan used repeatedly in referring to Siegmund. Later in the same act, both Gutrune and Gunther use this word with regard to Siegfried. Yet if Hagen represents a dark, sinister, and twisted form of the same heroism that Wagner attributes to Siegmund and Siegfried, he is also unlike them in one important way. Their *messianic* heroism is motivated by a preference for love over worldly power. Hagen's motives are quite the opposite.

In *Jesus of Nazareth* Wagner says that

> Every creature loves, and Love is the law of life for all creation; so if Man made a law to shackle love, to reach a goal that lies outside of human nature (—namely, power, dominion—above all: the *protection of property*), he sinned against the law of his own existence, and therewith slew himself.[237]

The messianic hero reveals how one may be redeemed by offering an alternative to this fate. " . . . Law itself could not make-up for Love, for it was the constraint, the compulsion to benefit the commonality. . . . [Love] can only be accomplished of free will . . . . Free Love could only manifest itself outside the law, and thus against it."[238] For this very reason, the messianic hero must be an "outlaw." By contrast, Hagen and Hunding, though infinitely more *evil* than Siegmund, display an almost slavish respect for the laws and customs of their society.

Wotan's Second Attempt at Creating a Hero

Perhaps the most characteristic feature of Wagner's musical leitmotivs is that they are rarely static; they develop thematically. For instance, we saw how Wagner transforms one motive into another, as when the theme of the mature Siegfried (Example 19) grows out of his theme as a young hero (Example 9). This same type of thematic development may also be found among Wagner's "leitmotivs of character." After Wotan's first attempt at creating a hero has failed, the high god finds that he has been given a second opportunity. Wotan's renewed effort to fulfill his plan by means of a hero both develops and improves on the qualities of the first. The character who stands at the center of this second attempt at redemption is none other than Siegmund's own son, Siegfried.

The important passage in which Siegfried observes that children bear certain similarities to their parents has already been noted. Accordingly, Wagner is careful to give this character many parallels to other members of his family.

1. Like his father, Siegfried is placed in several tableaus that echo familiar scenes with Wotan. In *Das Rheingold* 3, Wotan laughs uncontrollably at a "frightening" dragon (really Alberich, transformed through the power of the Tarnhelm). In *Siegfried* 2.2, the younger hero also laughs uncontrollably when confronted by the dragon Fafner. Just as the dragon theme (Example 8) links these two scenes musically, so do the parallel images of Wotan and Siegfried link the scenes in terms of character.

2. The power of both Wotan and Siegfried is revealed when they cause the weapon of another hero to shatter. Wotan

destroys Notung in Siegmund's hands in *Die Walküre*
2.3. Siegfried, in turn, uses the restored Notung to
shatter Wotan's spear in *Siegfried* 3.2.[239]

3. In further association with weapons, both Wotan and
   Siegfried are destroyed through the agency of a spear.
   Moreover, the spear, in both cases, has been one on
   which an oath or treaty has been sworn. By the end of
   Siegfried, Wotan can no longer prevent his grandson
   from achieving his destiny—and he realizes, at last,
   that his own end must come—when his spear, bearing
   the runes of the law, falls to pieces in his hands. In
   Götterdämmerung 3.2, Siegfried is treacherously stabbed
   in the back by Hagen who uses the same spear on
   which Siegfried had previously sworn honesty and loyalty to Gunther.

4. Wotan and Siegfried are both "wanderers." Wotan assumes the identity of "the Wanderer" in his travels
   throughout the third opera of the cycle. Siegfried similarly speaks of "wandering on" or of "becoming a wanderer" in the moments immediately before his encounter
   with Wotan (*Siegfried* 3.2). This verbal parallel is symbolic of what will happen in the cycle: Siegfried will
   inherit Wotan's mantle as "the Wanderer" just as he
   inherits the rest of his patrimony, the world itself (as
   Wotan declares in *Siegfried* 3.1).

5. Brünnhilde falls asleep and then awakens through the
   kisses of Wotan and Siegfried. By means of Wotan's
   kiss Brünnhilde loses both consciousness and her immortality at the end of *Die Walküre*. Conversely, a kiss
   from Siegfried awakens her to a new role as a mature,
   mortal woman in *Siegfried* 3.3.

6. Both Wotan and Siegfried are heard to call out *"Erwache!
   Erwache!"* when they attempt to awaken a sleeping
   woman. The proximity of these two scenes in *Siegfried*
   3, as Wotan cries out to Erda (a former lover) and as

Siegfried uses the same words to Brünnhilde (his future lover) makes this association particularly strong.

7. Both Wotan and Siegfried are described as having felled a great ash tree. According to the Second Norn, Wotan ordered his heroes to split the World Ash into kindling so as to set all of Valhalla ablaze. In his first forging song, the young Siegfried speaks of having felled an ash tree that he then burned into charcoal.

8. Both Wotan and Siegfried possess the ring momentarily. In *Das Rheingold* 4, Wotan wears it briefly before he surrenders it, at Erda's urging, to Fafner. Siegfried retrieves the ring from the dragon's hoard but soon offers it to Brünnhilde as a token of his love.

9. Fricka calls Brünnhilde the "bride of [Wotan's] will" (*Die Walküre* 2.1) and, in the interval between *Siegfried* and *Götterdämmerung*, Brünnhilde becomes Siegfried's bride in reality.

10. Finally, for members of the audience familiar with the Wagner's mediæval sources, the test of three riddles that Wotan passes during his encounter with Mime (*Siegfried* 1.2) is strikingly similar to the three contests that Siegfried, who lends invisible aid to Gunther, passes in order to win Brünnhilde in the seventh episode of the *Nibelungenlied*.

These similarities explain why Wotan tells Brünnhilde, "I find myself in everything I have made!" (*Die Walküre* 2.2). Like Siegmund, Siegfried is portrayed by Wagner as Wotan's second self. When the young hero dies, the high god may once again be said to die symbolically like Achilles, the figure who suffers a similar twin death by surrogate in the *Iliad*. This second death reminds Wotan that he, like everything that has ever existed, must someday pass into oblivion.

Nevertheless, in one sense Siegfried's death may be said to be an even greater loss to Wotan than Siegmund's. For Wotan's second attempt at creating a hero came far closer to fulfilling the god's "great idea" than did his first. Much more than his father, Siegfried had been the free and independent hero that Wotan originally intended. He was one generation further removed from Wotan, reared independently of him, and did not receive the same sort of divine protection that, according to Fricka, had been given to Siegmund. In recognition of Siegfried's true independence Wagner has Wotan say, in his farewell speech to Brünnhilde, that the former Valkyrie will someday be awoken by one who is far "freer than I, the god!" That same spirit of autonomy is inherent in Wotan's words to Alberich: "He whom I love I leave to fend for himself. Whether he stands or falls, he is his own master. I have use only for heroes." (*Siegfried* 2.1). This passage reinforces several themes that had been introduced earlier in the cycle. Siegfried, in accordance with Wotan's "great idea," is left to act on his own initiative, neither instructed nor abetted by the god himself.

Siegfried also possesses certain attributes that make him particularly well suited to retrieve the ring for Wotan. Though earlier in the cycle Wagner had never mentioned any exceptions to Alberich's curse, several such exceptions are later introduced, each specifically designed to suit Siegfried. For instance, in *Siegfried* 3.1, Wotan tells Erda that Siegfried is not subject to the curse because he is a stranger to fear. In *Götterdämmerung* 2.1, Alberich reveals to Hagen that, because Siegfried is unaware of the ring's value and makes no use of its power, the curse can have no effect on him. Siegfried, the one figure in the cycle who has no greed for the ring, is thus the one figure who may safely retrieve it.

The Perfection of the Messianic Hero

Despite all his positive attributes, Siegfried fails in his heroic mission because he has a slight imperfection. Wotan describes the hero that he envisions during his long speech to Brünnhilde in *Die Walküre* 2.2.

> Where can I find this friendly foe, this hero who,
> while opposed to the god, still fights for him?
> How can I create someone
> free—someone whom I've never protected—
> who, by defying me, will become dearest to me?
> How can I make that "other," no longer myself,
> who will do my will of his own accord?

While Siegfried may certainly be said to *oppose* Wotan, especially during their one, climactic encounter (*Siegfried* 3.2), he cannot really be said to *defy* him because he knows neither who Wotan is nor what the god has willed. Though he very nearly succeeds in fulfilling Wotan's "great idea," he does so completely by accident.

In order for Wotan's hero to be truly independent, it is not enough for him to act alone, as Siegmund did, or unprompted, as Siegfried did. The independent hero must, of his own free will, violate the command of Wotan and face his wrath. To put it more precisely, only by defying what Wotan *wills* can the hero bring about what Wotan *desires*. And what Wotan desires—what he has always desired even though he was not aware of it—is the end of a world that has been built on illusion, deception, and false oaths. We recall that Wotan told Brünnhilde the only thing he truly desired was "the end" (*Die Walküre* 2.2). By the final scene of the cycle, one character does fulfill this supreme desire of the god. This same figure is the hero whom Wotan had unconsciously invoked when he was first inspired by his "great idea." Moreover, by fulfilling the god's plan through a supreme act of self-sacrifice, this character will be revealed as the perfection of the *messianic* hero, a model of spiritual freedom comparable to Wagner's Jesus of Nazareth.

The character who embodies Wotan's "great idea" is an individual whom the god had consistently overlooked as he searched for his hero elsewhere in the cycle. The child/hero/redeemer/Messiah for whom Wotan had been looking since the final moments of *Das Rheingold* proves to be none other than Brünnhilde.[240] Like Siegmund and Siegfried, Brünnhilde is an offspring of Wotan. Like them, she resembles her father closely, pursues his desire without compulsion, and acts as his representative. Yet Brünnhilde also fulfills her role in a way that was not possible for either Siegmund or Siegfried. For, although given the chance, they do not go *willingly* to their deaths. Siegmund is struck down defiantly as he resists Hunding to the last and Siegfried remains innocently unaware of the treachery that surrounds him. Only Brünnhilde provides a perfect offering, an acceptable self-sacrifice because, like Wagner's Jesus, she is fully conscious of her choice and willing to accept whatever is required of her.

As in the case of the cycle's other heroes, Wagner takes great care to establish a close connection between Brünnhilde and Wotan. She is not merely his daughter. She is his Will personified. As Brünnhilde herself says to Wotan, "You are speaking to Wotan's will when you tell me what you want. Who am I if not your will?" (*Die Walküre* 2.2). Later in the same scene, Wotan admits the truth of Brünnhilde's statement by chastising her, "What are you but the blindly approving tool of my will?" In the following act, he calls her "the fertile womb of my will." No one else in the cycle is described as knowing Wotan's thoughts as completely as is Brünnhilde. Adopting a term used elsewhere to describe the other Valkyries, Wotan calls Brünnhilde a "maid of his will" [*Wunschmaid*].

What Wotan had required for his plan to be accomplished was a hero who could act independently and yet do what the god himself desired. For Brünnhilde, this role is inevitable since her will and Wotan's are the same. So completely does Brünnhilde embody Wotan's will that she pursues it even when he no longer recognizes that it *is* his will. Wotan himself admits this to his daughter at the end of *Die Walküre*, saying "You did what I myself longed to do." To Erda he reveals that "what the ruler of battles longed to do but restrained himself against his will, all too confidently the defiant maid dared on her own to do" (*Siegfried* 3.1). In *Götterdämmerung*, Brünnhilde echoes the god's words when she tells her sister Waltraute that she was fulfilling Wotan's own will when she protected Siegmund against the god's wrath. From his readings in Greek literature, Wagner knew the fifth line of the *Iliad* in which the poet described that epic as a tale of how a high god's will (*boulê*) had been accomplished. In Wagner's own epic cycle, the plot similarly moves towards the fulfillment of a god's will. Yet Wagner's story is more ironic—and some viewers may feel that it is more tragic— because, in order for that will to be accomplished, it became necessary for the god himself to be resisted and ultimately destroyed.

Far more than Siegmund or Siegfried, Brünnhilde becomes the perfect surrogate, the "second self" that Wotan had been seeking all along. Suggestions of this appear throughout the cycle. In *Die Walküre* 2.2, Wotan tells Brünnhilde that, when he speaks to her, he is speaking only to himself. The ironic punishment that Wotan imposes on Brünnhilde for her disobedience is an irresistible sleep—yet, by this very action, Wotan underscores the similarity between his daughter and himself, the character who is first introduced in *Das Rheingold* in a state of deep sleep. Brünnhilde *sees* for Wotan when his back is turned or his blindness hampers him (*Die Walküre* 3.3); she is the "eye" that he lost in drinking from the spring of eternal wisdom. Finally, just before Brünnhilde awakens as a mortal woman in the final scene of *Siegfried*, there occurs a reference to Siegfried's cutting of her breastplate and the severing of her iron mail. Earlier we noted how the mortality of both Wotan and Siegmund had been depicted through the destruction of weapons. In Brünnhilde's case, this also occurs, but the symbolic bond between hero and weapon exists here on an even more complete level. The German word that Wagner chooses for "breastplate" or "coat of mail" is *Brünne*, a self-conscious echo of Brünnhilde's name.

Embodying the high god's will, and yet independent enough to defy him, Brünnhilde alone can accomplish Wotan's "great idea" and restore harmony to the world. In *Götterdämmerung* 1.3, Waltraute tells Brünnhilde how she may redeem the world: Alberich's curse may yet be eliminated if Brünnhilde will return the ring to the Rhinemaidens. Though it is sometimes overlooked, this is precisely what Brünnhilde does at the end of the cycle. Even before that time, however, Wagner makes it clear that Brünnhilde is the one who will turn back the curse of the ring. Brünnhilde tells Waltraute that she will not accede to her sister's request because she will never renounce love. Yet by that very statement, Brünnhilde reverses the choice that Alberich had made in the opening scene of *Das Rheingold*. She chooses love over the world. Having proven herself in this way, Brünnhilde is able to complete her redemptive role by purging the world with fire and then by washing it—one might almost say by *baptizing* it—in the flood waters of the Rhine. She ends Wotan's cherished illusion of permanence by permitting his mythic world to sink back into nothingness.

In *Jesus of Nazareth*, Wagner had described the role that figures like Brünnhilde play and the lesson that characters like Wotan must

learn: " . . . the creature that fulfils this offering [i.e., death] with consciousness, by attuning its free will to the necessity of this offering,
becomes a co-creator,—in that it further devotes its free will to the
greatest possible moral import of the sacrifice, however, it becomes
God himself."[241] Throughout the cycle, Wotan had tried to preserve his
divinity by preserving his life. In the end, however, he learns that only
by willingly surrendering his life can he truly become a "god." For it is
only when a life is complete, when no more struggle remains, that life
can be said to be "perfect."

> Through death . . . my individuality is at like time per-
> fected, by the rounding-off of my personal being. So long
> as a man lives, he belongs (wittingly or unwittingly) to the
> movement of the generality. . . . Wherefore his ultimate
> death is . . . thus a last creation in itself, to wit the up-
> heaval of all unproductive egoism, a making place for life.
> If we are conscious of this, and act upon that conscious-
> ness, we are even God himself, namely the energising of
> eternal Love.[242]

Brünnhilde offers this perfection to Wotan at the same moment that
she embodies it herself, thus providing a model that the rest of the
world may follow. God and heroine, who had so long resembled one
another, eventually merge.

The proof of this may be seen in that sublime and magnificent
theme with which the cycle ends. Because of the redemptive quality of
Brünnhilde's action, critics have traditionally dubbed this theme "Redemption by Love." (Example 39) It should be remembered, however,
that this was one of the very few motives in the *Ring* for which Wagner
himself provided a tag, calling it "The Theme of Praise for
Brünnhilde."[243] In this cycle that begins at dawn and ends at twilight,
Wagner uses praise for Brünnhilde to offer his message of hope for the
world. As Wagner's own title for the final theme of the *Ring* suggests,
Wotan has at long last found his hero.

CHAPTER 7

Spectacle

Light and Color in the *Ring*

There is between music and light a mysterious affinity: as
H.S. Chamberlain so aptly expresses it, 'Apollo was not only
the god of song, but also of light.'

—Adolphe Appia[244]

The *Ring* is a story told in song and in light. In the preface that accompanied the first edition of the work's poems, Wagner said that his text was merely the skeleton of a future drama; the *Ring* as he imagined it could only exist as a "finished whole, whereto its music and scenic show are indispensable."[245] For this reason, when the cycle finally came to be staged at its first festival in Bayreuth, Wagner insisted that his score be accompanied with specific images of staging, costumes,[246] lighting, props, and gesture, all the *visual* elements that Aristotle called the "spectacle" of a drama.[247]

In 1872, as those first rehearsals were about to begin, Wagner asked his friend, the author and music critic Heinrich Porges, to record all the instructions he gave his performers. On page after page of Porges' notes,[248] Wagner returns to the drama's visual appearance, providing advice on everything from general scenic design to the most minor gestures of his actors.[249] For instance, in *Das Rheingold* 2, as Wotan tells Fricka that he values other women more than she might wish, "Wagner asked Fricka to turn away ashamed, and insisted that, whenever appropriate, her gestures should reinforce the meaning of the words. Thus at 'Dort schreiten rasch die Riesen heran' Fricka should point to the back of the stage: the gesture would have the effect of elucidating the powerfully rhythmic motive of the double basses and percussion" in the musical theme of the Giants.[250] Later, Wagner offered a similar suggestion, noting that "[t]he singer [portraying Loge] should make a point of accompanying his speeches with gestures and movements suggestive of the restlessness of his nature as a fire-god. . . . When Loge replies to Wotan's urgent pressure in tones of injured innocence—'Immer ist Undank Loge's Lohn . . . '—Wagner instructed him to reinforce the words with swaying movements of his upper body."[251]

To some extent, of course, Wagner's instructions merely reiterate the traditional actors' advice to "Suit the action to the word, the word to the action." (*Hamlet* 3.2) Porges continues, for instance, that "every change of position and indeed bodily movements must be dictated by the events."[252] Yet on another level, Wagner wanted what an audience witnessed during a performance to reinforce and bring an added dimension to the score he had composed. After Brünnhilde wakes in *Siegfried* 3.3, "[h]er excitement is expressed by a slight trembling of her fingers that corresponds with the figure of the harps."[253] Just as the rhythm of a character's speech is always reflected in the rhythms of the orchestra, so did Wagner want both of these rhythms to be reflected in the actions and images that were depicted on the stage.

At other times, Wagner used dramatic spectacle to associate images in the *Ring* with scenes familiar to his audience from literature, painting, or folklore. Immediately after Fricka's "nagging speech" in *Die Walküre* 2.2, for example, Brünnhilde approaches Wotan and "trustingly, timidly, lays her head and hands on the god's knees and breast." Brünnhilde's pose in this scene recreated a close visual parallel to the encounter of Zeus and Thetis in the *Iliad* (1.497-502, 511-513, 528-530).

> At first light Thetis went up to celestial Olympus
> and there she found the thunderer, the son of Cronus, as apart
> from all the rest he sat upon the height of deep-ridged Olympus.
> Thetis sat down before him, grasping his knees with her left hand,
> while with her right she took hold of his chin and
> made her prayer to lord Zeus, the son of Cronus.

. . . .

When she had finished, Zeus the cloud-gatherer did not reply
but sat long in silence. So Thetis, even as she had
grasped his knees,
continued to cling fast and began to plead with him again.

. . . .

Finally the son of Cronus nodded his dark brow in assent.
The lord's ambrosial locks waved from his immortal head
and set mighty Olympus quaking.

Because of the familiarity of Homer's text to nineteenth-century European audiences, a significant number of those who originally viewed
Die Walküre would have caught the illusion. Moreover, those who did
not know the episode from literature may well have encountered it in
art. In 1811, Jean-Auguste-Dominique Ingres completed a painting of
Jupiter, Thetis, and Hera that now appears in the Musée Granet of Aix-
en-Provence.

Jupiter and Thetis by Jean-Auguste-Dominique Ingres (1811)

Although it does not treat a particularly common subject for paint-
ers,[254] Ingres' work contains an uncanny parallel to the imagery that
Wagner wished to recall during Wotan's encounter with Brünnhilde.
Hera, Zeus' nagging wife and Fricka's counterpart, looms threateningly
in the extreme left of Ingres' painting. Thetis adopts the same humble
pose that Brünnhilde assumes when approaching the implacable father
of gods and men. Zeus sits in regal grandeur, a mythical parallel to
Ingres' earlier (1806) portrait of Napoleon enthroned.[255] The high god's
relaxed left arm, casually propped upon a billowing cloud, evokes the
Homeric epithet "cloud-gatherer," used twice in this very scene (*Iliad*
1.511 and 517). The god's right arm bears the spear that serves as his
symbol of authority. Beside him, an eagle provides further evidence of
Zeus' majesty; this is the form that the god traditionally assumed on
his travels throughout the world. Replace Zeus' eagle with Wotan's raven
and, *mutatis mutandis*, Ingres' painting conveys precisely the symbolism that Wagner wished to evoke in *Die Walküre* 2.2.

Wagner thus used visual imagery in the *Ring* for several distinct
purposes: to reinforce the meaning of his text, to enhance the rhythms
of his music, and to remind his audience of images they may have
encountered elsewhere. Yet far more important than any other use of
spectacle in the *Ring* was the *thematic* role that Wagner occasionally
assigned to the actions and images depicted on the Bayreuth stage. In
Das Rheingold 4, the giants Fasolt and Fafner measure their gold with
the body of the goddess Freia (*Freias Gestalt*). Wagner wanted this particular scene to lend visual expression to a theme repeated throughout
the cycle: the notion that greed, like the lust for power, obliterates love.
Sack after sack of gold is heaped before the goddess until finally love
herself (Freia) disappears from view. A similar visual image occurs in
Das Rheingold 3 and 4 when Alberich demonstrates the power of the
ring. On both of these occasions, according to Wagner's original stage
directions, Alberich "draws the ring from his finger, kisses it, and
extends it in a threatening gesture" or "touches the ring with his lips."
These images suggest that, in the world of the *Ring* where all traditional
values have been turned upside-down and where love has been renounced for power, kisses do not convey love or passion but are ges-

tures of sheer violence. That same implication is repeated later in the cycle when Wotan and Siegfried use kisses to exert *their* power by ending the immortality of a Valkyrie and by shattering the charm of a magic sleep.

Spectacle as Visual Leitmotif

Whenever Alberich kisses the ring in *Das Rheingold* 3 and 4, a motive known as "The Power of the Ring" is heard in the orchestra. (Example 40) Similarly, whenever Wotan or Siegfried kisses Brünnhilde, the audience is reminded of earlier instances in the cycle when that gesture, traditionally associated with love, has been corrupted to symbolize power. We have already seen parallels to Wagner's musical leitmotivs in the sound of his text, in the plot and thought of his drama, and in his manner of developing characters. Not surprisingly, then, Wagner's leitmotivic method of construction extends to the spectacle of the drama as well. Like musical leitmotivs, repeated visual images serve to reinforce similarities between successive episodes in the drama, provide continuity throughout a massive and complicated work, and reiterate themes the author has already introduced.

In fact, several different aspects of setting, costume, or staging may be regarded as having a leitmotivic function in the *Ring*. The Swiss theatrical designer Adolphe Appia (1862-1928), who studied both the theoretical and the practical aspects of producing the *Ring*,[256] viewed the setting of Brünnhilde's rock as something akin to a "visual leitmotif." As Appia put it, "[t]he last setting of *The Valkyrie* is used again in *Siegfried* and in *Götterdämmerung* and so not only represents for the eye the connecting link between these three parts but also leads it (the eye) time and again to the most sensitive moment of the drama."[257] Functioning, therefore, like one of Wagner's musical themes, the visual form of Brünnhilde's rock associates different episodes with one another, allowing them to assume greater levels of meaning with each appearance.

Like the sets, the props carried by actors in the *Ring* are sometimes given a thematic function. We have already noted that the image of Wotan's spear symbolizes his authority no less than does the musical phrase known as "The Spear." (Example 2) The symbolic significance of Wotan's weapon becomes apparent in the stage directions to *Das Rheingold* 2 where Wagner directs Wotan to assert his authority by thrusting the spear between Donner and the giants, abruptly ending their quarrel. Again, in *Das Rheingold* 4, when Wotan finally decides to surrender the ring, Wagner's stage directions tell the actor to "grasp the spear firmly and make a gesture indicative of a courageous decision."

Similarly in *Die Walküre* 2.5, when Wotan imposes his will against the disobedience of Brünnhilde, the god takes up position "above Hunding and stretches out his spear against Siegmund." In *Die Walküre* 3.3, when Wotan announces that Brünnhilde will be freed from her rock by only the bravest of men, he "holds out his spear in confirmation of his words." Shortly therafter, Wotan's sorrow is also illustrated by means of the spear: "at the words, 'Denn so kehrt der Gott sich der ab, so küsst er die Gottheit von dir', one must for the first time see Wotan's spear slipping from his hand."[258] Later in the cycle (*Siegfried* 1.2), "[a]fter Mime's frightened dismissal [of the Wanderer's words], 'Dir Weisem weis' ich den Weg', [Wotan] strikes his spear on the floor to the accompaniment of a fortissimo delivery of the Treaty motive and then seats himself by the hearth."[259] Finally, in one of the *Ring*'s most memorable scenes (*Siegfried* 3.2), the loss of Wotan's power is symbolized by the shattering of the god's once-indestructible spear.

A more consistently negative visual image in the *Ring* may be found in the symbol of the shield, an object usually associated with doom, hopelessness, and impending destruction. In *Die Walküre* 2.5, for instance, Brünnhilde protects Siegmund with her shield immediately before that character's death. The same image is recalled for the audience in *Götterdämmerung* 2.5 when, shortly after Siegfried and Gunther have formed a pact that will lead to their deaths, both are raised on shields carried by their admiring followers. Perhaps the most striking association of death with a shield occurs in *Götterdämmerung* 3.2 when, according to the stage directions, at the moment of Siegfried's death, "Siegfried lifts his shield high with both hands in order to throw it at Hagen: his strength leaves him; he collapses on the shield."

The similarity that we have seen between Wagner's visual leitmotivs and his musical themes may be illustrated in yet another way. We have examined how Wagner's musical "motives of memory" develop in complexity, undergoing numerous transformations and progressing just as the characters, images, and ideas associated with them progress. In precisely this way, Wagner's visual leitmotivs are fluid, developing and becoming more complex as the cycle continues. In order to illustrate how this process of visual transformation takes place, it is necessary to examine two examples of spectacle in some detail: the image of light and its antithesis, the image of darkness as suggested by the use of mist, smoke, dusk, and clouds.

The Image of Light

In his discussion of stagecraft in Wagner's cycle, Appia noted that, whatever else it might be, *Das Rheingold* is fundamentally an *elemental* work.[260] He notes, for instance, that the universe is created from a primal substance at the beginning of the cycle, the central images of water, air, and fire[261] recur throughout the drama, and the musical motives in *Das Rheingold* have an inchoate nature from which all the themes of the later dramas are ultimately derived. Thus Loge, the personification of fire, says in *Das Rheingold* 2, that he has searched the whole world—"water, earth, and sky"—for something dearer than love without finding it. Combined with his own fiery nature, Loge expresses in these words all the elements that Empedocles and other presocratics believed to exist. More than this, however, *Das Rheingold* introduces in embryonic form all the major components from which the cycle's later *conflicts* will be drawn: life and death, masculine and feminine, darkness and light, good and evil, love and power, Valhalla and Nibelheim. We are back in the world of Anaximander. A perfect unity, split into all the elements and qualities of existence, allows the perceptible universe to emerge.

Wagner referred to the highly elemental quality of *Das Rheingold* when he said that, with this work, "I was starting on the new path, where I had first to find the plastic nature-motives which, in ever more individual evolution, were to shape themselves into exponents of the various forms of Passion in the many-membered Action and its characters."[262] The composer conceived of the *Ring* as a progression from raw elements to complex creation, from the wholly divine world of *Das Rheingold* to the wholly human world of *Götterdämmerung*. Moreover, in Wagner's conception of his cycle, these two types of progression were intimately related: "Man is the completion of god. The eternal gods are the elements for the begetting of men. In man, therefore, creation finds its end. Achilles is higher and more perfect than elemental Thetis—"[263]

To all the other elements of music, character, plot, and nature that appear in *Das Rheingold*, one other ingredient must be added: the prelude to the *Ring* contains all the elemental qualities of *light* from which the three successive dramas will be constructed. Each scene in *Das Rheingold* is filled with a different hue. According to Wagner's stage directions, the watery domain of the Rhinemaidens is bathed in "a greenish twilight" (*grünliche Dämmerung*: *Das Rheingold* 1). As the gods descend to the fiery depths of Nibelheim, "dark red light dawns at a distance" (*dämmert aus der Ferne dunkelroter Schein auf*: *Das Rheingold*, stage directions at the end of 2). When Wotan threatens to retain the ring, the earth itself opens and a "bluish light (*bläulicher Schein*) bursts from the cleft in the rock at one side" (*Das Rheingold* 4). This blue light heralds the appearance of Erda, a figure who remains associated with the color blue throughout the cycle.[264] *Das Rheingold* thus presents a world split apart like light through a prism. Water, fire, and earth (three of the four basic elements)—green, red, and blue (the three primary colors of the additive spectrum)—have all been rent asunder, and the cycle continues until they are fused again into that final, great conflagration, a single burst of brilliant white light.

As the prelude to the cycle, *Das Rheingold* ends on a falsely positive note. The gods enter majestically into Valhalla and the music swells in supreme grandeur. The strife described in the opening scenes appears to have been completely cleansed by the blow of Donner's hammer. But a few traces of discord remain. Loge announces that he may yet incinerate these "most godlike gods" (*göttlichste Götter*): "Who knows what I'll do?" The Rhinemaidens reprise their formerly joyous "Rheingold!" theme in a minor key, concluding that all who live on earth are false and cowardly. Most important of all, however, the bridge of light that Froh creates to lead the gods to their new abode is still refracted. A pleasant discovery that Wagner made in one of his ancient sources (the *Gylfaginning* ["The Deluding of Gylfi"] section of the *Prose Edda*) was that the Norse gods entered Valhalla on Bifrost ("Trembling Roadway"), a *rainbow* bridge that glowed with fire.[265] According to Snorri Sturluson in the *Prose Edda*, Bifrost was a structure cunningly made of pure elemental light in three colors.[266] The image of the spectrum, alluded to throughout *Das Rheingold*, thus becomes emblazoned before the audience in one last vivid image. Though the final moments of the prelude appear to be joyous, it is clear that Wotan's world and its elements are still divided.[267]

In an image familiar to Wagner's audience from a variety of Christian, classical, and pagan sources, pure white light served as an image of goodness and represented the power of the gods. Darkness, on the other hand, was associated with evil. We have already seen that this contrast leads Wotan to refer to himself as "*Licht*-Alberich" in *Siegfried* 1.2 while his nemesis is often called "*Schwarz*-Alberich" or "*Nacht*-Alberich." In a similar way, Fasolt refers to Wotan in *Das Rheingold* 2 as "son of light" [*Lichtsohn*] while Alberich is often depicted as a creature of darkness. According to Wagner's stage directions, for instance, when Alberich emerges from his cave in *Das Rheingold* 1, he arises out of "a dark chasm" [*finstern Schlucht*] or "abyss" [*Abgrund*] and is said to be "still surrounded by darkness" [*Dunkel*]. As soon as Alberich seizes the gold, "dense night [*dichte Nacht*] suddenly falls everywhere" and "the rocks disappear in complete darkness [*dichtester Finsternis*]. The entire stage is filled with black waves [*schwarzem Gewoge*] from top to bottom." This contrast between the brightness of the gods' heavenly realm and the dank gloom of Nibelheim is established at the very beginning of the cycle. As *Das Rheingold* 1 emerges in the increasing light of the theater, Wagner says that the stage is "brighter towards the top, darker towards the bottom."

Wagner's association of light with good and darkness with evil

continues in the other dramas. Just as *Das Rheingold* ends with a lightning flash dispelling a dark mist, *Die Walküre* begins with a storm that
draws Siegmund into the dark heart of the forest, the realm of evil.
Much as *Das Rheingold* is a drama of elemental light, *Die Walküre* proves
to be a drama of *reflected* light. The moon of the "Wintersturme" scene
reflects the light of the sun. The gleam of Notung, embedded in the
trunk of Hunding's ash tree, reflects the light of a fire burning in the
hall. The eyes of the lovers Siegmund and Sieglinde reflect the light of
their increasing passion for one another. Since the light of *Die Walküre*
is only a weakened, reflected light, it proves to be no match for the
intense darkness that surrounds the characters. For example, just before the climactic battle between Siegmund and Hunding (*Die Walküre*
2.4), Wagner says that "the stage has gradually darkened [*verfinstert*];
heavy storm-clouds descend at the rear of the stage and begin to conceal the cliffs, ravine, and ridge." In the following scene (*Die Walküre*
2.5), as Siegmund joins the battle that will bring about his death, "he
runs upstage and, as he reaches the pass, disappears into the dark
storm-clouds [*in finstrem Gewittergewölk*], from which flashes of lightning may immediately be seen." Moments later "as Siegmund falls, the
bright lights on both sides of the stage vanish; profound darkness [*dichte
Finsternis*] descends, extending to the front of the stage."

The possibility that dark evil will overcome the brilliant power of
the gods is a theme repeated throughout *Die Walküre*. In *Die Walküre*
3.2, for instance, Wagner describes the setting where Wotan's angry
encounter with Brünnhilde will take place. "During the following scene,
twilight falls and the weather grows calm, followed at the conclusion by
nightfall." Furthermore, at the beginning of *Siegfried* 3.1, when Wotan's
anguish leads him to consult Erda once again, the stage is described as
filled with "night, storm, rain, lightning, and heavy thunder. The thunder slowly subsides, while the lightning continues to flash across the
clouds for some time." At the conclusion of this scene, when Wotan
dismisses the goddess to endless sleep, Wagner notes that Erda's "cave
is once again covered in darkness. Dawn lights the stage. The storm is
over."

Like Erda's cave, Fafner's lair is a place of darkness. In the initial description of the scene where it appears (*Siegfried* 2.1), Wagner says that the audience sees "a dark night with the deepest gloom upstage" [*finstere Nacht, am dichtesten über dem Hintergrunde*]. As the episode continues, darkness still surrounds the lair of the dragon while brilliant light illuminates Siegfried and the gods.[268] Later, in *Siegfried* 3.2, when the hero splinters Wotan's spear and effectively ends the high god's reign, Wagner says of Wotan that "he suddenly disappears into total darkness" [*Er verschwindet plötzlich in völliger Finsternis*]. Again, in *Götterdämmerung* 1.3, as Waltraute approaches Brünnhilde's rock with her grim news of the gods' distress, "a dark storm-cloud looms near the rocky platform's edge." When Siegfried, disguised as Gunther, later returns to Brünnhilde, another "storm-cloud rises out of the forest" (*Götterdämmerung* 1.3).[269] Then, after Siegfried's death, Wagner's stage directions include the following terse description of *Götterdämmerung* 3.2: "Night has fallen" [*Der Nacht ist hereingebrochen*].[270]

In contrast to these moments of grief and sadness, Wagner wanted the scenes of joy in his cycle to be brightly illuminated. For instance, at the moment when the gold awakens in *Das Rheingold*, the composer specified that his audience should see "a steadily strengthening ray of light that has penetrated the waters from above; at a point high up on the central reef it kindles and gradually brightens until it becomes a dazzling, brilliant golden glow; from it a magical golden light suffuses the water." Within a few moments, "the entire mass of water shimmers in the bright glow of gold." Opposites, in Wagner's mythic world, apparently attract. Alberich, that creature of darkness, is "powerfully drawn by the glow."

As might be expected, one of the most joyous episodes in the *Ring*—the encounter and growing passion of Siegmund and Sieglinde— is represented as a scene of ever increasing light. When Siegmund first meets his sister, he gazes at her "with increasing warmth" (*mit wachsender Wärme*: *Die Walküre* 1.1). Hunding notices the resemblance of the two Wälsungs and says that a snakelike *gleam* shines from their eyes (*Der gleissende Wurm glänze auch ihm aus dem Auge*: *Die Walküre* 1.2). Moreover, light draws Siegmund to Notung. When Siegmund notices the sword that Wälse had thrust through the tree in Hunding's hall, he immediately associates its light with the gleam he has observed in Sieglinde's eyes.

> What glows so brightly there in the flickering light?
> What is the spark that leaps from the trunk of the ash tree?
> The flash blinds my eyes
> so heartily does the flickering light laugh!
> How vividly the gleam scorches my heart!
> Is it the glance of that radiant woman?

Siegmund's lines contain numerous terms for "light," "radiance," "glow," and "gleaming."[271] The "Winterstürme" scene begins when "the full moon shines into the house and its light falls on the lovers, so that all at once they can see each other properly." In symbolic recognition of their growing love, Wagner notes that "the moonlight gradually becomes brighter."

The Light of the Gods

The same intense light with which Wagner symbolizes joy in the *Ring* is also, by extension, associated with the domain of the gods. At the beginning of *Das Rheingold* 2, for instance, he describes the gods' heavenly realm: "The light of breaking day strengthens and is reflected off the battlements of a castle standing on a rocky peak in the background." The parallel between light and divinity is made even clearer in *Das Rheingold* 4 when the gods' regain their superhuman strength. "The foreground is now quite bright again; with the return of the light, the gods' appearance regains its original vitality." *Das Rheingold* concludes with similar images. Valhalla, the gods' new home, is seen "gleaming in the evening sunlight," and Wotan instructs the Rhinemaidens to console themselves for the loss of their gold by contemplating "the gods' new radiance" [*der Götter neuem Glanze*].

In Wagner's cycle, the power of the gods is always represented by brilliant light. In *Die Walküre* 2.5, as Sieglinde observes the climactic battle between Siegmund and Hunding, "she runs toward the slope, but a flash of light suddenly dazzles her [*Schein blendet aber plötzlich*], so that she staggers to one side as if blinded. Brünnhilde is seen in the glaring light [*Lichtglanze*], hovering above Siegmund and covering him with her shield." Later, in *Die Walküre* 3.2 when Wotan angrily dismisses the Valkyries, "a vivid flash of lightning rends the cloud and reveals the Valkyries galloping away at full speed." Porges reported Wagner's desire to have the Wanderer's arrival in *Siegfried* 2.1 indicated with a light: "Immediately before Alberich's words, 'Banger Tag, bebst du schon auf?', a flash of light is seen through the thick foliage of the forest."[272] This is the light that Alberich notices when he asks "What gleam is shining there? A bright spark is glistening ever nearer." [*Welcher Glanze glitzert dort auf? Näher schimmert ein heller Schein.*] Within a few moments, however, Alberich notices that the light has faded and night has returned to its former darkness. For the moment at least, the power of evil has proved stronger than the dawn of the gods. When the Wanderer finally appears onstage, "a shaft of moonlight suddenly falls on the scene, as if the clouds have parted."[273]

Building on the splintered world of *Das Rheingold*, the light of the gods in the later dramas occasionally loses its brilliance or is tinged with color. For instance, in *Die Walküre* 2.5 when Siegmund draws back his sword intending to deal Hunding a deathblow, Wagner says that "a fiery *red* glow [*ein glühend rötlicher Schein*] breaks through the cloud on the left and Wotan is seen standing above Hunding." Later, the stage directions note that "an ever increasing fiery light [*wachsender Feuerschein*] is seen." Red, the color of Alberich and Nibelheim, reminds the audience that, like his antagonist, Wotan too renounced love for power when he sacrificed his son Siegmund. As we have seen on several different levels, the Nibelung who stole the gold of the Rhinemaidens and the supreme god who stole the bough of the World Ash are more alike than they are different.

Red is also the color associated with danger and sorrow in the *Ring*. In the prologue to *Götterdämmerung*, Wagner's stage directions note that, after the Rope of Fate has been torn, "the red of dawn becomes stronger in the sky as the light from the fire below fades." In *Götterdämmerung* 2.2 after Siegfried has deceived Brünnhilde and carried off the ring by force, Wagner notes that "the Rhine is dyed red by the steadily increasing glow of the dawn."[274]

A final example of color imagery in the cycle is associated with
Wotan. In *Siegfried* 1.2 when the high god enters Mime's cave disguised as the Wanderer, he is "dressed in a long, dark blue [*dunkelblauen*]
cloak." At the beginning of *Siegfried* 2.1 when the Wanderer encounters Alberich near Fafner's cave, the stage directions note that "a bluish
light [*bläulicher Glanz*] shines." Blue, it must be remembered, is the
color of Erda, the earth. It is appropriate, therefore, that this would be
the color that Wotan assumes whenever he walks the earth, demon-
strating the wisdom that he has gained from the goddess Erda herself.
Moreover, in the original Bayreuth production of 1876, Wagner's costume designer Carl Emil Doepler, adopted blue as a "family color" of
the Wälsungs. In response to a critic who asked him "why I had
symbolised so much with the colour blue," Doepler replied that he had
"used it only with all those figures to do with the Wälsungs, and besides
the Master himself is demanding a blue coat for Wotan."[275] Clara Steinitz,
who wrote the descriptions when Doepler's sketches were later published, described Siegfried's "blue cloak" as the "symbol of Wotan's
blood" in keeping with the Doepler's original imagery.[276] Color imagery, it is clear, was keenly in the mind of both the composer and his
designer as these original plans for the cycle came to be created.

The Image of Light in the Immolation Scene

Each drama of the *Ring* ends with a spectacular image of light. The
final scene of *Das Rheingold* presents Donner dispelling the mist as
Froh reveals the rainbow bridge leading to Valhalla. *Die Walküre* ends
with the "magic fire" with which Wotan surrounds Brünnhilde to guard
her in its protective sheath of flame.[277] *Siegfried* returns to this setting,
surrounding the hero and his beloved with flames that will soon ignite
the entire world. Yet, of all the dramas in the cycle, *Götterdämmerung*
ends with the most climactic light. Siegfried's funeral pyre spreads its
flames from Nibelheim all the way to the gods' home in Valhalla. The
visual imagery of this final scene was so important to Wagner's conception of the *Ring* that he described it in elaborate detail. As Wagner
imagined the end of the cycle, all the elements of his mythic universe,

rent apart and scattered since their first appearance in *Das Rheingold*, were restored to a single, organic whole. Just as Wagner saw the immolation scene as a way of reintroducing and recombining musical leitmotivs in a new intensity, so do Wagner's visual leitmotivs attain new levels of meaning when reprised in the work's culmination. As Brünnhilde prepares Siegfried's funeral pyre, she mentions light repeatedly. The former Valkyrie commands the fire to blaze high and bright [*Hoch und hell lodre die Glut*] and consume the body of the man whose pure light shone on her like the sun [*wie Sonne lauter strahlt mir sein Licht*]. She then casts the massive torch that ignites the final conflagration. Returning to her earlier comparison of Siegfried to the sun, she tells her horse Grane that the hero lies shining on the pyre [*im Feuer leuchtend*]. She wonders whether Grane feels beckoned by the laughing flames. Wagner thus draws an explicit parallel between what the audience now sees and the final act of *Siegfried* when, awakened by her lover, Brünnhilde's first action was to greet the light of the sun. Together, she and Siegfried laughed at the fires that would one day destroy their world. Now that time has come.

Siegfried's burning pyre is also reflected in the heat of Brünnhilde's breast which seems to burn, a brilliant fire taking hold of her heart [*wie sie entbrennt; helles Feuer das Herz mir erfasst*]. As Brünnhilde then disappears, riding Grane into the center of the blaze, Wagner's stage directions note that the flames rise up instantly and begin to fill the entire stage. For many viewers of the *Ring*, this climactic image of fire is so striking that they speak of it as though it were the last scene of the cycle. But many more images follow. Wagner says that this fire should immediately be extinguished, leaving only a dense billow of smoke [*Dampfgewölk*] hanging over the scene. Suddenly, the waters of the Rhine spill over their banks, inundating the area where the fire was moments before [*hat seine Flut über die Brandstätte gewälzt*]. The Rhinemaidens recover the ring, carrying Hagen to his doom, when suddenly a red light—that repeated symbol of grief in the cycle—begins to shine with growing intensity [*bricht ein rötlicher Glutschein mit wachsender Helligkeit aus*]. The fiery glow then spreads across the heavens, reaching even the hall of the gods. Wagner directs that, as soon as the image of the gods becomes completely obscured by the light of the growing flames, the curtain should fall. The cycle thus ends as it began . . . with waves set against the flickering flames of Loge, a Nibelung scrambling frantically among the rocks of the Rhine, and the sudden appearance of a light that breaks through the surface of the waves.

THE TWILIGHT OF THE GODS

PATTERN:	order	⇒	chaos	⇒	existence	⇒	non-existence
MUSIC:	"Magic Fire"	⇒	"The Rhinemaidens'"	⇒	"Redemption by Love"/ "Praise for Brünnhilde"	⇒	D♭
SIGHT:	the Gibichungs' castle	⇒	flames	⇒	the Rhine River	⇒	darkness
THOUGHT:	the universe	⇒	fire	⇒	water	⇒	nothing
SPEECH:	dialogue	⇒	monologue	⇒	speech without song	⇒	silence

Parallel Developments at the End of *Götterdämmerung*

Fire and water, heat and cold, earth and heaven, the primary colors of the spectrum—all of Heraclitus' opposing qualities that were severed like Anaximander's primal substance at the beginning of the cycle—merge as the *Ring's* final notes are heard. Through Brünnhilde's messianic self-sacrifice, the world has become whole again.

The Image of Darkness: Mist, Smoke, Dusk, and Clouds

Against the imagery of light that appears throughout the *Ring*, Wagner places parallel images of darkness to symbolize evil, suffering, and the absence of the gods. As the immolation scene suggests, one particular form of darkness assumes special meaning in the cycle: the gloom caused, not merely by the absence of light, but by its unnatural *obliteration*. Mist, for example, has been used to conceal the light of the gods ever since the opening of *Das Rheingold*.[278] As Wagner says in his description of the first scene, the home of the Rhinemaidens is one where "waves dissolve into an increasingly fine, damp mist." At the beginning of the cycle, there appears to be nothing noticeably sinister about this image. But as the strength of the gods begins to fade in the second scene of the drama, Wagner says that a mist surrounds them, representing as it were the onset of their mortality. Both in the original stage directions and in Porges' notes, we are told that " . . . a pale mist fills the stage and the gods are seen to grow increasingly old and pallid."[279]

Like mist, smoke has negative connotations in the *Ring*. When Wotan and Loge descend into Nibelheim, "a puff of sulphurous smoke at once bursts forth. . . . The sulphurous smoke emitted by the fissure spreads out over the entire stage and rapidly fills it with a thick cloud" (*Das Rheingold* 2). This smoke is intended to remind the audience of "Nibelheim," a term that Wagner chose to suggest both "home of the Nibelungs" and "land of *Nebel* [mist or fog]."[280] To reflect its infernal nature, Wagner made sure that Nibelheim's representation at Bayreuth was suitably horrific. Porges states that the "scenery contributed to the [vision inspired by the composer's music]: the enormous rocky ravines stretching so far into the distance that the eye could hardly follow them aroused in the spectator feelings of fear and dread completely in harmony with the atmosphere created by the music."[281] Moreover, as the Nibelheim scene (*Das Rheingold* 3) continues, smoke, mist, and the darkness of evil become specifically associated with Alberich. Thus, when Alberich vanishes during his first test of the Tarnhelm, Wagner notes that "where he stood a moment before is a column of mist [*Nebelsäule*]" (*Das Rheingold* 3). Shortly thereafter, "the column of mist vanishes towards the background."

Alberich's darkness and evil haunt the gods and follow them to their heavenly domain. According to Porges, as *Das Rheingold* 4 begins (using the same setting as scene 2), "We are back on the open mountain heights, still shrouded by a pale mist."[282] This symbolic association of the mist, Alberich, and evil is repeated later in the scene when

Alberich returns to his subterranean home: "The dense mist [*dichte Nebelduft*] in the foreground gradually clears." Soon, "Donner, Froh, and Fricka appear out of the dispersing mist [*immer mehr zertheilenden Nebel*]." The cloud of evil begins to lift . . . though not entirely. Wagner notes that "a veil of mist [*Nebelschleier*] still hangs over the background . . . so that the distant castle remains hidden." This is the haze that Donner's thunderous hammer will soon clear away. The god draws back his weapon and "the mist collects around him during what follows." Within a few moments "Donner disappears completely as the thundercloud thickens and darkens round him." The storm raised by the god dispels this gloom, and his fellow deities, deceived by their illusions of happiness, cross the rainbow bridge into Valhalla.

Just as *Das Rheingold*'s other "elements" recur throughout the cycle, so does this association of mist with evil. In *Die Walküre* 2.5, for instance, Wagner describes a haze that is present at the death of Siegmund: "The cloud at once divides in the center, so that Hunding becomes clearly visible." Shortly thereafter, the stage directions note that "Wotan, surrounded by clouds [*von Gewölk umgeben*], stands at the back of the scene leaning on his spear." In *Die Walküre* 3.1 during the famous ride of the Valkyries—a scene that, for all its excitement, results in Wotan's condemnation of Brünnhilde for her disobedience—Porges notes that "a thick cloud looms."[283] Wagner's own scenic description adds that "traces of cloud race past the edge of the rocky platform, driven on by the storm-wind." This darkness intensifies as Wotan nears the scene. "Black thunderclouds have gathered around the peak; a fearsome storm-wind is sweeping in from the rear, to the right of which a fiery red light is glowing ever more intensely." All the images of foreboding are present: the darkness of evil, the red glow of Nibelheim, and a cloud so thick that it obscures the light of divine goodness. With the spectacle of the drama supporting Wagner's evocative music, the audience cannot fail to sense the threatening forces that surround the characters. The resulting tension explodes one scene later (*Die Walküre* 3.2) when Wotan announces the nature of Brünnhilde's punishment. As he hands down his daughter's sentence, "a thick black cloud [*schwarzes Gewölk*] hangs at the edge of the precipice."

The clouds and mist that appear throughout the *Ring* are examples of the "pathetic fallacy," the literary device in which nature assumes the emotions of various characters. The sky is "angry" because Wotan is angry. Dark clouds echo the dark wrath that furrows his brow. The cycle's most explicit instance of the pathetic fallacy appears in *Die Walküre* 2.1 when Brünnhilde announces the angry arrival of Fricka. She says that Wotan must endure a powerful storm [*harten Sturm*] because his wife is coming. Though the parallels are not drawn as openly, other uses of nature imagery in the cycle also serve as examples of the pathetic fallacy, a literary device common in both Classical and Romantic literature.

Viewed from another perspective, however, smoke, clouds, and mist form part of the same imagery of light that we have seen repeatedly in the *Ring*. The characters most closely associated with cloud and mist—Wotan and Alberich—are precisely those who are most guilty of sacrificing love for power. Their actions create, not the natural darkness of evening or twilight, but an unnatural gloom, capable of obscuring even the life-giving rays of the sun. It is this artificial darkness that other characters—from Donner and Froh in *Das Rheingold* to, most dramatically, Brünnhilde in the final moments of *Götterdämmerung*—must seek to dispel.

The Implication of Spectacle in Productions of the *Ring*

Wagner's use of spectacle as a form of visual leitmotif has several important consequences for productions of the *Ring*. To begin with, it means that departing from his scenic conception is quite a different thing from, for instance, staging *Norma* or *La bohème* in modern dress. In most operas, the director and the set designer collaborate with the composer and the librettist. All these artists combine their insight to create a new work, interpretation or, at the very least, a revised emphasis. This is possible in other operas because visual symbols are not bound to the text and music in the way that Wagner envisioned them for the *Ring*. In a "total work of art," however, spectacle, music, theme, character, and speech all have a certain relationship with one another. Changing the work's visual imagery would distort an aspect of the drama that the composer depended on to convey his ideas.[284] To put it another way, altering the *Ring*'s spectacle would be comparable to setting Wagner's libretto to an entirely new score or performing his music to a different plot or set of words. The result might be quite interesting. It might even be a work of great artistic merit. But it would not be the *Ring*.

Such a view has always had its critics. No less an authority than Wieland Wagner rejected visual conservatism and concluded that

> The actual staging—and it alone—is subject to change. To avoid change is to transform the virtue of fidelity into the vice of rigidity .... Thus, in modern times, change becomes merely a question of taste; only those who are ahead of their time are accused of infidelity.[285]

This perspective has influenced a number of recent productions. What is the harm, many feel, in altering the appearance of the *Ring*? Perhaps a revised scenic conception could even enhance Wagner's composition by making its images more familiar to a modern audience.

Unfortunately, departures of this sort deprive Wagner's creation of something vital. If, as we have seen, the composer has given the *Ring*'s appearance the same thematic function that he assigned to his text, characters, and music, then altering the work's spectacle can only undermine its symbolism. As Appia concluded, an author or composer "cannot achieve a unity unless the *entire* production is in harmony with his original conception."[286] That unity of conception is precisely what makes the *Gesamtkunstwerk* different from an ordinary theatrical production. Moreover, that unity was Wagner's fundamental goal: it was through this quality in his drama that he hoped to restore social unity to Germany, much as the "unified" tragedies of Aeschylus, he believed, created a harmonious society in classical Athens. To those who ask, therefore, "Does an audience really miss anything if they do not see Alberich kiss the ring to invoke its power or Siegfried and Gunther raised up on the shields of the Gibichungs? Will anything be lost if the drama is transported from the Rhine to a modern hydroelectric dam or recast as an apocalyptic fantasy in some imaginary world?" we should answer "Perhaps so." At the very least the audience will miss the delicate web of poetry, music, and visual art that makes the *Ring* an unparalleled work of imagination. They will miss experiencing a set of images developed on multiple artistic levels simultaneously. They will miss understanding how the composer's visual cues always expand on and reinterpret the symbols that he introduces in his music and his text. In short, they will miss the *Ring*.[287]

Finale

Wagner, who made the most heroic of all attempts to originate a new form of expression from the ashes of Greek
drama, observed that it was the 'folk' who created art; the
Greek unity of author and spectator had been shattered,
and modern society had degenerated from 'national community' into 'absolute egoism.'[288]

We have seen that Wagner sought to give the *Ring* a high degree of
thematic and structural unity by creating parallel thematic associations
on every level of his drama. He approached his text in the same way as
his music, his imagery in the same way as his text, his characters in the
same way as his imagery, and his staging in the same way as his characters. One may speak of a "leitmotif of sleep," not only in the score,
but also in the sound of Wagner's language and the symbols of his
libretto. "Light, life, and awakening" have thematic associations in the
spectacle of the drama, the imagery of its poetry, and the themes of its
music. This type of highly unified focus, Wagner believed, was characteristic of ancient Greek drama and instrumental in attaining a sense
of "national community" among the ancient Greek city-states. In the
Theater of Dionysus, Wagner imagined lovers of poetry discovering
how much they had in common with lovers of dance, just as the aristocracy learned that their tastes were not really different from those of
the peasants. This artistic unity, Wagner believed, would be transformed
into a civic unity, if only he could recreate "a total work of art" for his
own society.

That the very existence of a "national community" in ancient Greece
was itself merely one of Wagner's romantic illusions helps define the

nature of the composer's "classicism." Wagner's classical ideals owed at least as much to the values of his own time as they did to the works of ancient authors.[289] In the poems he read (usually in translation) by Homer, Aristophanes, and Aeschylus, Wagner believed he found evidence of an idealized world in which the troubles of his own society no longer existed. What he actually found was but a reflection of his own romantic dreams. At its core, Wagner's classical world was not really classical at all but a distillation of romantic images wrapped in a thin veil of classical form. He may have spoke often of Achilles, Oedipus, and Antigone but the values he attributed to them were his own.

Nevertheless, though Wagner may have been mistaken in many of his notions about the Greeks, we should not conclude that he was insincere about what he believed. To restore the classical harmony he attributed to ancient Athens, he truly believed dramatists needed to restore complete unity between author and spectator. To do this entailed developing an entirely new type of drama in which every aspect of creative endeavor—theater, music, ballet, painting, and sculpture—worked together perfectly as a "total work of art." From his reading in Aristotle's *Poetics*, Wagner also knew that all six of Aristotle's constituent elements of tragedy—plot, character, speech, thought, spectacle, and song—needed to work together as a single unit, functioning according to the same basic principles.

In this way, a single line of development may be traced from Wagner's Romantic ideas about the Classical past to his concept of the *Gesamtkunstwerk*, from the *Gesamtkunstwerk* to his principle of thematic association or *leitmotivs*, and from his *leitmotivs* to similar repeated patterns throughout the other aspects of his drama. The true impact of Wagner's romantic classicism should thus be sought, not in the composer's borrowing of bits of plot and character from the *Iliad* or the *Oresteia*, but from his entire approach to how form and meaning come together in a major work of art. Wagner hoped that the *Ring* would unite citizens of all classes and tastes, showing them an example of a perfect unity in art. As Homer and Aeschylus had done before him, Wagner believed that he could use his art to bring about a new age of peace, harmony, and social order.

We now know, of course, that Homer and Aeschylus never achieved the goals Wagner attributed to them. Even more tragically, neither did Wagner. In the years after his death, the *Ring* and its images became co-opted, not by the supporters of peace and brotherhood, but by the proponents of a nationalism that divided the very nation Wagner hoped to unite. The pure and selfless love of Brünnhilde was eclipsed by Alberich's lust for power. Like so many romantic dreams, Wagner's idealism proved impossible to translate into reality.

Sufficient time has now elapsed that it is possible to examine Wagner's ambitious dreams objectively. Despite the composer's many faults, the boy who loved the *Odyssey* still became the man who dreamt of gods and heroes, who imagined epic journeys to distant lands, and who believed that giants, impervious to force, could still be conquered by cleverness. It is significant that Wagner's Wotan, like Homer's Odysseus before him, ultimately returns home to die, having learned the only courage that really matters is acceptance of the truth Erda taught him before his story ever began: *Alles was ist, endet!*

MUSICAL EXAMPLES

Example 1: Nature

Example 2: The Spear

Example 3: The Ring

Example 4: Valhalla

Example 5: The Gold

Example 6: Hagen

Example 7: Donner

Example 8: The Dragon

Example 9: Siegfried the Hero

Example 10: Alberich's Curse

Example 11: Erda

Example 12: "Du bist der Lenz"

Example 13: The Sword

Example 14: Notung

Example 15: Rheingold!

Example 16: Wehe!

Example 17: The Giants

Example 18: The Twilight of the Gods

Example 19: The Mature Siegfried

Example 20: Brünnhilde the Woman

Example 21: Brünnhilde the Valkyrie

Example 22: Fafner the Dragon

Example 23: Brünnhilde's Love for the Volsungs

Example 24: Song of the Forest Bird

Example 25: "Weia! Waga!"

Example 26: The Need of the Gods

Example 27: Wotan's Frustration

Example 28: The Primal Element or Primal Substance

Example 29: The River Rhine

Example 30: Water

Example 31: Sleep

Example 32: Loge's Fire

Example 33: Brünnhilde's Sleep

Example 34: Siegfried's Indomitable Vitality

Example 35: Awakening

Example 36: The Awakening of the Gold

Example 37: Fate

Example 38: "Heil dir, Sonne!"

Example 39: Redemption By Love / Praise for Brünnhilde

Example 40: The Power of the Ring

WORKS CITED

Aberbach, Alan David. *The Ideas of Richard Wagner*. New York: University Press of America, 1988.

Appia, Adolphe. *Music and the Art of the Theatre*. Trans. Robert W. Corrigan, Mary Douglas Dirks, and Walter R. Volbach. Coral Gables, Florida: University of Miami Press, 1962.

Bailey, Robert. "Wagner's Musical Sketches." *Report of the Eleventh Congress of the International Musicological Society*. Vol. 1. Copenhagen: 1972. Pp. 240-46.

Barnes, Jonathan. *The Presocratic Philosophers*. 2 vols. London: Routledge and Kegan Paul, 1979.

Barth, Herbert; Mack, Dietrich; and Voss, Egan, eds. *Wagner: A Documentary Study*. Trans. P.R. Ford and Mary Whittal. New York: Oxford University Press, 1975.

Borchmeyer, Dieter. *Richard Wagner: Theory and Theatre*. Trans. Stewart Spencer. Oxford: Clarendon Press, 1991.

Butler, E.M. *The Tyranny of Greece Over Germany*. New York: Macmillan, 1935.

Chamberlain, H.S. *Richard Wagner*. Trans. G. Ainslie Hight. London: L.M. Dent, 1897.

Cicora, Mary A. *Mythology as Metaphor*. Westport, Connecticut: Greenwood Press, 1998.

Cook, Peter. *A Memoir of Bayreuth 1876*. London: Peter Cook, 1979.

Cooke, Deryck. *I Saw the World End: A Study of Wagner's Ring*. 1979: rpt. London: Oxford University Press, 1992.

_____. *An Introduction to Der Ring Des Nibelungen*. 1969: reissue on CD. London: Decca Recording Company, 1995. First issued as *Weaving the Ring: An Introduction to Der Ring Des Nibelungen*. London: Decca Recording Company, 1969. (Still available on cassette from the Wagner Society of New York, 1989).

Cord, William O. *An Introduction to Richard Wagner's Der Ring des*

Nibelungen: A Handbook. Athens, Ohio: Ohio University Press, 1983.

Corse, Sandra. *Wagner and the New Consciousness.* London: Associate University Presses, 1990.

Crossley-Holland, Kevin. *The Norse Myths.* New York: Pantheon Books, 1980.

Dahlhaus, Carl, ed. *Richard Wagner: Werk und Wirkung.* Regensburg: G. Bosse, 1971.

Darcy, Warren. "'*Alles was ist, endet!*' Erda's Prophecy of the World's Destruction," *Programmheft 2 (Das Rheingold) der Bayreuther Festspiele* (1988). Pp. 67-92.

_____. "'*Creatio ex Nihilo*': The Genesis, Structure, and Meaning of the *Rheingold* Prelude." *19th Century Music.* Vol. 13 (1989) Pp. 79-100.

_____. "'Everything That Is, Ends!' The Genesis and Meaning of the Erda Episode in *Das Rheingold.*" *Musical Times.* Vol. 129 (1988). Pp. 443-47.

Davidson, H.R. Ellis. *Gods and Myths of Northern Europe.* Harmonsworth, Middlesex: Penguin, 1964.

Deathridge, John. "The Nomenclature of Wagner's Sketches." *Proceedings of the Royal Music Association.* Vol. 101 (1974-75). Pp. 74-89.

_____. "Wagner's Sketches for the *Ring.* Some Recent Studies." *Musical Times.* Vol. 118 (1977) 387. Pp. 383-89.

Deathridge, John and Dahlhaus, Carl. *The New Grove Wagner.* New York: Norton, 1984.

DiGaetani, John L. *Penetrating Wagner's Ring.* New York: Da Capo Press, 1978.

Donington, Robert. *Wagner's 'Ring' and its Symbols.* New York: St. Martin's Press, 1974.

Ellis, William Ashton. *Life of Richard Wagner.* London: Kegan Paul, Tench, Trübner, 1900. 6 vols.

Ewans, Michael. *Wagner and Aeschylus.* Cambridge: Cambridge University Press, 1982.

Fay, Stephan. *The Ring: Anatomy of an Opera.* London: Secker and Warburg, 1984.

Fischer-Dieskau, Dietrich. *Wagner and Nietzsche*. Trans. Joachim Neugroschel. New York: Seabury Press, 1976.

Förster-Nietzsche, Elizabeth. *The Nietzsche-Wagner Correspondence*. Trans. Caroline V. Kerr. New York: Liveright, 1921.

Freeman, Kathleen. *Companion to the Pre-Socratic Philosophers*. 3rd. ed. Cambridge, Massachusetts: Harvard University Press, 1966.

Fricke, Richard. *Wagner in Rehearsal, 1875-1876: The Diaries of Richard Fricke*. Trans. George R. Fricke. Ed. James Deaville and Evan Baker. *Franz Liszt Studies #7*. Stuyvesant, New York: Pendragon Press.

Gillespie, Iris. "Richard Wagner and the Heroic Mystique." *Wagner*. Vol. 12. No. 3 (September, 1991). Pp. 99-115.

Glasenapp, C.F. *Das Leben Richard Wagners*. 6 vols. Fourth edition. Leipzig: Breitkopf und Härtel, 1905.

Glass, Frank W, *The Fertilizing Seed: Wagner's Concept of the Poetic Intent*. Ann Arbor, Michigan: UMI Research Press, 1981, 1983.

Gregor-Dellin, Martin and Mack, Dietrich, eds. *Cosima Wagner's Diaries*. 2 vols. Trans. Geoffrey Skelton. New York: Harcourt Brace Jovanovich, 1980.

Grey, Thomas S. *Wagner's Musical Prose*. Cambridge: Cambridge University Press, 1995.

Gutman, Robert W. *Richard Wagner: The Man, His Mind, and His Music*. New York: Harcourt, Brace, and World, 1968.

Hegel, Georg Wilhelm Friedrich. *Hegel's Lectures on the History of Philosophy*. 3 vols. Trans. E.S. Haldane. 1892: rpt. London: Routledge and Kegan Paul, 1963.

Holman, J.K. *Wagner's Ring: A Listener's Companion and Concordance*. Portland, Oregon: Amadeus Press, 1996.

Hueffer, Francis, trans. *Correspondence of Wagner and Liszt*. 2 vols. New York: Greenwood Press, 1969.

James, Burnett. *Wagner and the Romantic Disaster*. New York: Midas Books, 1983.

Jenkyns, Richard. *The Victorians and Ancient Greece*. Cambridge, Massachusetts: Harvard University Press, 1980.

Kaufman, Walter. *Basic Writings of Nietzsche*. New York: Modern Library, 1968.

_____. *Nietzsche: Philosopher, Psychologist, Antichrist.* 3rd. ed. Princeton: Princeton University Press, 1968.

Knapp, J. Merrill. "The Instrumentation Draft of Wagner's *Das Rheingold.*" *Journal of the American Musicological Society.* Vol. 30 (1977), pp. 272-95.

Koheil, Ruth and Richardson, Herbert. "Why Brünnhilde is the True Hero of the *Ring* Cycle: An Analysis of Her Psychological Development." *New Studies in Richard Wagner's "The Ring of the Nibelungen."* Ed. Herbert Richardson. Lewiston, New York: Mellen, 1991. Pp. 177-89

Lee, M. Owen. *The Olive-Tree Bed and Other Quests.* Toronto: University of Toronto Press, 1997.

_____. *Wagner's Ring: Turning the Sky Round.* 1990: rpt. New York: Summit Books, 1991.

Lloyd-Jones, Hugh. *Blood for the Ghosts.* Baltimore: Johns Hopkins University Press, 1982.

_____. "Wagner and the Greeks." *London Times Literary Supplement.* January 9, 1976. Pp. 37-39.

Magee, Bryan. *The Philosophy of Schopenhauer.* Oxford: Clarendon Press, 1983.

Magee, Elizabeth. *Richard Wagner and the Nibelungs.* Oxford: Clarendon Press, 1990.

Marchand, Suzanne L. *Down From Olympus: Archaeology and Philhellenism in Germany, 1750-1970.* Princeton: Princeton University Press, 1996.

McCreless, Patrick. *Wagner's Siegfried: Its Drama, History and Music.* Ann Arbor: UMI Research Press, 1982.

Millington, Barry. *Wagner.* New York: Random House, 1984.

_____, ed. *The Wagner Compendium.* New York: Schirmer, 1992.

Millington, Barry and Spencer, Stewart, eds. *Wagner in Performance.* New Haven: Yale University Press, 1992.

Nattiez, Jean-Jacques. *Wagner Androgyne.* Trans. Stewart Spencer. Princeton: Princeton University Press, 1993.

Newman, Ernest. *The Life of Richard Wagner.* 4 vols. New York: Alfred A. Knopf, 1937.

————. *Wagner As Man and Artist.* 1924: rpt. New York: Limelight Editions, 1989.

————. *Wagner Nights.* 1949: rpt. London: The Bodley Head, 1988.

Nietzsche, Friedrich. *Philosophy in the Tragic Age of the Greeks.* Trans. Marianne Cowan. New York: Gateway, Regnery: 1962.

————. *Werke in drei Bänden.* Munich: Carl Hanser Verlag, 1966.

Osborne, Charles. *The Complete Operas of Wagner.* 1990: rpt. London: Grange Books, 1995.

Plantinga, Leon. *Romantic Music.* New York: Norton, 1984.

Porges, Heinrich. *Wagner Rehearsing the 'Ring.'* Trans. Robert L. Jacobs. Cambridge: Cambridge University Press, 1983.

Rather, L.J. *The Dream of Self-Destruction.* Baton Rouge: Louisiana State University Press, 1979.

————. *Reading Wagner: A Study in the History of Ideas.* Baton Rouge: Louisiana State University Press, 1990.

Roller, Duane W. "Wagner and the Classics," *Euprhosyne* 20 (new series 1992) 231-52.

Russell, James Earl. *German Higher Schools.* New York: Longmans, Green, and Co., 1899.

Sabor, Rudolph. *The Real Wagner.* London: Cardinal, 1987.

Schopenhauer, Arthur. *Parerga and Paralipomena.* Trans. E.F.J. Payne. 2 vols. Oxford: Clarendon Press, 1974.

————. *The World as Will and Representation.* Trans. E.F.J. Payne. 2 vols. New York: Dover Publications, 1966.

Schuler, John. *The Language of Richard Wagner's Ring des Nibelungen.* Lancaster, Pennsylvania: Steinman and Foltz, 1908.

Shaw, George Bernard. *The Perfect Wagnerite: A Commentary on the Nibelung's Ring.* 1923: rpt. New York: Dover, 1967.

Skelton, Geoffrey. *Wagner in Thought and Practice.* Portland, Oregon: Amadeus Press, 1991.

Srocke, Martina. *Richard Wagner als Regisseur.* Munich: Emil Katzbichler, 1988.

Spotts, Frederic. *Bayreuth: A History of the Wagner Festival.* New Haven: Yale University Press, 1994.

Stein, Jack M. *Richard Wagner and the Synthesis of the Arts.* Detroit: Wayne State University Press, 1960.

Sturluson, Snorri. *The Prose Edda.* Trans. Jean I. Young. Berkeley: University of California Press, 1964.

Swain, Joseph P. *Musical Languages.* New York: Norton, 1997.

Taylor, Ronald. *Richard Wagner: His Life, Art, and Thought.* New York: Taplinger, 1979.

Trevelyan, Humphrey. *Goethe and the Greeks.* New York: Octagon Books, 1972.

Wagner, Cosima. *Die Tagebücher.* Ed. M. Gregor-Dellin and D. Mack. 2 vols. Munich: Piper, 1976.

Wagner, Richard. *Mein Leben.* Ed. Martin Gregor-Dellin. 2 vols. Munich: List, 1969.

————. *My Life.* Trans. Andrew Gray. Ed. Mary Whittall. 1983: rpt. New York: Da Capo Press, 1992.

————. *Richard Wagner's Prose Works.* Trans. William Ashton Ellis. 8 vols. 1892: rpt. New York: Broude Brothers, 1966.

————. *Sämtliche Schriften und Dichtungen.* 12 vols. Leipzig: Breitkopf and Härtel, 1928.

————. *Selected Letters of Richard Wagner.* Trans. Stewart Spencer and Barry Millington. New York: Norton, 1987.

Wallace, William. *Richard Wagner As He Lived.* New York: Harper and Brothers, 1925.

Wapnewski, Peter. *Der traurige Gott: Richard Wagner in seinem Helden.* Munich: Beck, 1978.

Waterman, John T. *A History of the German Language.* Rev. ed. Seattle: University of Washington Press, 1973.

Watson, Derek. *Richard Wagner: A Biography.* New York: Schirmer, 1979.

Von Westernhagen, Curt. "Über die Bedeutung von Kompositionsskizzen" in *Die Entstehung des Ring.* Zürich: Atlantis, 1973. Pp. 13-24.

————. "*Das Rheingold*: Das Einzelskizzenblatt" in *Die Entstehung des Ring.* Zürich: Atlantis, 1973. Pp. 31-45

————. *Wagner: A Biography.* Trans. Mary Whittall. 2 vols. Cambridge: Cambridge University Press, 1978.

White, Chappell. *An Introduction to the Life and Works of Richard Wagner.* Englewood Cliffs: Prentice-Hall, 1967.

Williams, Simon. *Richard Wagner and Festival Theatre*. London: Greenwood Press, 1994.

Winkler, Franz E. *For Freedom Destined*. Garden City, New York: Waldorf Press, 1974.

ENDNOTES

1 Porges, *Wagner Rehearsing the 'Ring,'* p. 130.

2 Wagner's costume designer, Carl Emil Doepler, does note that he had "exhaustively studied Tacitus" before preparing his sketches of the costumes to be used in the *Ring*. See Cook, *Memoir of Bayreuth*, p. 25. Nevertheless, Doepler's recollections were published only after those of Porges.

3 "Classical Elements in Richard Wagner's *Der Ring des Nibelungen*" there retitled "Plot: Classical Form and Meaning in Wagner's *Ring*"), *Opera Quarterly* 11.1 (1994/95), pp. 79-94; "The Thematic Role of *Stabreim* in Richard Wagner's *Der Ring des Nibelungen*" (here retitled "Speech: the Thematic Role of Stabreim in the *Ring*"), *Opera Quarterly* 11.4 (1995), pp. 59-76; "Sleep in the *Ring*" (here retitled "Thought: Sleep in the *Ring*"), *Opera Quarterly* 12.2 (winter 1995/96), pp. 3-22; "The Messianic Hero in Wagner's *Ring*" (here retitled "Character: The Messianic Hero in the *Ring*"), *Opera Quarterly* 13.2 (winter 1996/97) 21-38; and "Spectacle in the *Ring*" (here retitled "Spectacle: Light and Color in the *Ring*"), *Opera Quarterly* 14.4 (summer 1998) 41-57. Reprinted with written permission from Oxford University Press.

4 See "*Der Ring des Nibelungen* in seinen Beziehungen zur griechischen Tragödie und zur zeitgenössischen Philosophie," *Richard-Wagner Jahrbuch*, vol. 2 (Berlin: Hausbücher, 1907), pp. 284-330.

5 Lloyd-Jones, "Wagner and the Greeks" in *Blood for the Ghosts*, pp. 126-42.

6 Roller, "Wagner and the Classics," pp. 231-52.

7 Chamberlain had married Wagner's daughter Eva in 1908.

8 Chamberlain, *Richard Wagner*, p. 36.

9 These sites included Rome, Naples, Pompeii, Herculaneum, Baiae, Pozzuoli, the cave of the Cumaean Sibyl, Lake Avernus, the Phlegraean Fields, and even the crater of Vesuvius. See Leopold

Mozart's letter to his wife written in Naples on June 16, 1770 in Wilhemn A. Bauer and Otto Erich Deutsch, eds., *Mozart: Briefe und Auszeichnungen*, vol. 1 (Basel: Bärenreiter Kasell, 1962), pp. 360-62, letter 191. A translation of this letter appears at Emily Anderson, ed. and trans., *The Letters of Mozart and His Family*, vol. 1, 2nd ed. (New York: St. Martin's, 1966), pp. 144-45, letter 98.

10 Wallace, *Wagner As He Lived*, pp. 266, 265.

11 One of the best short analyses of H.S. Chamberlain appears in William L. Shirer, *The Rise and Fall of the Third Reich* (New York: Fawcett Crest, 1950, 1960), pp. 152-59. See also John Toland, *Adolf Hitler* (New York: Anchor/Doubleday, 1976), p. 147, and David C. Large and William Weber, eds., *Wagnerism in European Culture and Politics* (Ithaca, New York: Cornell University Press, 1984) 116-17, 130-32.

12 One instance of Wallace's manipulation or distortion of the facts is as follows. Wallace cites the following passage from the authorized translation of *Mein Leben*, published in 1911: "Droysen's eloquent commentaries in particular helped to bring before my imagination the intoxicating effect of the production of an Athenian tragedy, so that I could see the *Oresteia* with my mind's eye, as though it were actually being performed, and its effect upon me was indescribable. Nothing, however, could equal the sublime emotion with which the *Agamemnon* trilogy inspired me, and to the last word of the *Eumenides* I lived in an atmosphere so far removed from the present day that I have never since been really able to reconcile myself with modern literature." [Richard Wagner, *My Life*, authorized translation (New York: Dodd, Mead and Company, 1911), p. 415.] Wallace uses this passage to claim that he has caught Wagner in a serious error: "The *Oresteia* and the *Agamemnon* trilogy which Wagner alluded to as two different groups of plays, are ONE AND THE SAME THING. As well say that *Twelfth Night* is one play and *What You Will*, another." (Wallace, *Wagner As He Lived*, p. 268.) Nevertheless, the real problem here lies in the translation that Wallace was using, not in Wagner himself. Wagner's

original text reads: "Namentlich die beredten Didaskalien *Droysens* halfen mir, das berauschende Bild der athenischen Tragödienaufführungen so deutlich meiner Einbildungskraft vorzuführen, daß ich die »Oresteia« vorzüglich unter der Form einer solchen Aufführung mit einer bisher unerhört eindringlichen Gewalt auf mich wirken fühlen konnte. Nichts glich der erhabenen Erschütterung, welche der »Agamemnon« auf mich hervorbrachte: bis zum Schluß der »Eumeniden« verweilte ich in einem Zustande der Entrücktheit, aus welchem ich eigentlich nie wieder gänzlich zur Versöhnung mit der modernen Literatur zurückgekehrt bin." (Wagner, *Mein Leben*, p. 356.) It is the authorized translation's misleading insertion of the term "however" that incorrectly made Wallace believe that Wagner was changing topics at this point and beginning to speak of a new work. Wagner was not. The Gray and Whittal translation makes the composer's sequence of thought much clearer: "…that I could see the *Oresteia* with my mind's eye as if actually being performed, and its impact on me was indescribable. There was nothing equal to the exalted emotion evoked in me by *Agamemnon*; and to the close…" (Wagner, *My Life*, p. 342.)

13 Both are wild and natural young men who respond more from instinct than from habits they have learned. Both are tutored by creatures (Chiron and Mime) who are less than human in appearance and more than human in knowledge. Both are endowed with weapons forged by the gods that, in the end, prove unable to save them.

14 Both lose sight in this world to symbolize the extent of their wisdom on a higher plane. Both demonstrate their wisdom through their skill at answering riddles. Both are first elevated, then destroyed by the very same quality of their personalities.

15 Both characters refuse to submit even when that decision costs them their lives. Both dispute with a sister who temporizes and seeks to advocate a more moderate position. Both walk undeterred into their own tomb or pyre as a final indication of how

inflexible they are in their principles. See Cicora, *Mythology as Metaphor*, pp. 67-68, 81-84.

16 Wagner himself felt that "all myths were variations from a common origin, and that Germanic and Greek legends were in all essentials the same: he compared the Nibelungen with Oedipus and Antigone, Siegfried with Apollo ..." Butler, *Tyranny of Greece Over Germany*, p. 311.

17 Jenkyns, *Victorians and Ancient Greece*, p. 95.

18 Wagner, *My Life*, p. 6.

19 Wagner, *My Life*, p. 6.

20 Wagner, *My Life*, p. 16.

21 James Earl Russell notes that the written examination for graduation from a German Gymnasium in the nineteenth century included "(1) a German essay; (2) a translation from German into Latin; (3) a translation from the Greek, and (4) from the French into German; and (5) four problems in mathematics—one each from plane geometry, solid geometry, trigonometry and algebra. The oral examination includes Latin, Greek, religion, history and mathematics." Russell, *Higher Schools*, p. 182.

22 Wagner, "To Friedrich Nietzsche" in *Prose Works*, vol. 5, p. 292.

23 Wagner, *My Life*, p. 14.

24 Wagner, "Autobiographical Sketch" in *Prose Works*, vol. 1, p. 4.

25 Wagner, *My Life*, p. 339.

26 Wagner, "Autobiographical Sketch" in *Prose Works*, vol. 1, p. 4.

27 Wagner, *My Life*, p. 22. (Emphasis added.)

28 The title of Chapter 2, section 2 of Wallace, *Wagner As He Lived*, pp. 12-18.

29 See Wallace, *Wagner As He Lived*, p. 15.

30 Russell, *German Higher Schools*, p. 247. For more on Johannes Schulze, see Marchand, *Down From Olympus*, p. 22.

31 Hugo Münsterberg, *American Traits from the Point of View of a German* (1901: rpt. Port Washington, New York: Kennikat Press, 1971), p. 47.

32 Friedrich Paulsen, *German Education Past and Present*, trans. T. Lorenz (London: T. Fisher Unwin, 1908), pp. 201-02.

33 Stefan Zweig, *The World of Yesterday* (1943: rpt. Lincoln, Nebraska: University of Nebraska Press Press, 1964), p. 28.

34 See Raymond V. Scoder and Vincent C. Horrigan, *A Reading Course in Homeric Greek* (Chicago, Illinois: Loyola University Press, 1985) and Frank Beetham, *Beginning Greek With Homer: An Elementary Course Based on Odyssey V* (London: Bristol Classical Press, 1996). Clyde Pharr's *Homeric Greek: A Book for Beginners* (1920: rpt. Norman, Oklahoma: Oklahoma University Press, 1959) takes a similar approach, but uses the *Iliad* rather than the *Odyssey* for material.

35 Glasenapp's examination of the records took place while performing research for *Das Leben Richard Wagners*. See Wallace, *Wagner As He Lived*, p. 13.

36 Wagner, *My Life*, p. 22.

37 See Wagner, *My Life*, p. 35.

38 Wagner, *My Life*, p. 38.

39 Wagner, *My Life*, p. 23.

40 Wagner, *My Life*, p. 23.

41 Rather, *Reading Wagner*, p. 7.

42 Rather, *Reading Wagner*, p. 14. It should be noted that, although a Roman slave and Roman emperor, Epictetus and Marcus Aurelius actually wrote in Greek, despite Rather's listing.

43 This assumption is made by Wallace among others. "As for Wagner's 'voluminous works,' let us hope that his 'library' was not like that of one other, a worshiper, too, the pages of whose favorite author (in twelve volumes) were uncut!" Wallace, *Wagner As He Lived*, pp. 269-70.

44 Sabor, *Real Wagner*, p. 243.

45 Wagner, *My Life*, p. 261.

46 Wagner, *My Life*, p. 339.

47 Wagner, *My Life*, pp. 342-43.

48 Wagner, "Zukunftsmusik," in *Prose Works*, vol. 3, pp. 306-07.

49 According to the entry in Cosima Wagner's diaries dated December 31, 1880. See Borchmeyer, *Theory and Theatre*, p. 77.

50 See Rather, *Reading Wagner*, pp. 25-26, Sabor, *The Real Wagner* 243. Cosima's reference to Wagner omitting "quite a few passages in

order to be able to read me these plays" appears in *Tagebücher*, vol. 1, p. 303 (entry of October 23, 1870).

51 See Aberbach, *Ideas of Richard Wagner*, 120 and Newman, *Life*, vol. 4, p. 325. The text for "A Capitualation," may be found in *Prose Works*, vol. 5, pp. 5-33. The German text appears as *Eine Kapitulation* in *Sämtliche Schriften*, vol. 9, pp. 1-41.

52 Wagner, "To Friedrich Nietzsche," *Prose Works*, vol. 5, pp. 293-95.

53 Wagner, "To Friedrich Nietzsche," *Prose Works*, vol. 5, p. 295. "Nietzsche appreciated Wagner's support, but quickly recognized that Wagner's letter would in fact produce effects amongst the philologists contrary to those intended. Consequently, he joyfully accepted his friend Erwin Rohde's offer to write a scholarly defense of *The Birth of Tragedy* to be circulated within the guild." Marchand, *Down From Olympus*, p. 130.

54 Wagner, "To Friedrich Nietzsche," *Prose Works*, vol. 5, p. 297.

55 See Wagner, "To Friedrich Nietzsche," *Prose Works*, vol. 5, p. 297.

56 Wagner, "Art and Revolution," *Prose Works*, vol. 1, p. 54. Compare E.M. Butler's summary of Wagner's approach to classical myth and literature: "… Wagner was not creating myths, nor even recreating them, as the Greek tragic dramatists had done. He was merely adapting ancient legends to suit a philosophy of life they had not been created to express; at times even, as in *The Rhinegold*, using them for purposes of political propaganda. He did not believe in Wotan, Loki or Brunhild; he turned them into symbols …" Butler, *Tyranny of Greece Over Germany*, p. 312.

57 Wagner, "Art and Revolution," *Prose Works*, vol. 1, p. 52.

58 Wagner, "Art and Revolution," *Prose Works*, vol. 1, p. 53.

59 Wagner, "A Letter to Berlioz," *Prose Works*, vol. 3, pp. 289-90.

60 Fischer-Dieskau, *Wagner and Nietzsche*, p. 16.

61 *First Olympian Ode*, ll. 1-2. The translation is that of Richmond Lattimore, *The Odes of Pindar* (Chicago, IL: University of Chicago Press, 1947), p. 1.

62 Translated from Wagner, *Schriften und Dichtungen*, vol. 2, p. 156.

63 Sturluson, *Prose Edda*, p. 32. The beginning of this passage is a direct quotation by Sturluson of the third stanza of the "Völospá"

("The Sibyl's Prophecy"), the first poem included in most editions
of *The Poetic Edda*:

"When Ymir lived,   long ages ago
before there were seas,   chill waves or shore,
Earth was not yet   nor the high heavens
but a great emptiness   nowhere green."

From Patricia Terry, trans., *Poems of the Vikings: The Elder Edda* (India-
napolis: Bobbs-Merrill Co., 1969), p. 3. The original Norse text
may be found in Hans Kuhn, *Edda: Die Lieder des Codex Regius
nebst verwandten Denkmälern* (Heidelberg: Carl Winter
Universitätsverlag, 1962), p. 1.

64 Translated from Wagner *Schriften und Dichtungen*, vol. 5, p. 200.

65 Wagner, *My Life*, p. 499. The German text appears in Wagner,
Mein Leben, vol. 2, pp. 511-12.

66 Deathridge and Dahlhaus, *New Grove Wagner*, p. 39.

67 See Darcy, "'*Creatio ex Nihilo*'," p. 80.

68 Deathridge and Dahlhaus state that, despite the date on this draft,
it was actually written "much later" than the journey to La Spezia.
See Deathridge and Dahlhaus, *New Grove Wagner*, p. 39.

69 Curt Von Westernhagen appears to contradict this in *Wagner*, p.
187. "In the sketch the introduction is admittedly in Eb major
and in 6/8 time, it comprises variations that roll on, steadily
crescendoing, over the pedal point of the low Eb. The melodic
line of the very first horn motive is already indicated, developing
out of the Eb major triad." But the "sketch" to which Von
Westernhagen (or, more properly, his translator) refers here is actually the first continuous musical draft of *Das Rheingold* (to be
discussed below), not the isolated prose sketch of the prelude. On
the complicated issue of the terminology that scholars use to refer
to Wagner's numerous drafts, revisions, and sketches, see
Deathridge, "Nomenclature of Wagner's Sketches," pp. 74-89;
Bailey, "Wagner's Musical Sketches," pp. 240-46; and Knapp, "Instrumentation Draft of Wagner's *Das Rheingold*," pp. 273-74, n. 5.
A more complete discussion by Von Westernhagen of the sketches

JLL

may be found in "Über die Bedeutung von Kompositionsskizzen" and "*Das Rheingold*: Das Einzelskizzenblatt."

70 See Knapp, "Instrumentation Draft," p. 282.

71 Von Westernhagen *Wagner*, vol. 1, pp. 187-89.

72 Deathridge, "Wagner's Sketches for the *Ring*.," p. 387.

73 See Knapp, "Instrumentation Draft," pp. 276-80.

74 Wagner, *My Life*, p. 380.

75 Wagner, *My Life*, pp. 380-81. See Newman, *Wagner Nights*, p. 424.

76 Wagner, *My Life*, p. 380.

77 Deathridge and Dahlhaus, *New Grove Wagner*. p. 78.

78 With cycles that presented multiple stories and ended with comedy, the tetralogies of most ancient tragedians bore a closer resemblance to Puccini's *Il Trittico* than Wagner's *Ring*.

79 Though it initially seems strange that the giddy Rhinemaidens are termed "wise" by Brünnhilde, this remark must be interpreted in light of Wagner's concept of "true wisdom" in the cycle. The Rhinemaidens, like Siegfried, are blissfully unaware of the false distinction that is made by the *so-called* wise individuals of this world. They are thus free to act with perfect insight or intuition. (Cf. Siegfried's hatred of Mime: he loathes the dwarf, and rightly so, but cannot explain why. Similarly, the Rhinemaiden's at the end of *Das Rheingold* intuitively condemn everything that is "false and cowardly" on earth.) This is Wagner's version of the Adam and Eve motif. People are at their finest and are most pure when they do not know the difference between good and evil. Worldly knowledge corrupts.

80 In *Das Rheingold* 4, Erda says that the Norns nightly speak what she sees. In *Siegfried* 3.1, she says that they spin what she knows. In the Prologue to *Götterdämmerung*, the Norns speak of their own wisdom and eternal knowledge. Wagner himself recognized the parallel between the first appearance of the Rhinemaidens first scene and the Norns' scene, as indicated by Heinrich Porges in his rehearsal notes: "In this scene—the counterpart to that of the Rhinemaidens in that here it is the 'dark side of nature' that is being revealed—the Fate motive, which is the tragic motto of

Götterdämmerung, is often sounded." Porges, *Wagner Rehearsing the 'Ring',* p. 117.

81 The most thorough treatment of ring composition in archaic poetry appears in W.A.A. Van Otterlo's "Untersuchungen über Begriff, Anwendung und Entstehung der griechischen Ringkomposition," *Meded. der niederländischen Akademie afdeeling Letterkunde* 7.4 (1944), pp. 131-76. See also Robert L. Fowler, *The Nature of Early Greek Lyric* (Toronto: University of Toronto Press, 1987), pp. 61-82, and Bernhard Abraham Van Groningen, *La composition littéraire archaïque grecque* (Amsterdam: Noord-Hollandsche Uitg. Mij., 1958), pp. 51-55.

82 The works of Aeschylus and Pindar held special importance to Wagner. See, for instance, the following comment made by Nietzsche to the classicist Erwin Rohde: "Dearest friend, it is impossible to tell you all that I learn and see, hear and comprehend during these visits [to Wagner]. Schopenhauer and Goethe, Aeschylus and Pindar still live—I give you my word for it." Förster-Nietzsche, *Nietzsche-Wagner Correspondence,* p. 19. In fact, all four authors mentioned by Nietzsche had a strong influence on Wagner's mature work. Compare also Ewans, *Wagner and Aeschylus,* p. 16.

83 Laomedon, the king of Troy, invited Poseidon and Apollo to build the walls of his city. In return, he agreed to offer them a splendid sacrifice. Upon completion of their work, however, Laomedon refused to honor his part of the bargain. To punish Laomedon, the two gods sent a sea monster that would ravage Troy unless the king permitted it to consume his daughter, Hesione. Heracles agreed to kill the sea monster in return for Hesione but, upon completion of this task, Laomedon once again reneged. (See *Iliad* 21.443-60). Wagner uses the following parallels in developing his story about the creation of Valhalla in *Das Rheingold*: Laomedon (Wotan), Poseidon, Apollo, and Heracles (Fasolt and Fafner), Hesione (Freia).

84 Like Fafner, both Patroclus and Hector prophesy (correctly) moments before their deaths. See *Iliad* 16.852-54, 22.356-60.

85 A combination of Alberich's ring and the Tarnhelm, the ring of Gyges could make the wearer invisible and thus conveyed power without responsibility. See Plato, *Republic* 2.359 d — 360 e.

86 "A candidate for the priesthood could only succeed to office by slaying the priest, and having slain him, he retained office till he was himself slain by a stronger or a craftier." Sir James Greorge Frazer, *The Golden Bough*, abridged edition (1922: rpt. New York: Macmillan, 1950) 1.

87 See Trevelyan, *Goethe and the Greeks*, pp. 1-14.

88 See "*Der Ring des Nibelungen* in seinen Beziehungen zur griechischen Tragödie und zur zeitgenössischen Philosophie," *Richard-Wagner Jahrbuch*, vol. 2 (Berlin: Hausbücher, 1907), pp. 284-330.

89 See *Wagner und die Antike* (Bayreuth: L. Ellwanger, 1905).

90 See *Wagner's Dramas and Greek Tragedy* (New York: Columbia University Press, 1919).

91 The influence of Aeschylus on Wagner was also the subject of Ewans' fascinating *Wagner and Aeschylus* and of Arthur Drews' article "Wagner and the Greeks" in *Wagner* 1 (1980), pp. 17-21. On the general topic of classical literature and its influence on Wagner, see Roller, "Wagner and the Classics," 231-252.

92 The essay appears as Chapter 10 in *Blood for the Ghosts*, pp. 126-42. It was originally published in the *London Times Literary Supplement*, January 9, 1976, pp. 37-39.

93 See Lloyd-Jones, *Blood for the Ghosts*, p. 133.

94 See Ewans, *Wagner and Aeschylus*, p. 60.

95 See Ewans, *Wagner and Aeschylus*, p. 60.

96 Christian August Brandis, *Handbuch der Geschichte der griechisch-römischen Philosophie* (Berlin: G. Reimer, 1835). At about the same time that Wagner was composing the *Ring*, Brandis released *Geschichte der Entwickelungen der griechischen Philosophie und ihrer Nachwirkungen im römischen Reiche* (Berlin: G. Reimer, 1862).

97 Hegel, *Hegel's Lectures on the History of Philosophy*. These lectures, first delivered between 1805 and 1830, appeared in print in 1834 and then were reissued in a revised edition in 1840.

98 Heinrich Ritter and Ludwig Preller, *Historia Philosophiae Graeco-*

Romanae ex fontium locis contexta (Hamburg: F.A. Perthes, 1838).

99 *Die Fragmente der Vorsokratiker griechisch und deutsch* (Berlin: Weidmannsche Buchhandlung, 1903).

100 On the availability of classical texts in the nineteenth century and the German approach to classicism, see Lloyd-Jones, *Blood for Ghosts*, pp. 126-81, and Trevelyan, *Goethe and the Greeks*, pp. 1-14.

101 This passage is discussed in G.S. Kirk and J.E. Raven, *The Presocratic Philosophers* (Cambridge: Cambridge University Press, 1971), p. 87. See also Hegel *History of Philosophy*, vol. 1, pp. 174-85; Freeman, *Companion*, pp. 549-55; and Barnes, *Presocratic Philosophers*, vol. 1, pp. 5-16.

102 See Wagner, *My Life*, pp. 429-30.

103 The passage of the *Metaphysics* just cited is translated and discussed by Hegel in *History of Philosophy*, vol. 1, pp. 174-75.

104 Wagner, *My Life*, p. 54.

105 See Fischer-Dieskau, *Wagner and Nietzsche*, p. 104.

106 Nietzsche, *Philosophy in the Tragic Age of the Greeks*, p. 38. The original German text appears as "Die Philosophie im tragischen Zeitalter der Griechen" in Nietzsche, *Werke in drei Bänden*, vol. 3, p. 361.

107 Cowan translation, p. 45; German text (*Werke in drei Bänden*), p. 365.

108 On this philosophy, see Hegel, *History of Philosophy*, vol. 1, pp. 185-89; Freeman, *Companion*, pp. 55-64; Barnes, *Presocratic Philosophers*, vol. 1, pp. 19-37; and Charles H. Kahn, *Anaximander and the Origins of Greek Cosmology* (New York: Columbia University Press, 1960), pp. 119-65.

109 An excellent discussion of this scene appears in Darcy's "'*Alles was ist, endet!*' Erda's Prophecy of the World's Destruction," pp. 67-92. Briefer, but more widely available, is the same author's summary of this Bayreuth essay in "'Everything That Is, Ends!' The Genesis and Meaning of the Erda Episode in *Das Rheingold*," pp. 443-47.

110 Deathridge and Dahlhaus, *New Grove Wagner*, p. 150.

111 Nietzsche, *Tragic Age*, p. 50. The German text appears in *Werke in*

drei Bände, vol. 3, p. 369.

112 In a note jotted alongside section 408 of *Mixed Opinions and Maxims* (1979): see Kaufman, *Basic Writings of Nietzsche*, p. 159, n. 8.

113 In *Ecce Homo*, "Birth of Tragedy" section 3, a passage that appears in Kaufman, *Basic Writings*, p. 729. On the influence of Heraclitus on Nietzsche, see Kaufman, *Nietzsche: Philosopher, Psychologist, Antichrist*, p. 241.

114 Heraclitus fragment 90 which appears in Plutarch, *De E apud Delphos* 8.388d.

115 See, for instance, Newman, *Wagner Nights*, p. 510.

116 From both *Mein Leben* (English translation, *My Life*, p. 508) and Wagner's notes we can conclude that this occurred on September 26, 1854.

117 See Wagner, *My Life*, p. 508.

118 Wagner, *My Life*, p. 510.

119 Schopenhauer, *Parerga and Paralipomena*, vol. 1, pp. 227-309.

120 On the influence of these ideas on Wagner, see Gutman, *Wagner*, p. 294.

121 Schopenhauer's theories also seem to have influenced Wagner's description of Erda's wisdom as arising out of dreams in *Siegfried*: "*Mein Schlaf is Traümen, mein Traümen Sinnen, mein Sinnen Walten des Wissens.*" ["My sleep is dreaming, my dreaming contemplation, my contemplation the control of wisdom."]

122 See Gutman, *Wagner*, p. 294; Magee, *Philosophy of Schopenhauer*, p. 335; and Newman, *Life of Richard Wagner*, vol. 2, p. 431, n. 8.

123 Schopenhauer, *Parerga*, vol. 1, pp. 31-136.

124 Wagner, *My Life*, p. 509.

125 See, for instance, Cooke, *I Saw the World End*, pp. 88-131.

126 *Wagner's Ring: Turning the Sky Round*, p. 18.

127 Plantinga, *Romantic Music*, pp. 406-07.

128 White, *Wagner*, p. 141.

129 On Schopenhauer's disdain for "descriptive music," see Magee, *Philosophy of Schopenhauer*, pp. 182-83 and 240, Frederick Coplestone, *Arthur Schopenhauer: Philosopher of Pessimism*

(Andover: Burns Oates and Washbourne, 1947), p. 139, and Michael Fox, *Schopenhauer: His Philosophical Achievement* (Totowa, New Jersey: Barnes and Noble, 1980), pp. 144-45.

130 Schopenhauer, *Parerga and Paralipomena*, vol. 2, p. 430.

131 Schopenhauer, *Parerga and Paralipomena*, vol. 2, p. 432.

132 Schopenhauer, *World as Will and Representation*, vol 2, p. 448.

133 Schopenhauer, *World as Will and Representation,* vol 2, p. 449.

134 Wagner, "On Liszt's Symphonic Poems," *Prose Works*, vol. 3, p. 247.

135 Later in life, Wagner even ridiculed his own early symphonic compositions, calling his "Philadelphia March," for instance, "only parade-ground music." Fricke, *Wagner in Rehearsal*, p. 81.

136 Plato, *Laws* 2. 669 d 6 — 670 a 2. Translated by A.E. Taylor in Edith Hamilton and Huntington Cairns, eds., *The Collected Dialogues of Plato* (Princeton, New Jersey: Princeton University Press, 1963), p. 1266.

137 Henry George Liddell, Robert Scott, Henry Stuart Jones, and Roderick McKenzie, *A Greek-English Lexicon* (1940: rpt. Oxford, Clarendon Press, 1968), p. 1148 [hereafter "LSJ"]. LSJ note that, while *mousikê* implies "esp., poetry sung to music," it is not limited to this sense. It is used by Plato to signify the arts and letters in general (*Timaeus* 88 c and *Phaedo* 61 a) and, in its adjectival form *mousikos* is used by Aristophanes to mean a "man of letters and accomplishments, scholar" (*Knights* 191).

138 Wagner, "On Musical Criticism," *Prose Works*, vol. 3, p. 68.

139 Readers who desire such a listing should consult Holman, *Wagner's Ring*, pp. 103-69.

140 Grey, *Wagner's Musical Prose*, p. 319.

141 See, for instance, William Mann, "Down with Visiting Cards" in DiGaetani, *Penetrating Wagner's Ring*, pp. 303-06.

142 For a psychological interpretation of the role that memory plays in Wagnerian leitmotivs, see Morton F. Reiser, "Wagner's Use of the Leitmotif to Communicate Understanding" in *Psychoanalytic Explorations in Music*. (Madison, Connecticut: International Universities Press, 1993), pp. 217-28.

143 On certain aspects of Wagner's "linguistic" use of leitmotivs, see Swain *Musical Languages*, pp. 58-61. Note also Swain's conclusion (on p. 174) that "Richard Wagner has shown us that the semantics of music can be downright propositional—if the context is just right."

144 "The orchestral accompaniment following Siegmund's last note contains a proposition: 'Siegmund's father is Wotan.'" Swain, *Musical Languages*, p. 48.

145 This story is well known. Wagner was disappointed with this moment in the drama after having seen it onstage during rehearsals for the *Ring*'s first Bayreuth performance in 1876. Believing that the sword motif alone would not convey to the audience the substance of Wotan's great idea, he directed Franz Betz, the actor playing Wotan, to hold up a sword that had "accidentally" been left behind by Fafner. This stage direction is missing from the Schott and Schirmer scores but appears as early as the Breitkopf score of 1910. See Cooke, *I Saw the World End*, pp. 234-35.

146 See Cooke, *I Saw the World End*, p. 296.

147 See Cooke, *Introduction to Der Ring Des Nibelungen*, CD 1, tracks 2-4.

148 Henderson, "The Music of the Trilogy" in DiGaetani, *Penetrating Wagner's Ring*, p. 296.

149 Cooke, *Introduction to Der Ring Des Nibelungen*, CD 1, track 5.

150 The function of formulae, not as poetic devices, but as vital elements of the oral tradition would not, of course, have been known to Wagner. The oral nature of the *Iliad* and the *Odyssey* was not discovered until the work of Milman Parry and Alfred Lord in the twentieth century.

151 *Zu Schutt gebrannt der prangende Saal, zum Stumpf der Eiche blühender Stamm.* ["Our shining hall was burnt to ashes. The flourishing trunk of our oak burnt to its roots."]

152 Oscar Wilde, "Preface" to *The Picture of Dorian Gray* in *The Picture of Dorian Gray and Other Writings* (New York: Bantam, 1982), p. 3. *Dorian Gray* is also the novel that contains the passage "I like Wagner's music better than anybody's. It is so loud

that one can talk the whole time without other people hearing what one says." (*Ibid.*, p. 42) A few lines later, however, the title character himself implies that Wagner's works are "good music."

153 Waterman, *History of the German Language*, p. 73.

154   "Sithen the sege and the assault was sesed at Troye,
         The borge brittened and brent to brondes and askes,
         The tulk that the trammes of tresoun ther wroght
         Was tried for his tricherie, the trewest on erthe."

Book 1, ll. 1-4. *Sir Gawain and the Green Knight*, ed. R.A. Waldron (Evanston, IL: Northwestern University Press, 1970), p. 29.

155   "In a somer seson whan soft was the sonne
         I shope me in shroudes as I a shepe were;
         In habite as an hermite unholy of workes
         Went wyde in this world wondres to here."

Prologue, ll. 1-4. William Langland, *Piers Plowman*, ed. J.A.W. Bennett (Oxford: Clarendon Press, 1972), p. 1.

156 For the history of this term, see Dietrich Hofmann's entry "Stabreimvers" in Klaus Kanzog and Achim Masser, eds., *Reallexikon der deutschen Literatursgeschichte*, 2nd ed., vol. 4 (Berlin: Walter de Gruyter, 1984), pp. 183-93.

157 For instance, an early academic use of the term "Stabreim" for alliteration appears in Wilhelm Jordon, *Der epische Vers der Germanen und sein Stabreim* (Frankfurt: Jordon, 1868).

158 Though the word "Buchstabe" originally meant "beech stick," it later assumed the sense of "letter" or "character" from the beechwood upon which ancient runes were carved.

159 While Wagner did read parts of the Eddas in the original, he was most familiar with these poems in their 1837 translation into German Stabreim by Ludwig Ettmüller [*Die Lieder der Edda von den Nibelungen* (Zürich: Orell, Füssli and Company, 1837).] Wagner also owned Ettmüller's 1830 translation of the *Völuspá* (Leipzig: Weidmann, 1830), a work that contained both the original text and a German translation, as well as an introduction, notes, and a glossary. See W.J. Henderson, "The Sources of the Poems" in DiGaetani, *Penetrating Wagner's Ring*, pp. 257-69; Cord, *Introduc-*

tion, pp. 49-66; Cooke, *I Saw the World End*, pp. 74-131; Rather, *Dream of Self-Destruction*, p. 3; and Magee, *Richard Wagner and the Nibelungs*, p. 29.

160 Robert W. Gutman [in *Wagner*, p. 139] thus described Wagner's use of Stabreim as a deliberate attempt to "return to language's simplest roots" after the "elegant diction" of *Lohengrin*.

161 As in the melodious lament of the Rhinemaidens near the end of *Das Rheingold*: *Rheingold! Rheingold! Reines Gold! / O leuchtete noch in der Tiefe dein lautrer Tand!*

162 As in the harsh words of Alberich when he vainly scrambles on the rocks to reach the Rheinmaidens in *Das Rheingold* 1: *Garstig glatter glitschriger Glimmer!*

163 On this theory, see Wagner, *Prose Works*, vol. 2, pp. 224-36. The German text appears in Wagner, *Schriften und Dichtungen*, vol. 4, pp. 91-103. See also Reinhard Gerlach, "Musik und Sprache in Wagners Schrift *Opera und Drama*" in Dahlhaus, *Werk und Wirkung*, pp. 9-39 and McCreless, *Wagner's Siegfried*, p. 86.

164 For instance, this is the approach taken by Paul Herrmann in *Richard Wagner und die Stabreim* (Hagen: Risel and Company, 1883). More recent discussions of the historical and musical functions of Stabreim appear in McCreless, *Wagner's Siegfried*, pp. 37 and 56, and Cooke, *I Saw the World End*, pp. 74-78. The relationship of Stabreim to Wagner's theories of language has been discussed in Gerlach, "Musik und Sprache" (in Dahlhaus, *Werk und Wirkung*, pp. 9-39); Newman, *Man and Artist*, pp 202-15; and Borchmeyer, *Theory and Theatre*, pp. 149-56. The poetic function of Stabreim is discussed in Gutman, *Wagner*, p. 139 and Schuler, *Language of Ring*, pp. 50-63. Hermann Wiessner's *Der Stabreimvers in Richard Wagners 'Der Ring des Nibelungen'* (Berlin: Ebering, 1924) [now widely available as a Kraus Reprint (Lübeck: Matthiesen, 1967)] offers the most comprehensive treatment of Stabreim in the *Ring* from a poetic perspective. Most interesting is Wiessner's statistical analysis of the frequency with which Wagner adopted various types of alliterative patterns (pp. 86-98).

165 Borchmeyer, in a rare scholarly reference to the thematic function

of Stabreim, does *mention* (in *Wagner: Theory and Theatre*, p. 156) that "there was a clear analogy in Wagner's mind between alliteration on the one hand and the web of leitmotivs on the other" but offers no examples or further explanation. Earlier (p. 150) Borchmeyer refers to Stabreim as the "microstructural counterpart" to leitmotif. In a similar fashion, Stein mentions (in *Wagner*, pp. 72-74, 92-93, 104-106) the general similarity that Stabreim bears to the musical leitmotif. Sandra Corse (in *Wagner and the New Consciousness*, p. 53) notes that "the usefulness of *Stabreim*, [Wagner] feels, is that it allows the poet to establish relationships between particular words and concepts simply through the way words sound. Verse written in *Stabreim* is thus similar to music . …" The remainder of Corse's discussion makes it clear, however, that she has in mind *rhythmic* similarities between Stabreim and music, not parallels between alliteration and leitmotivs.

166 Wagner, *Prose Works*, vol. 2., p. 227.

167 *Opera and Drama* in *Prose Works*, vol. 2., p. 291. See also Stein, *Wagner and the Synthesis of the Arts*, pp. 71-72.

168 See David A. White, *The Turning Wheel* (London: Associated University Presses, 1988), p. 56.

169 Cf. Wagner's own stage directions at this point of the drama: *Aus der Felskluft zur Seite bricht ein bläulicher Schein hervor: in ihm wird plötzlich Erda sichtbar, die bis zu halber Leibeshöhe aus der Tiefe aufsteigt.* "At one side of the stage, a bluish light shines forth from a cleft in the rock. Suddenly Erda appears, rising from the depths to half her height."

170 Dated January 25, 1854, and discussed by Cooke in *I Saw the World End*, p. 266.

171 This becomes especially apparent in the following lines, spoken by Siegmund in *Die Walküre* 1.2: *Gehrt' ich nach Wonne, weckt' ich nur Weh! / drum musst' ich mich Wehwalt nennen; / des Wehes waltet' ich nur.* ("If I sought joy, I aroused only woe. / Thus must I be called Woeful, / I am filled only with woe.")

172 Cf. Wotan's later reference to Brünnhilde with these words: *Wachend*

wirkt dein wissendes Kind / erlösende Weltentat. ("Waking, the child of your wisdom will perform a deed that will redeem the world.")

173 On the historical use of Stabreim in family names, see Waterman, *History of the German Language*, p. 23.

174 Recall that these groups of characters are also said to *look alike*: thus Hunding immediately notices the similarity between Siegmund and Sieglinde, and Fasolt and Fafner are almost always depicted on stage as barely distinguishable.

175 Schopenhauer, *Parerga and Paralipomena*, vol. 1, pp. 227-309. On the influence of these ideas on Wagner, see Gutman, *Wagner*, p. 294.

176 If it appears strange that the Rhinemaidens, like Erda, should be referred to as "wise women," recall Brünnhilde's reference to these three sisters as *Der Wassertiefe weise Schwestern* during the immolation scene to Wotan's description of Erda as *der Welt weisestes Weib* in *Siegfried* 3.1.

177 Initial "s," if followed by an unvoiced stop ("p" or "t"), is indistinguishable from "sch."

178 The boast appears in *Götterdämmerung* 3.1. Siegfried, of course, does not know that the Norns' thread of fate has *already* been torn.

179 Examples of this theme include:

Das Rheingold 1: Alberich attempts to lure the Rhinemaidens

He he! Ihr Nicker!
Wie seid ihr niedlich, neidliches Volk!
Aus Nibelheims Nacht naht'
ich mich gern,
neigtet ihr euch zu mir.
[Hey! You nymphs!
What a lovely, desirable group you are!
I'd gladly come up
from the darkness of Nibelheim
if only you'd come down to me!]

For a discussion of Wagner's use of Stabreim in this passage, see Rather, *Reading Wagner*, pp. 49-50.

Das Rheingold 3: Alberich tries out the magic of the Tarnhelm

Niblungen all, neigt euch nun Alberich!

[All you Nibelungs, now bow down to Alberich!]

Das Rheingold 3: Alberich does not trust Wotan

Nach Nibelheim führt euch der Neid.

[Envy led you to Nibelheim.]

Das Rheingold 3: Loge tries to trick Alberich

So neidlichen sah ich noch nie.

[I never saw anyone so enviable.]

Die Walküre 1.3: Siegmund names Notung

Notung! Notung! So nenn ich dich, Schwert.

Notung! Notung! neidlicher Stahl!

[Needful! Needful! I name you, sword!

Needful! Needful! Glorious steel!]

Die Walküre 2.2: Alberich plots vengeance against Wotan

Mit neidischem Grimm grolt mir der Niblung.

[With envy and anger the Nibelung

bears his grudge against me.]

Siegfried 1.1: Mime reveals that Notung alone can help him win the
     ring

Nur Notung nützt meinem Neid.

[Only Notung serves my envy.]

Siegfried 1.1: Mime says that greed is not enough to repair Notung

Des Niblungen Neid,

Not und Schweiss nietet mir Notung nicht.

[A Nibelung's envy,

need and sweat will not rivet Notung together for me.]

Siegfried 1.3: On three separate occasions, Siegfried calls out the same
     words to Notung during his "forging songs"

Notung! Notung! Neidliches Schwert!

[Needful! Needful! Enviable sword!]

Siegfried 2.3: Alberich refuses to share any of the gold with Mime

Nichts von allem!

Nicht einem Nagel sollst du dir nehmen!

[Nothing at all!

Not a nail shall you take!]

Götterdämmerung, Prologue: the second Norn retells the story of the
  gold
Aus Not und Neid
ragt mir des Niblungen Ring.
[From need and envy
arose the ring of the Nibelungen.]
180 Examples of this theme include:
Das Rheingold 4: Alberich warns Wotan about seizing the ring
Des Unseligen, Angstversehrten
fluchfertige, furchtbare Tat,
zu fürstlichem Tand soll sie
fröhlich dir taugen,
zur Freude dir frommen mein Fluch? ...
Frevelte ich, so frevelt' ich frei an mir.
[Must the curse-laden, frightful deed
of one who is unlucky and fear-ridden
serve your pleasure
as a princely toy,
permitting you to laugh at my curse? ...
If I did wrong, I wronged only myself.]
Das Rheingold 4: Wotan is shocked by the murder of Fasolt
Furchtbar nun erfind' ich des Fluches Kraft!
[I find the curse's power frightful!]
Die Walküre 2.2: Wotan realizes that he cannot save Siegmund
In eigner Fessel fing ich mich,
ich Unfreiester aller!
[I find myself in fetters that I devised myself,
I, the least free of all!]
Die Walküre 2.2: Wotan explains his decision to Brünnhilde
Der Fluch, den ich floh,
nicht flieht er nun mich.
[The curse that I fled
still has not left me.]
Siegfried 3.1: the Wanderer tells Erda that he will yield to the curse
Froh und freudig führe frei ich nun aus.

[Now I shall do it freely, willingly and happily.]

181 Examples of this theme include:

Die Walküre 1.2: Hunding warns Siegmund to treat his home with
   respect

Heilig ist mein Herd:

heilig sei dir mein Haus!

[My hearth is sacred.

Let my house be sacred to you, too!]

Die Walküre 2.3: Sieglinde warns Siegmund of Hunding's approach

Horch! die Hörner, hörst du den Ruf? …

Horch, o horch! Das ist Hundings Horn!

[Listen! The horns! Do you hear the call?…

Listen! Listen! That's Hunding's horn!]

Siegfried 1.1: Mime tells Siegfried how he found Sieglinde

Zur Höhle half ich ihr her,

an warmen Herd sie zu hüten.

[I helped her into the cave

to watch over her by the warm hearth.]

182 For instance, this is what occurs in the "toad formula" (*Krum und
   grau krieche Kröte: Das Rheingold* 3), a phonetic pattern that introduces a musical theme *also* heard only in this passage and thus not
   technically a leitmotif.

183 Opening of Poem 87. Heinrich Heine, *Buch der Lieder* (*Die
   Heimkehr*, 1823-1824).

184 Cf. Wellgunde's phrase *Durch den grünen Schwall den wonnigen
   Schläfer sie grüsst* ("Through the green billows [the sun] greets the
   blissful sleeper.") later in the first scene of *Das Rheingold*.

185 Schopenhauer, *Parerga and Paralipomena*, vol. 1, p. 435.

186 "Each day is a little life; every waking and rising a little birth; every
   fresh morning a little youth; every going to rest and sleep a little
   death." [From Schopenhauer's "Unser Verhalten gegen uns selbst
   betreffend" section of "Paränesen und Maximen" in *Aphorismen
   zur Lebensweisheit* (Stuttgart: Alfred Kröner, 1968), p. 175. The
   translation is that of T. Bailey Saunders in *Essays of Arthur
   Schopenhauer* (New York, NY: A.L. Burt, 1892), p. 130.] "Our

life might be regarded as a loan received from death; sleep would then be the daily interest on that loan." [From the essay entitled "On the Doctrine of Indestructibility" in *Parerga and Paralipomena*, vol. 2, p. 275.] On these ideas, see D.W. Hamlyn, *Schopenhauer: the Arguments of the Philosophers* (London: Routledge and Kegan Paul, 1980), pp. 158-59.

187 Letter to Franz Liszt in Weimar, written on January 15, 1854, just after Wagner had completed *Das Rheingold*. See Wagner, *Selected Letters*, p. 299, letter 170.

188 Letter to Mathilde Wesendonck in Zürich, written on August 21, 1858. See Wagner, *Selected Letters*, p. 416, letter 217.

189 Number 81 in the *Wagner Werk-Verzeichnis*. See Millington, *Wagner Compendium*, pp. 321-22.

190 For instance, Odysseus is suddenly overcome with sleep just after leaving the island inhabited by Aeolus, keeper of the winds (*Odyssey* 10.31-32), just before his crew slaughters the cattle of Hyperion (12.338), after he arrives on the island of Scheria (5.491-493), and as the Phaeacians return him to Ithaca (13.79-80: this sleep is specifically said to be "sweet, most like death"). On the level of metaphor, the poem suggests that, just as Odysseus succumbs to sleep despite his intelligence and heroic deeds, so must he some-day succumb to death. Only when Odysseus begins to realize this truth is he allowed to return home, resume his life, and die. The death of Odysseus is explicitly foretold at *Odyssey* 11.119-137.

191 The use of sleep as an image of death is common throughout early European and Near Eastern epic. In the Mesopotamian *Epic of Gilgamesh*, translated at the British Museum only near the end of Wagner's life, the hero's quest for immortality ends with a contest against sleep. If Gilgamesh can remain awake for six days and seven nights, Utnapishtim, who survived the primeval flood, will make him immortal. No sooner is this offer made, however, than Gilgamesh falls asleep, proving symbolically that he is a creature of death.

192 See, for instance, Matthew 9.4, Mark 5.5, Luke 8.6, and (in a slightly different context) John 11.7.

193 Wagner, "Jesus of Nazareth" in *Prose Works*, vol. 8, p. 286.

194 In his famous letter to Franz Liszt written on February 11, 1853, just after the text of the *Ring* had been completed, Wagner wrote: "Mark well my new poem—it contains the world's *beginning* and its end!" (*emphasis added*) Wagner, *Selected Letters*, p. 281, letter 158.

195 For the Freemasons, this is also the German word meaning "initiation," with all of its attendant implications of "dedication" and "rebirth." The same root appears in a variety of terms concerned with holiness or ordination, including *Weihwasser* (holy water), *Weihebecken* (font), and *Weihnacht* (Christmas).

196 Wagner, "To Friedrich Nietzsche" in *Prose Works*, vol. 5, p. 297.

197 See Millington, *Wagner*, p. 213.

198 Lee, *Turning the Sky Around*, p. 73.

199 Donington, *Wagner's 'Ring' and its Symbols*, p. 37.

200 In the *Iliad*, both Patroclus (16.849-854) and Hector (22.358-360) foretell the future as they are dying. In the *Ring* itself, Fafner develops similar prophetic powers only moments before his death (*Siegfried* 2.2).

201 Schopenhauer *Parerga and Paralipomena*, pp. 227-309. See also Gutman, *Wagner*, p. 294.

202 Wagner, "Beethoven" in *Prose Works*, vol. 5, pp. 68-69.

203 In the third scene of *Das Rheingold*, sleep is again presented as a threatening and dangerous loss of awareness. Loge deceitfully asks Alberich how he would protect himself if a thief should attempt to steal the ring while he was asleep (*im Schlaf*).

204 Lee, *Turning the Sky Around*, p. 11.

205 With this potion, Mime hopes, *sinnlos sinkt er in Schlaf* ("Siegfried will sink unconscious into sleep"): *Siegfried* 1.3.

206 This expression is to be taken in both a literal and figurative sense. The literal "tree of the Wälsungs" is the giant ash tree in the hall of Hunding; this is the tree into which Wotan had inserted Notung for Siegmund later to recover. In its symbolic sense, the tree represents the family itself which is "rooted" in Wälse/Wotan. Cf. Mime's reply to the Wanderer in *Siegfried* 1.2: *Siegmund und*

Sieglind' stammten von Wälse. The German word *Stamm* can mean both "tree trunk" and "race."

207 See Cooke, *Introduction to Der Ring Des Nibelungen,* CD 2, track 10.

208 Cooke, *Introduction to Der Ring Des Nibelungen,* CD 1, track 5.

209 Cooke, *Introduction to Der Ring Des Nibelungen,* CD 1, track 5.

210 Cooke, *Introduction to Der Ring Des Nibelungen,* CD 2, track 15.

211 Wotan's appearance in this scene, *lying on the ground,* symbolically places him in close proximity to the earth, Erda, and the prophetic power of nature.

212 This staging may result from a misinterpretation of the later stage directions *leise, ohne sich zu rühren, so daß er immerfort zu schlafen scheint, obwohl er die Augen offen hat* ("gently, without moving, so that he *appears* to sleep even though his eyes are open"). The context makes it clear, however, that what Wagner meant by these words is that Hagen should appear *to the audience* to be asleep, not merely to Alberich.

213 Rather, *Dream of Self-Destruction,* p. 107. The italics appear in Rather's original.

214 Barth, Mack, and Voss, *Documentary Study,* p. 184. On this theme, see Linda Hutcheon and Michael Hutcheon, "'Alles was ist, endet': Living with the Knowledge of Death in Richard Wagner's *Der Ring des Nibelungen,*" *University of Toronto Quarterly* 67.4 (1998) pp. 789-811

215 Wagner, *Selected Letters,* p. 626, letter 314

216 Compare also Siegfried's description of Gunther in *Götterdämmerung* 3.2: *"Ihm glich ich auf ein Haar."*

217 The date of *Jesus of Nazareth* can be determined by a reference to it in "A Communication to my Friends" in Wagner, *Prose Works,* vol. 1, pp. 378-80. The German edition of the sketch may be found in *Schriften und Dichtungen,* vol. 11, pp. 273-324.

218 *Wagner's Prose Works,* vol. 8, p. 297. *Schriften und Dichtungen,* vol. 11, p. 284.

219 "When he came to writing *Opera and Drama,* Wagner replaced Christ with another paradigmatic figure: Siegfried, the sun god,

supplants the Christian hero with his promise of redemption through death." Nattiez, *Wagner Androgyne*, p. 31.

220 An excellent discussion of this essay appears in Gutman, *Wagner*, pp. 425-26. See also Watson, *Wagner: A Biography*, pp. 303-05 and Borchmeyer, *Wagner: Theory and Theater*, p. 410.

221 The essay bears the more awkward title "Hero-dom and Christendom" in *Prose Works*, vol. 6, pp. 277-78. *Schriften und Dichtungen*, vol. 10, pp. 277-79.

222 Gregor-Dellin and Mack, *Cosima Wagner's Diaries*, vol. 2 (1878-1883), p. 1007. This is the entry of February 9th, 1883; Wagner died on February 13th.

223 *Wagner's Prose Works*, vol. 8, p. 306. *Schriften und Dichtungen*, vol. 11, p. 293.

224 (The italics appear in Wagner's original text.) Both passages are from *Wagner's Prose Works*, vol. 8, p. 335. *Schriften und Dichtungen*, vol. 11, pp. 319-20. A large number of similar passages appear. See, for instance, "God is the Father and the Son and the Holy Ghost: for the father begetteth the son throughout all ages, and the son begetteth again the father of the son to all eternity." *Wagner's Prose Works*, vol. 8, p. 300. *Schriften und Dichtungen*, vol. 11, p. 287.

225 See *Wagner's Prose Works*, vol. 8, pp. 291, 299. *Schriften und Dichtungen*, vol. 11, pp. 279, 286.

226 On these ideas see Borchmeyer, *Wagner: Theory and Theatre*, pp. 399-401 and Taylor, *Wagner*, p. 92.

227 Fasolt speaking to Wotan in *Das Rheingold* 2 summarizes this origin of Wotan's power: "You are what you are only through treaties. / The extent of your power has been stipulated and set forth." See also: the Wanderer's reply to Mime's third question in *Siegfried* 1.2; Alberich's comments to the Wanderer in *Siegfried* 2.1; and the Second Norn's first long speech in the prologue to *Götterdämmerung*.

228 See note 145 above.

229 Hueffer, *Correspondence of Wagner and Liszt*, vol. 2 (1854-1861), letter #200, p. 117.

230 On the general concept of heroism in Wagnerian music drama, see Gillespie, "Wagner and the Heroic Mystique," pp. 99-115.

231 Other passages also explore the nature of Wotan's plans for the hero in the *Ring*. For instance, in *Siegfried* 2.1 Alberich says to the Wanderer [= Wotan]: "Have you reared a boy who will cunningly pluck the fruit that you dare not grasp?"

232 Gutman provides an intriguing summary of the relationship between fathers and sons throughout Wagnerian music drama in *Wagner*, p. 9. A less persuasive—and more jargon-laden—analysis appears in Donington, *Wagner's 'Ring' and Its Symbols*, pp. 39-40, 270.

233 See Millington, *Wagner*, pp. 226-27 and Newman, *Wagner Nights*, pp. 667-69.

234 James B. Prichard, ed., *The Ancient Near East: An Anthology of Texts and Pictures*, vol. 1 (Princeton: Princeton University Press, 1958), p. 49 (Old Babylonian tablet 2, section 5.15).

235 Wagner was also aware of the parallels between these two scenes, as indicated by Porges' notes: "The brothers' struggle for the ring—'the giants' struggle in *Das Rheingold* is repeating itself', Wagner remarked—and Gunther's death quickly follow." Porges, *Wagner Rehearsing the 'Ring'*, p. 143.

236 This is such a "defining moment" for Alberich that, as Deryck Cooke has suggested, the dwarf's personal leitmotif is developed from the instrumental accompaniment to this scene. See Cooke, *Introduction to Der Ring Des Nibelungen*, CD 2, track 12 and Cooke, *I Saw the World End*, pp. 40-41.

237 *Wagner's Prose Works*, vol. 8, p. 301. *Schriften und Dichtungen*, vol. 11, p. 288.

238 *Wagner's Prose Works*, vol. 8, p. 321. *Schriften und Dichtungen*, vol. 11, p. 306.

239 What lapse of consistency, one wonders, has allowed Wagner to describe this sword as weaker than Wotan's spear at one moment and yet stronger later in the cycle? It should be remembered that these weapons are symbols of their respective hero's vitality and, like the mythical image of the "external soul," are linked to the

strength of these figures; when a weapon shatters, it suggests that the hero's own fate has been sealed.

240 Ruth Koheil and Herbert Richardson reach much the same conclusion, but from a Jungian perspective, in "Why Brünnhilde is the True Hero of the *Ring* Cycle," pp. 177-89.

241 *Wagner's Prose Works,* vol. 8, p. 313. *Schriften und Dichtungen,* vol. 11, p. 299.

242 *Wagner's Prose Works,* vol. 8, pp. 316-17. *Schriften und Dichtungen,* vol. 11, p. 303.

243 Lee, *Turning the Sky Around,* p. 61. W.J. Henderson noted in "The Music in the Trilogy," reprinted in Di Gaetani, ed., *Penetrating Wagner's Ring,* that in this theme "we … recognise its significance as an embodiment of the glorious divinity of Brünnhilde, the divinity of ideal womanhood, ennobled by love and sanctified by sacrifice" (p. 292). Nevertheless, until the publication of the documents in which Wagner's own interpretation of the theme was revealed, the use of this theme at the end of *Götterdämmerung* baffled some critics. Thus Chappell White (in an essay also reprinted in Di Gaetani's *Penetrating Wagner's Ring*) says, "What does this motive tell us? Not much, for those who want the associations and intentions neat and clear. The motive was introduced in Act 3 of *Die Walküre,* when Sieglinde learned of her pregnancy and addressed words of ecstatic wonder and gratitude to Brünnhilde. It has not been heard since. Evidentally Wagner wished to suggest the connection between Sieglinde's coming sacrifice for the birth of Siegfried and Brünnhilde's sacrifice for the rebirth of the world, but the association is neither decisive nor clear" (p. 364). Yet when one understands that the motive is a celebration of Brünnhilde's heroism—a heroism indicated at the two moments of the cycle when her willingness to undergo self-sacrifice is most pronounced—the use of this theme at the cycle's conclusion becomes both "decisive and clear."

244 Appia, *Music and the Art of the Theatre,* p. 73. The Chamberlain quotation appears in Chamberlain, *Richard Wagner,* p. 196.

245 Wagner, "Preface to the 'Ring' Poem" in *Prose Works,* vol. 3, p.

282. On Wagner's belief in the need for fidelity to his original vision, see Fay, *Ring: Anatomy of an Opera*, pp. 5-6, 203.

246 On Wagner's views regarding the appearance of costumes in the *Ring*, see Srocke, *Richard Wagner als Regisseur*, pp. 86-88 and also Cook, *Memoir of Bayreuth*, 24-25.

247 "... [T]he composer himself supervised and approved every aspect of the 1876 'Ring' performances. This included the scenery, the stage effects and the costumes as well as the coaching of the singers, the acting and the musical performance. He sat on the stage himself during rehearsals and watched everything, correcting singers, discussing the staging and indicating how he wished his text to be presented and his music to be played." Cook, *Memoir of Bayreuth*, p. 15.

248 Later published as *Die Bühnenproben zu den Bayreuther Festspielen des Jahren 1876* in the *Bayreuther Blätter* between 1881 and 1896. An English translation is available as Porges, *Wagner Rehearsing the 'Ring.'*

249 See also Fricke, *Wagner in Rehearsal*, pp. 32, 46, 80 and Cook, *Memoir of Bayreuth*, pp. 34-35 for examples of Wagner's careful attention to the gestures of his actors. The choreographer Fricke claims, however, to have overruled many of Wagner's suggestions.

250 Porges, *Wagner Rehearsing the 'Ring,'* p. 15.

251 Porges, *Wagner Rehearsing the 'Ring,'* p. 21. Numerous other examples may be cited, including "Fricka's cries for help were accompanied by eloquent gestures" (p. 16) and a lengthy discussion of the gods' gestures and body language after the Giants carry off Freia: "As the music expresses the feeling of mortality, so the positioning and gestures of the actors must convey their feeling of being in the grip of a magical spell threatening their lives." For instance, Wotan's eyes should be "downcast, his spear lowered, its tip pointing downwards." (p. 26) Just as Wagner's musical leitmotivs often contain ascending scales when associated with growth and development, but descending scales when dealing with destruction, so did Wagner want the actors' gesture to reflect either the positive or negative emotion of a scene.

252 Porges, *Wagner Rehearsing the 'Ring,'* p. 66.

253 Porges, *Wagner Rehearsing the 'Ring,'* p. 109.

254 One of the few instances of a parallel to this scene was a 1779 drawing by George Romney now in the Fitzwilliam Museum, Cambridge.

255 This painting, now in the Musée de l'Armée at Les Invalides in Paris, is a companion piece to Ingres' *Jupiter and Thetis.* Napoleon's arms and legs are held in the same position as Jupiter's. A sceptre is placed at the same angle as Jupiter's spear. Napoleon's expression anticipates the imperial aloofness of the later Jupiter.

256 An excellent summary of Appia's approach to design (and more readable than many of Appia's own writings) appears in Patrick Carnegy, "Designing Wagner: Deeds of Music Made Visible?" in Millington and Spencer, *Wagner in Performance*, pp. 53-57. A discussion of Cosima Wagner's intense opposition to Appia's ideas appears at p. 61. See also Williams, *Wagner and Festival Theatre*, pp. 151-54 and Frederic Spotts, *Bayreuth: A History of the Wagner Festival* (New Haven, Yale University Press, 1994), pp. 106-7.

257 Appia, "The Staging of *The Ring*," in DiGaetani, *Penetrating Wagner's Ring* , p. 387-88. Like Appia's work on lighting, this essay is taken from Appia's *Music and the Art of the Theatre*, pp. 209-219.

258 Porges, *Wagner Rehearsing the 'Ring,'* p. 76.

259 Porges, *Wagner Rehearsing the 'Ring,'* p. 87.

260 Appia, "The Staging of *The Ring*," in *Music and the Art of the Theatre*, p. 214.

261 It is surprising that Appia pays so little attention to the fourth Empedoclean element—earth—in a drama that twice progresses through the various layers of the earth, contains scenes on both the summit and depths of the earth, and introduces a goddess who is herself a personification of the earth.

262 Wagner, "Epilogue to the 'Nibelung's Ring'," in *Prose Works*, vol. 3, p. 266.

263 Wagner, "Sketches and Fragments," in *Prose Works*, vol. 8, pp. 367-68.

264 Compare, for example, *Siegfried* 3.1 when Erda again rises from

the earth: "Light gathers at the cave-vault, a bluish gleam illuminates the figure of Erda rising slowly out of the depths behind.
She appears to be covered in hoar-frost; her hair and clothing give
off an icy shimmer."

265 "The red you see in the rainbow is flaming fire." Sturluson, *Prose
Edda*, p. 44. See also Crossley-Holland, *Norse Myths*, pp. 6, 62-
63, 174, and Davidson, *Gods and Myths of Northern Europe*, pp.
26, 193.

266 "You will have seen it, [but] maybe you call it the rainbow. It has
three colours and is very strong, and made with more skill and
cunning than other structures." Sturluson, *Prose Edda*, p. 40.

267 The use of light in *Das Rheingold* helps account for what many
audiences otherwise feel to be the unnecessary presence of Donner
and Froh in the drama. Donner is the conqueror of darkness who
dispels the mist. Froh is the personification of nature who restores the light.

268 Thus the following scene description appears in *Siegfried* 2.2: "the
upstage area [i.e., Fafner's cave]…remains in heavy shadow, while
the higher ground center-stage is gradually lit more brightly by the
rising sun as the scene proceeds."

269 Contrast this occurrence to the first time that Siegfried approaches
Brünnhilde's rock in *Siegfried* 3.2: "He plunges into the billowing
fire." Soon, "the flames burn bright, then gradually begin to grow
dim and slowly turn into an ever finer cloud, which seems to reflect the flush of early morning." After Siegfried has appeared,
"the flames instantly recede so that once more only their light is
seen shining from below." Thus when Siegfried approaches
Brünnhilde with pure intentions, the flames burn brightly. When
he approaches in deceit, the imagery is that of storm-clouds and
darkness.

270 Cf. the parallel description in the following scene (*Götterdämmerung*
3.3): *Es ist Nacht*.

271 This vocabulary includes *gleisst, hell, Glimmerschein, Strahl, Blitz*,
and *Schein*.

272 Porges, *Wagner Rehearsing the 'Ring,'* p. 95.

273 Other examples of light and fire imagery in the *Ring* include the following:

Die Walküre 2.5, during the duel of Hunding and Siegmund: "A flash of lightning illuminates the ridge for an instant, revealing Hunding and Siegmund fighting."

Siegfried 1.3, as Siegfried forges Notung: "He has heaped coal on to the fire and encourages it to burn bright …" Siegfried then places the melting pot "on the glowing coals" and "pours the red-hot contents" into the mold.

Siegfried 3.2, when Siegfried splinters Wotan's spear with Notung: "a lightning flash leaps up from it in the direction of the mountaintop where, from this moment onward, the hitherto dull light begins to flicker and glow with increasingly bright flames."

Götterdämmerung 2:1, during Hagen's sleep scene and his conversation with Alberich: "It is night.…The moon comes out suddenly and casts a harsh light on Hagen and his immediate surroundings."

Götterdämmerung 3.2, after the death of Siegfried: "The moon breaks through the clouds and casts a growing light on the cortège as it reaches the crest."

Götterdämmerung 3.3, as Siegfried's funeral begins: "It is night. The moonlight is reflected on the surface of the Rhine." Soon "men and women with lamps and torches throng in great confusion round the procession of those returning with Siegfried's body."

274 The costume designer, Carl Emil Doepler, used red for a different symbolic purpose during the first complete cycle in 1876. In the published version of his sketches, Clara Steinitz said that the "red of [Fricka's] costume stands for the energy of Wotan's eternal wife." Cook, *Memoir of Bayreuth*, p. 58.

275 Cook, *Memoir of Bayreuth*, pp. 41, 42.

276 Cook, *Memoir of Bayreuth*, p. 66.

277 Note Wagner's scene description for the end of *Die Walküre* 3.3: After Wotan has struck the rock three times with his spear, "a jet of flame shoots out of the rock, then fans out to form a glowing fire that glows steadily brighter."

278 On the technical apparatus used to create fog, smoke, and steam

during the 1876 festival, see Evan Baker, "Wagner and the Ideal Theatrical Space" in Mark A. Radice, *Opera in Context* (Portland, Oregon: Amadeus Press, 1998), p. 269. On some of the problems created by this apparatus, see Fricke, *Wagner in Rehearsal*, p. 68.

279 Porges, *Wagner Rehearsing the 'Ring,'* p. 24. The phrasing is almost identical in Wagner's stage directions.

280 The German *Nebelheim* would thus be equivalent to the Norse *Niflheim*, the land of darkness and mist described in the Icelandic sagas. Davidson defines Nifleim as "the realm of mist and darkness" and "the abode of darkness" in *Gods and Myths of Northern Europe*, pp. 32 and 235. Cf. Crossley-Holland, *Norse Myths*, pp. xxi-xxii.

281 Porges, *Wagner Rehearsing the 'Ring,'* p. 28.

282 Porges, *Wagner Rehearsing the 'Ring,'* p. 33. A similar remark appears in Wagner's original stage directions: "The scene is still shrouded by a pale mist [*fahle Nebel*] as it was at the end of Scene Two."

283 Porges, *Wagner Rehearsing the 'Ring,'* p. 65.

284 This helps account, at least in a small way, for part of Cosima Wagner's extreme conservatism in the productions staged at Bayreuth after Wagner's death. See Williams, *Wagner and Festival Theatre*, pp. 150-151 and Spotts, *Bayreuth: History of the Wagner Festival*, pp. 90-110.

285 Wieland Wagner, "Tradition and Innovation" in DiGaetani, *Penetrating Wagner's Ring* , p. 389. See also Jean-Jacques Nattiez's essay, unfortunately marred by semiological jargon, "'Fidelity' to Wagner: Reflections on the Centenary *Ring*," in Millington and Spencer, *Wagner in Performance*, pp. 75-98.

286 Appia, "Staging of the *Ring*," in *Music and the Art of the Theatre*, p. 210.

287 Peter Cook was even more forceful in his dismissal of most modern productions of the *Ring*. "We do not experience 'Wagner' any more. What we are offered instead is a shoddy mixture of misguided and misinformed notions presented in an offensive and

often distracting manner, to be accompanied somehow by Wagner's words and music. I am beginning to think that the only solution will lie with a return to Wagner's original scenery and costumes or something very like them, and his written stage directions. ... It might be argued that this would lead to a 'Standard Wagner' production, but even this would be preferable to the unbridled licence of producers which has had to be endured in recent years." Cook, *Memoir of Bayreuth,* p. 12.

288 Jenkyns, *Victorians and Ancient Greece,* pp. 110-11.

289 See Herbert Samuel Lindenberger, "Wagner's *Ring* as Nineteenth-Century Artifact" in *Comparative Drama* 28.3 (fall 1994) pp. 285-310.

Index